Douglas
Heeyegan

SPIDER-MAN

THE ULTIMATE GUIDE

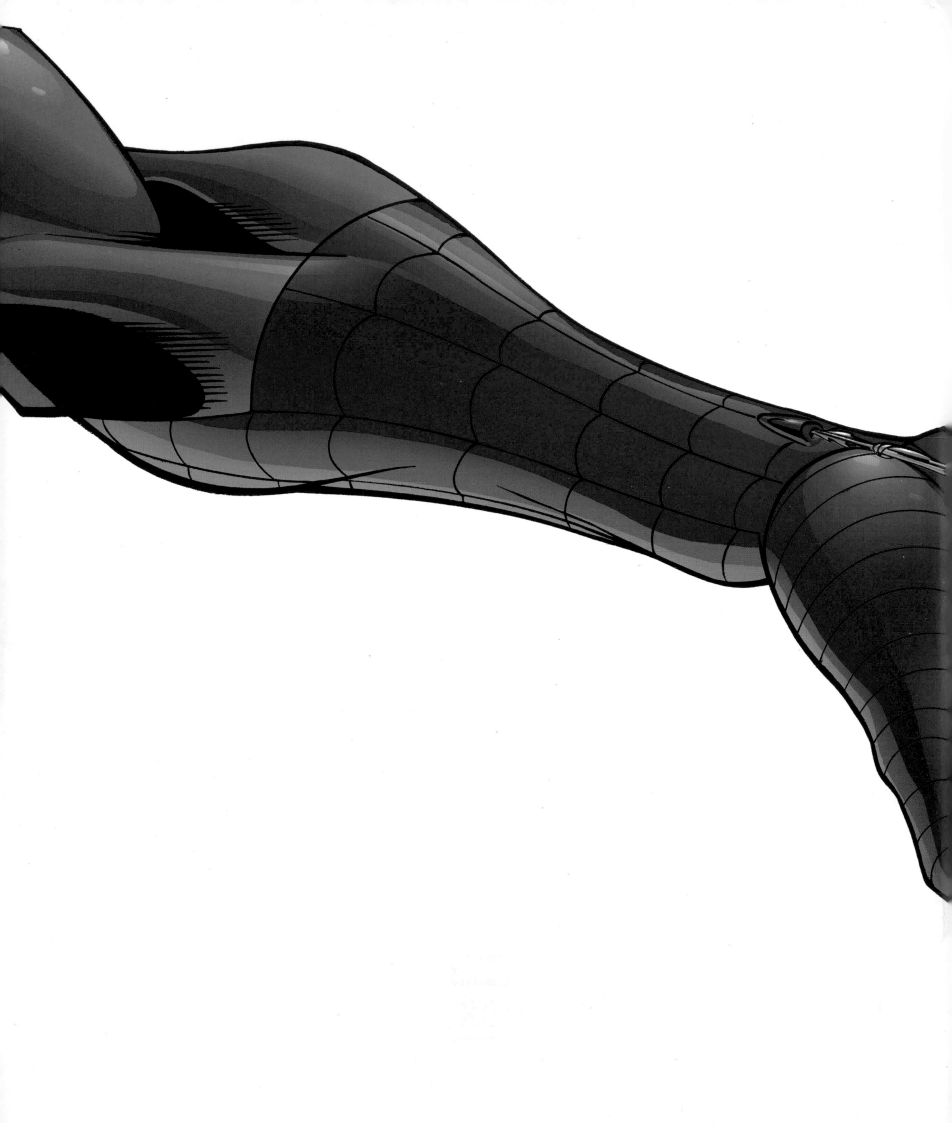

SPIDER-MAN®

THE ULTIMATE GUIDE

TOM DEFALCO

MARVEL

DK

A DORLING KINDERSLEY BOOK

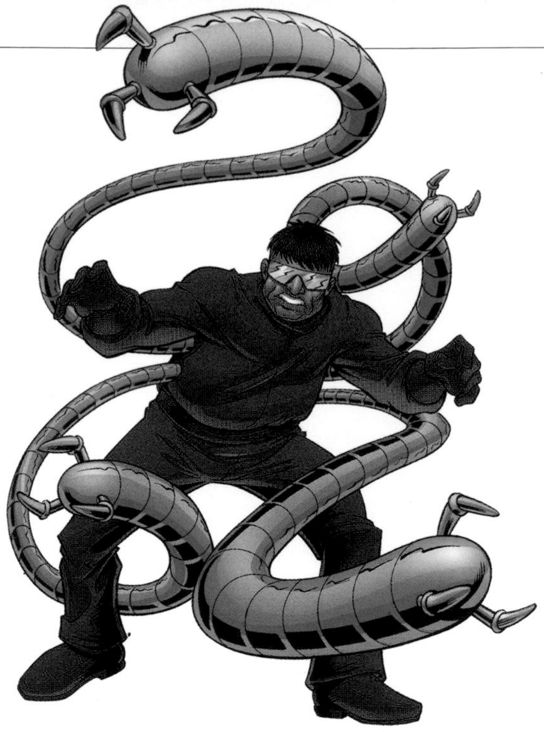

CONTENTS

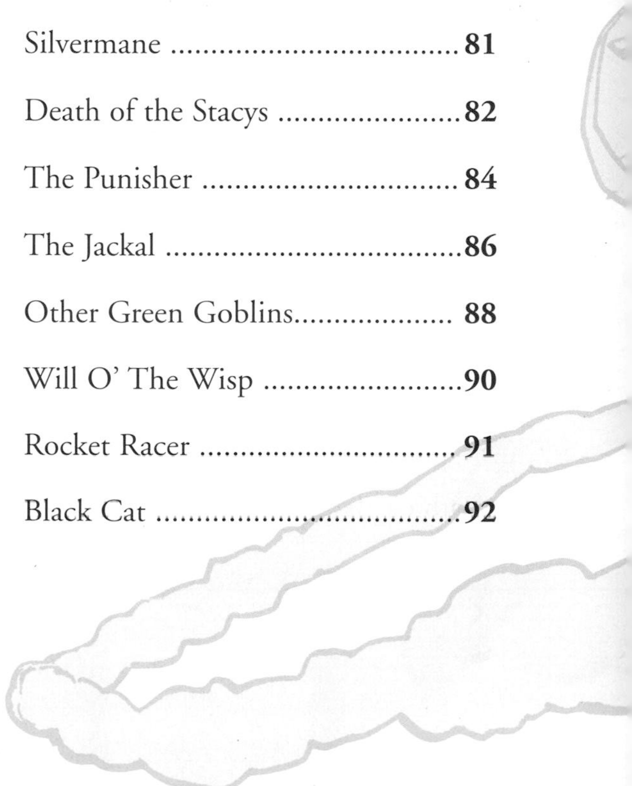

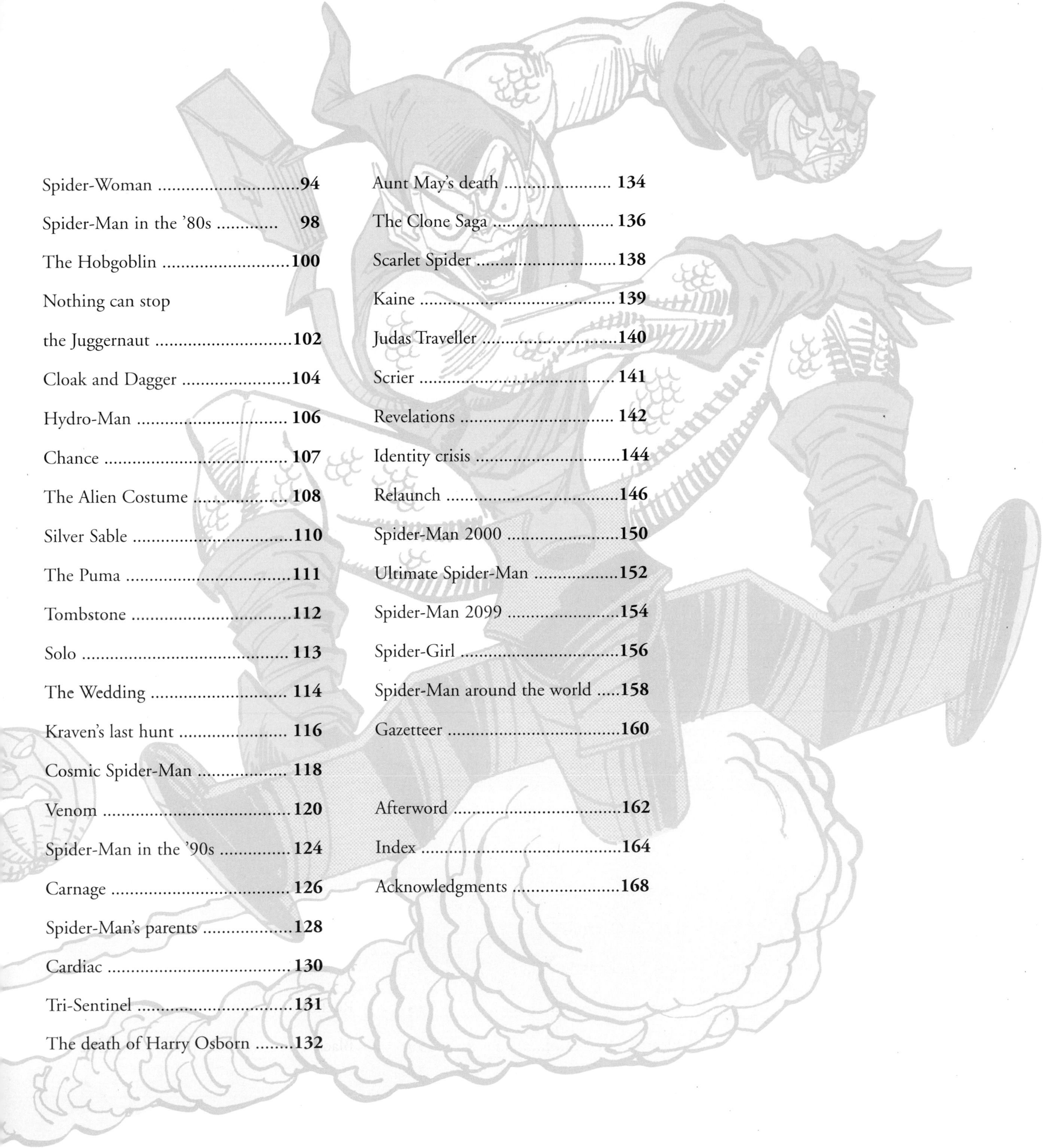

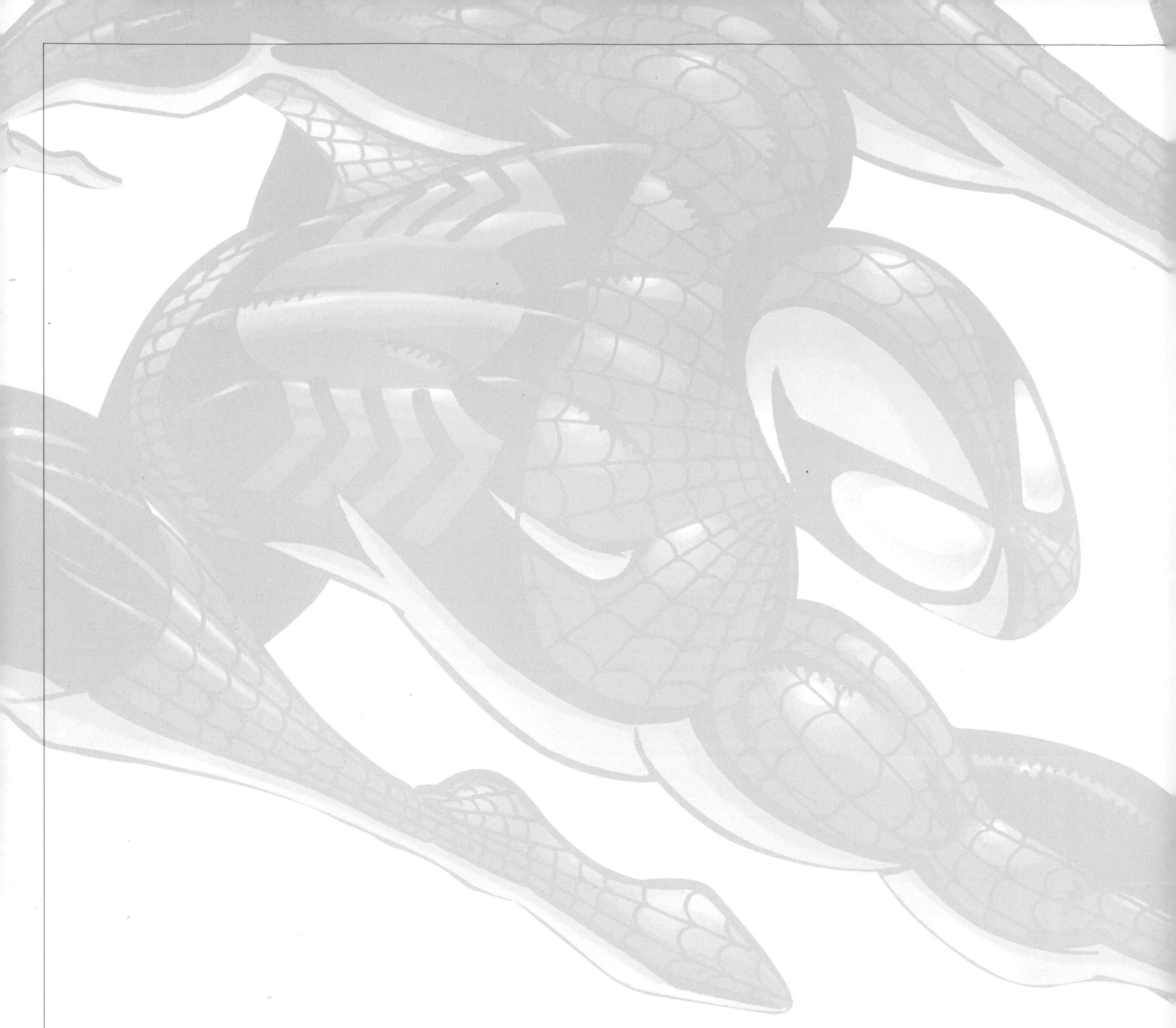

FOREWORD

LIFE IS FUNNY! (As if you didn't know). I don't mean "Ha ha funny." I mean in the sense of odd, peculiar, strange.

You're probably wondering what this has to do with Spider-Man. Well, I'm glad you asked.

You see, before coming up with the idea for everyone's favorite web-swinger, I had already created The Fantastic Four and the incredible Hulk. And, after doing Spidey, Marvel and I then generously gifted an appreciative world with such characters as the X-Men, Daredevil, Iron Man, The Avengers, and... well, you get the idea.

So here's the point. Why is it that every new person I meet usually says something like, "Hey, aren't you the one who wrote Spider-Man?" I mean, they hardly ever ask me if I wrote the Hulk, or The Silver Surfer, or even Sgt. Fury and the Howling Commandos (for those of you with really long memories)? Nope, it's always, "Aren't you the one who wrote Spider-Man?"

Now things like that make me think. Why is Spider-Man the first character that comes to mind when people mention Marvel or me? Over the years I've come up with a theory about that and now, because of my justly famed generosity, I'd like to share it with you.

I think Spidey has made such a lasting impression because he's possibly the most realistically human of all super heroes. He never has enough money, he's constantly beset by personal problems, and the world doesn't exactly applaud his deeds—in fact, most people tend to suspect and distrust him. In short, he's a lot like you and me.

There's another thing about Peter and his arachnid alter-ego. When his series first started, way back in 1963, Peter was just a teenager, still in school. Most of the comic book readers were teenagers as well, so that made it really easy for them to identify with him. You see, at that time all the comic book super heroes were adults. The only teenagers in comics were the heroes' sidekicks. Well, I figured, "Where is it written that teenagers can only be sidekicks?" The answer, of course, was "Nowhere!" So Spidey was probably the first comic book hero that teenagers themselves could identify with.

Whoa, I think I omitted another important point. You may have noticed that Peter Parker never lived in Gotham City, or Metropolis, or any place that was obviously a fictional city. Nope, his very first story planted him firmly in Forest Hills, a part of New York City. So readers could really visualize him web-swinging around the streets of New York and its environs. It was just another element that gave Spidey a feeling of reality even though he was actually part of an imaginative comic book universe.

Finally, there was the humor. I tried to make sure that our web-headed wonder was never without some sort of wisecrack or sharp retort, no matter how tense a situation might be. That, too, was an effort to be realistic because, as you know, most young people have a flip way of speaking. They're never as proper or pedantic as so many other heroes are portrayed. In fact, just between you and me, Spidey speaks a lot like I do. Or maybe I speak like he does. After a while, it's hard to tell who's imitating whom!

And there you have it. My take on the reason Spider-Man seems to have such an unshakable hold on the minds and emotions of so many readers. Even though I'm equally proud of the many other characters the mighty Marvel bull-pen and I have been associated with over the years, I now feel I can understand why our wondrous wall-crawler is the first one people think of when they talk comics to me. And I hope I've succeeded in making it clearer to you, too.

If I haven't succeeded, that's okay. It makes me resemble poor ol' Peter Parker even more. None of us ever seems to get anything totally right!

But don't waste time worrying about us. There's a lot of story waiting for you on the pages ahead. So wiggle your webs and plunge right in. You know how your friendly neighborhood Spider-Man hates to be kept waiting!

Excelsior!

Stan Lee

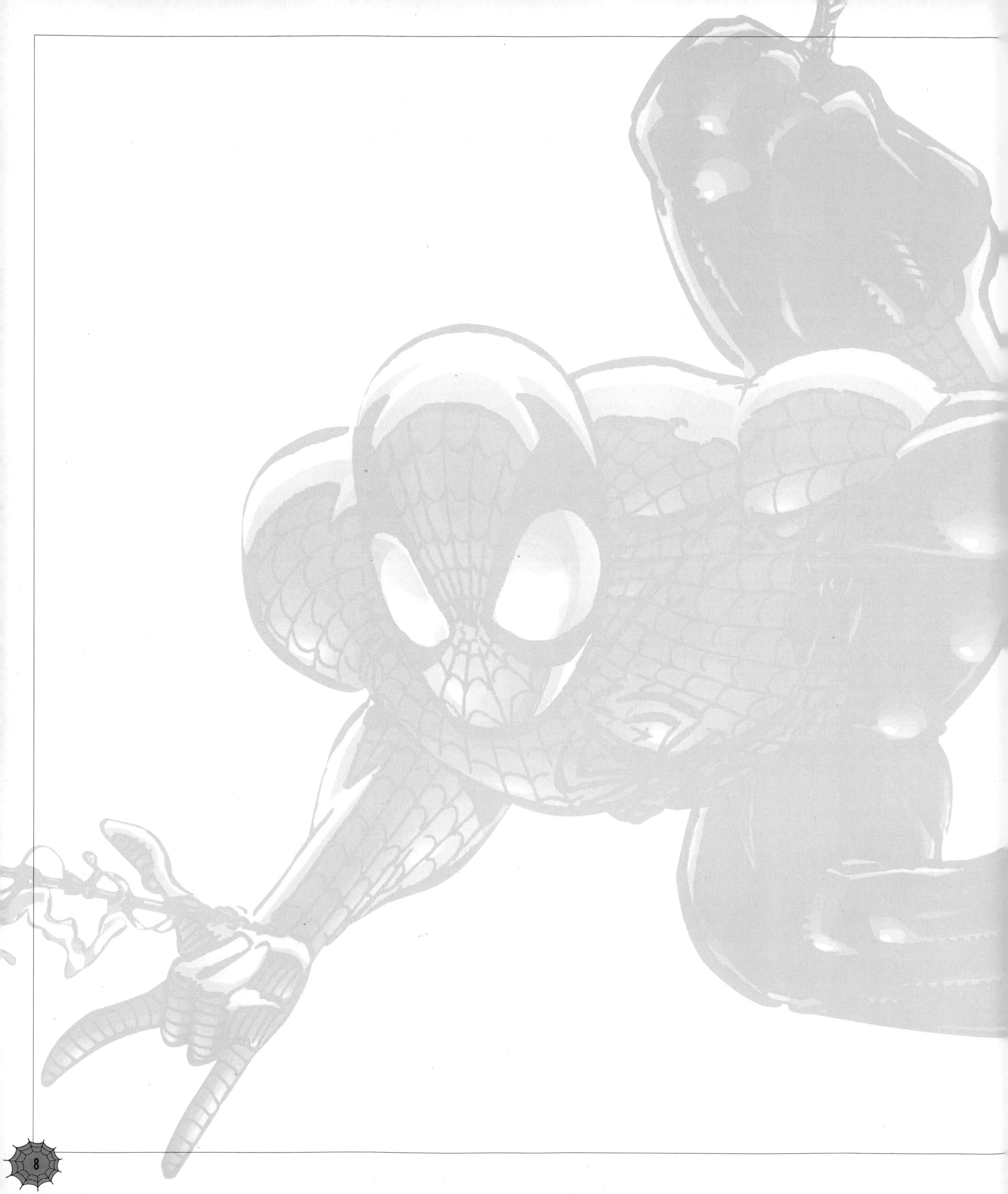

INTRODUCTION

WE LIVE in an age of polls and focus groups. Market research is king. Television shows and movies are screened before test audiences and are often changed because of bad reactions. No manufacturer would dare release a new product unless it had been blessed by the appropriate consumer survey reports. A thorough market analysis must be conducted before anything appears on the shelves of your local store.

If Spider-Man had been created in 2001, the odds are that he never would have made it past the research experts.

Things were different at Marvel Comics in 1962. Stan Lee only had to convince one man, a publisher by the name of Martin Goodman, to take a chance on a new character. Goodman looked at Spider-Man, carefully gauged the web-slinger's chances for success, and immediately said no.

Goodman understood his audience. The popular super heroes of the day all followed the same formula. They were adults with glamorous jobs or lifestyles. They were role models who believed in truth and justice. They were also handsome and muscle-bound. Within hours of receiving their powers, they designed a colorful costume and began to patrol the city.

Goodman also knew that most people hated spiders. He believed that teenagers could only be used as sidekicks or as the stars of humor stories. Most of all, Goodman was convinced that no one wanted to read about a wimpy crime fighter who shed tears and made mistakes.

Stan persisted. He had faith in Spider-Man and kept looking for a chance to sneak him into print. When Stan learned that *Amazing Adult Fantasy* was about to be canceled, he dropped a word out of the title and put Spidey on the cover. He figured that even Martin wouldn't care if the web-swinger was a failure.

But Stan wasn't sure about the look. He rejected the first version of the cover drawn by Steve Ditko and commissioned Jack Kirby to draw a second one, featuring a more heroic-looking Spider-Man.

The rest, as they say, is comic book history. *Amazing Fantasy* #15 hit the comic book racks and sold pretty well. Well enough for Spider-Man to be granted his own title nearly a year later. (The long gap is because of the way comic books were distributed in the United States in those days. It took a publisher nearly nine months to ascertain the sales on an individual issue.)

From his very first story, Spider-Man stood out from the other costumed crime fighters. They went into battle full of confidence. Not Peter Parker! He was always doubting and second-guessing himself. He assumed that he would lose every fight and that all his missions would end in failure. But he didn't let that stop him. No matter how hopeless the situation or overwhelming the odds, Spider-Man never quit. He refused to accept defeat or surrender to despair. His body could be broken, but his spirit was never conquered.

Spider-Man's message is simple. It's all about responsibility. If you want to be a good person, you have to be accountable for your actions. You can't blame others for your mistakes or failures. You also have a duty to use your talents to make this world a better place. If you have the power to stop something bad from happening, you need to step forward. One person can make a difference, especially if he or she acts in a responsible manner.

As it says in the comic books, "With great power, there must also come great responsibility."

PETER PARKER

PETER PARKER was only a young boy when his parents died in a plane crash. He immediately moved in with his father's older brother and wife. Ben and May Parker (*see pages 12-13*) were an elderly couple with no children of their own, and they raised Peter as if he were their son. They rarely spoke about Peter's real parents, so Peter became convinced that his parents had left him because of something he had done. Afraid of being abandoned, Peter worked hard to win his aunt and uncle's approval—though he didn't have to worry. Ben and May truly loved their nephew and would have done anything to please him.

HIGH SCHOOL

Peter was an honor student, and his teachers always thought very highly of him. He always came prepared for class, and completed all the assignments. The other students, however, had little time for a know-it-all like puny Parker. The girls thought he was too quiet, and the boys considered him a wimp. Peter was painfully shy, and some of his classmates misinterpreted his silence for snobbery. He had trouble making friends, but he never stopped trying. He often invited other students to join him at science exhibits or monster movies. But they usually responded with ridicule, and almost never asked him to join them.

Peter's glasses
May Parker insisted that Peter wear glasses, but after he became Spider-Man his eyesight improved. Flash Thompson broke Peter's last pair of glasses during a shoving match, and Peter never got around to buying a new pair.

Since Aunt May bought most of Peter's clothes, they were hardly stylish.

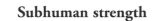

Subhuman strength
Before he gained his spider-powers, Peter Parker had considerably less than average strength for a boy of his age. Clumsy and uncoordinated, he also had no athletic ability. He had a fear of heights, too—even getting a book from the top shelf in the library resulted in his suffering severe symptoms of vertigo.

Peter often carried a backpack that contained all his school texts, plus books for his own reading pleasure.

Heroes on his mind
Peter always thought of his Uncle Ben as his best friend. Ben had an extensive collection of old comic books and science-fiction magazines that he enjoyed sharing with his nephew. Peter spent hours reading these comics and their stories about courageous heroes and their intriguing adventures. He dreamed of being a costumed adventurer like Captain America, striking terror into the hearts of criminals.

Peter always wore white socks, and polished his shoes every night before bed.

Graduation day

Peter Parker graduated from Midtown High with the highest scholastic average in the school's history, but he almost missed the ceremony. Instead of attending to last-minute graduation details, Peter was trading punches with a superhuman villain, the Molten Man (*see page 68*). He won his fight and arrived home just in time to change for the ceremony. Later, he was thrilled to discover that he had won a full scholarship to Empire State University.

No college degree

Spider-Man ruined Peter's college graduation. In the week before the ceremony, Spidey was battling the Green Goblin and the Rocket Racer. He couldn't graduate with the rest of his class since he'd missed a required gym class.

A serious student

Fascinated with science ever since Uncle Ben took him to his first monster movie, Peter Parker immersed himself in his studies. Despite web-swinging and a hectic social life, he was determined to be a success and to make his Aunt May proud.

COLLEGE LIFE
Peter was more self-confident in college than he had been in high school. Leaving home for the first time, he moved into a bachelor pad and even bought a motorcycle.

> ...TO BE AMONG THE BEST AND THE BRIGHTEST OF THE BIOCHEMISTS OF THE FUTURE, UNDERSTANDING EVERY FACET OF THE SCIENCE HE'S CHOSEN AS HIS LIFE'S WORK!

Postgraduate work

Peter finally got his degree from Empire State University, but he continued his studies as a graduate student and took a job as a teaching assistant. With all these activities, as well as being Spider-Man, Peter's life got a little too hectic. He decided he needed a rest, and he withdrew from the graduate program. Later, taking Aunt May's advice, he returned to college and continued working toward his master's degree.

The man behind the mask

Throughout his career as Spider-Man, Peter has always been torn between his sense of duty and the mixed feelings he has received from the public. This reception has varied from praise to outright condemnation, and it has left the teenager confused about his role. It has even driven him to the brink of despair, causing him to throw away his costume and renounce his alter ego. Nevertheless, his dedication to using his powers responsibly has always led to Peter donning his mask again in the hope that some day the world will learn to appreciate Spider-Man.

UNCLE BEN AND AUNT MAY

On learning that Jerome had shot a jewelry store clerk, Ben tried to stop May from running away with him.

BORN IN Brooklyn, New York, to a struggling working-class family, Ben Parker was a bright and happy child who was popular with both his teachers and his classmates. He had a vivid imagination, collected comic books, and read science fiction. He also loved a good practical joke, and he dreamed of becoming a professional comedian when he grew up. When his father died unexpectedly, Ben dropped out of high school to support his widowed mother and much younger brother, Richard. He took a series of menial jobs and was working at the amusement park in New York's Coney Island when he first met May Reilly.

A new responsibility
When Peter's parents were reported dead, Ben and May welcomed the orphaned child into their lives. The couple were living on a low income and had to make many sacrifices for the boy.

MAY'S CHOICE

SIMPLY THE BEST
Ben and May provided all the support that Peter needed, both financial and emotional.

Although she was attracted to Ben, May also dated Johnny Jerome, a young street hustler. Jerome suddenly proposed to May and asked her to leave town with him. Before she could answer, Ben arrived and told her that Jerome was a criminal who was wanted by the police. After Jerome was arrested, May started to appreciate Ben's sense of responsibility, and she agreed to marry him. Meanwhile, Ben's brother Richard had become an intelligence agent. He met and married Mary Slattery who was also an agent, and they had a son, Peter. When the couple were assigned to an overseas mission, Richard asked Ben and May to take care of Peter for a few months. Unfortunately, the mission went wrong, and Richard and Mary were apparently killed.

Ben and May looked after Peter when his parents were killed.

A friend in need
Recalling the popularity he enjoyed as a child, Ben was dismayed to see that Peter had few friends his own age. He did everything he could to encourage his nephew to come out of his shell and went out of his way to spend time with Peter.

Best friends

Ben tried to build up Peter's self-esteem by pushing him to participate in sports and often tried to teach him how to defend himself. When Peter failed to show any interest in physical activities, Ben earned May's disapproval by introducing him to monster movies, comic books, and science fiction novels. These journeys into the fantastic sparked Peter's imagination, and he started to develop a taste for science.

A secret tragedy

May was forever changed by the tragedy of losing her only child. She went from a vivacious young girl who lived for excitement, to a nervous and overprotective old woman. Constantly worried about the state of her nephew's health, she fusses over him to make sure he eats properly and dresses warmly. Peter accepts his aunt's coddling with wry humor. Though he has long since outgrown any need to be protected, he understands that she means well.

FRUSTRATED COMIC
Ben spent many hours telling jokes and pulling tricks on Peter. While a lot of his uncle's material was corny and dated, Peter didn't care. He developed a real appreciation for quips and pranks.

STRONG-WILLED WOMAN
May's spirit remains strong, and she holds on to her opinions stubbornly. She believes that Spider-Man is a masked menace and that Doctor Octopus is a charming gentleman.

A united front

After the murder of Ben, Peter and his aunt grew even closer. They genuinely love one another, and always watch each other's back.

DIVIDED LOYALTIES?
May Parker suffers from a weak heart and has had many serious health problems over the years. Peter is often torn between his duties as Spider-Man and helping his ailing aunt. He has even let a villain get away to go to May's bedside when she has become ill. But Peter's attempts at help can be misplaced. After receiving some of Peter's blood during a transfusion, May's body reacted badly with the radioactive particles in his system, and she went into a coma.

PETER'S FRIENDS

Flash Thompson often ridiculed Peter, unaware that his puny classmate was Spider-Man.

HOW'D BIG, BRAVE PETER HURT HIS POOR LITTLE ARM? DID YOU TRY TO TURN TOO MANY HEAVY PAGES AT ONE TIME, BOOKWORM? OR DID YOU DROP A NASTY LITTLE TEST-TUBE ON IT IN THE LAB?

SINCE PETER Parker was considered a nerd by most of his classmates, he didn't have any real friends in high school. He was an outsider who occasionally hung out with the more popular students. Peter had known one of them, Flash Thompson, ever since they were kids, but they never got along. An athlete who gained his nickname because of his speed, Flash had to struggle to complete his school assignments, so he had little use for a puny know-it-all. The young Flash was a troublemaker and a bully who stole comic books and baseball cards from the local newsstand, and who often extorted money from his classmates.

STAR ATHLETE

Life changed for Flash Thompson when he entered Midtown High. Thanks to his strength and speed, he became the star of the school's football team and led the baseball team in home runs. He stopped stealing and harassing his classmates, but he continued to bully Peter. Ironically, Flash was also one of Spider-Man's biggest fans and even formed a fan club to support his hero.

YEAH? WHEN I'M THRU LEANIN' ON YA, EVEN THE BRIDE OF FRANKENSTEIN WON'T GIVE YOU A SECOND LOOK!

WELL, DON'T WORRY ABOUT IT! SHE'S NOT MY TYPE, ANYWAY!

Trading insults
As he gained confidence with his spider-powers, Peter began to stand up to Flash Thompson and return insult for insult.

WELL, I'LL *TELL* YOU. I'VE BEEN THINKING LONG AND HARD, TRYING TO FIGURE OUT HOW TO *MAKE IT UP* TO YOU FOR BREAKING YOUR GLASSES.

The "In" crowd
Flash usually hung around with a fashionable crowd that included Jason Ionello, a wisecracking practical joker; Liz Allen, Midtown High's beauty queen; Tiny McKeever, a good-natured goliath; and Sally Avril, a bright and energetic cheerleader and gymnast.

THAT'S THE *SIZE* OF IT, PARKER! I'M GONNA SHOW YOU WHAT HAPPENS TO WISEGUYS WHO TRY TO MAKE TIME WITH MY GIRL!

YOUR GIRL??! YOU'VE AS MUCH CHANCE WITH LIZ AS *I* HAVE WITH SOPHIA LOREN!

Flash's father was a police officer. But Harrison "Harry" Thompson was also an alcoholic who often struck his children when he was drunk.

AN ALL-AMERICAN BOY
Flash attended Empire State University on a full football scholarship, but he dropped out to enroll in the United States Army. After he completed his tour of duty, Flash visited Peter and the two realized that they had a lot in common. To their surprise, they eventually became close friends.

Flash's real name is Eugene.

FLASH THOMPSON

JEALOUS
Though he seemed to be one of the most popular boys at Midtown High, Flash was very insecure. He was jealous of Peter's scholastic achievements. He also feared that his girlfriend Liz Allen had a thing for Peter and that she wanted to upgrade to someone smarter. When threats didn't convince Peter to stay away from Liz, Flash often resorted to punches.

HOW MANY MORE TROPHIES YOU *WANT*, SAL? HOW'D YOU LIKE TO DO SOMETHING ELSE --

-- SOMETHING THAT'LL MAKE US THE MOST *POPULAR* KIDS ON CAMPUS?

IS THIS ANOTHER ONE OF YOUR ATTEMPTS TO OUT-*FLASH* FLASH THOMPSON, JASON?

JASON AND SALLY
Jason Ionello wanted to be as idolized as Flash Thompson, but most of his jokes fell flat. Sally Avril was a gymnast who donned a costume and briefly became a crimefighter known as the Bluebird. Her life was cut short when she was killed in a car crash.

College friends?

Peter won a college scholarship for science and enrolled in New York's Empire State University after he graduated from Midtown High. Flash Thompson shared a few classes with Peter for a while, but the former football star eventually left school to join the army. Peter also met other students, such as Harry Osborn. Harry was the son of multimillionaire industrialist Norman Osborn, who later became the super-criminal, the Green Goblin (*see pages 54-55*). When they first met, Peter thought that Harry was a spoiled rich kid, and the two of them did not get along.

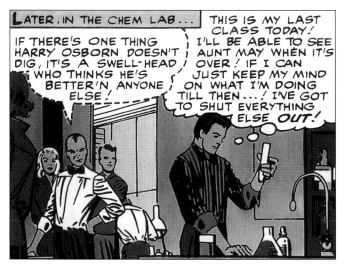

A misunderstanding

The night before Peter started college, Aunt May went into the hospital. He was so worried about her that he practically sleepwalked through his classes. He ignored everyone around him, including Harry, who thought Peter was just being rude. Harry eventually learned the truth, and, as the two got to know each other, their friendship slowly grew.

ROOMMATES
Eventually, Harry Osborn became Peter's best friend. They even decided to share an off-campus apartment together.

Peter's posse

After his lonely days in high school, Peter Parker came out of his shell when he went to college. He made friends and became quite popular. He started dating the beautiful Gwen Stacy and even formed a genuine friendship with Flash Thompson. He also established a close relationship with Mary Jane Watson.

POSTGRADUATE FRIENDS
After getting his college degree, Peter decided to continue his studies in biophysics. He briefly took a job as a teaching assistant where he made more new friends. Dr. Morris Sloan was his supervisor. Phil Chang, Steve Hopkins, and Marcy Kane were all fellow teaching assistants. Debra Whitman, Dr. Sloan's timid young secretary, dated Peter for a short period. Dr. Curt Connors was an old friend of Peter's who led a double life as the Lizard (see pages 48-49).

PHILIP
CHANG

MARCY
KANE

DR. MORRIS
SLOAN

STEVE
HOPKINS

DEBRA
WHITMAN

DR. CURT
CONNORS

PETER'S GIRLFRIENDS

PETER PARKER is living proof that being bitten by a radioactive spider can only help your social life. Before he gained his amazing spider-powers, Peter was just a shy and insecure young man. Popular girls like Liz Allen and Sally Avril hardly ever gave him a second glance, and they wouldn't even consider going out with him. There is no way he would have had the courage to ask his boss's secretary for a date, and he never would have approached anyone as pretty as Gwen Stacy. After he became Spider-Man, however, Peter started to come out of his shell, and a lot of women liked what they saw...

OUTSPOKEN
Betty Brant always treated J. Jonah Jameson with respect, yet she wasn't afraid to speak her mind.

Liz Allen

Liz Allen was one of the most popular girls at Midtown High. Though often in the company of Flash Thompson, Liz developed a crush on Peter Parker as he became less timid.

BETTY BRANT

Peter's job as a freelance photographer for the *Daily Bugle* led to his first serious romance. Betty Brant was J. Jonah Jameson's secretary. Peter first became attracted to Betty because she always wore a smile and was never flustered by her volatile boss. Peter and Betty also had a lot in common, since they both had very complicated lives. Betty had an ailing mother and a brother who was usually in trouble. In order to support her family, she had to drop out of high school and get a full-time job. Betty also shared Peter's insecurities and shyness. They started going out, and eventually fell in love.

NO LOVE FOR SPIDEY
Though she was infatuated with Peter, Betty Brant hated Spider-Man for failing to stop criminals from murdering her brother Bennett.

Dangerous liaisons

Peter Parker's dual identity may have helped bring him and Betty Brant together, but it was also responsible for separating them. Betty liked Peter because he seemed to be a quiet boy who didn't take unnecessary risks. As time went on, she began to fear that he enjoyed taking dangerous pictures for the *Daily Bugle*. She begged him to stop, but he needed the money and ignored her concerns. Fearing that Peter wasn't the man he pretended to be, Betty became involved with a reporter named Ned Leeds, whom she later married.

LIZ ALLEN

BETTY BRANT

Gwen Stacy

Peter met the lovely Gwen Stacy at Empire State University. Eventually they fell deeply in love. Unfortunately, the relationship was destined to end in tragedy (*see pages 82-83*).

Glory Grant was was J. Jonah Jameson's secretary after Betty Brant left. Glory and Peter were never an item, but they were always close friends.

GLORY GRANT

GWEN STACY

DEBRA WHITMAN

The best of intentions

As Liz Allen grew more interested in Peter Parker, she began to defend him to the other members of her group. Her acts of kindness backfired because they made Flash Thompson even more jealous of Peter.

ANYWAY, FORGET ABOUT PUNY PARKER! I'VE GOT BIG PLANS FOR MY SPIDER-MAN FAN CLUB! IT'S GONNA BE THE GREATEST FAN CLUB IN TOWN... BECAUSE SPIDEY'S THE GREATEST *GUY* IN TOWN!

AND *I'M* GOING TO FIND SOME WAY TO GET PETER PARKER *INTO* THAT CLUB!

After graduation

Once they graduated from high school, Liz realized that chasing Peter was a waste of time. She accepted the fact that they would never be a couple, and settled for his friendship. She also decided that she had outgrown Flash Thompson and broke up with him. Liz later became romantically involved with Peter's college roommate, Harry Osborn (*see page 15*), and they were eventually married.

IT'S OKAY, LIZ! DON'T WORRY ABOUT *ME!* THAT BIRDBRAIN DOESN'T SCARE ME!

I *KNEW* IT! YOU'VE BECOME AS BAD AS *FLASH* IS! AND I THOUGHT YOU WERE *DIFFERENT!*

HE *WILL* BE, WHEN *I'M* THROUGH WITH HIM!

How can she know?

In graduate school, Peter dated Debra Whitman, a girl with serious problems of her own who began to suspect that Peter was secretly Spider-Man.

DEB, PHOTOGRAPHING SUPER-CRIMINALS IS MY SPECIALTY-- IT'S WHAT I GET PAID FOR!

YOU'RE LYING TO ME, PETER!

YOU'RE NOT GOING TO PHOTOGRAPH SUPER-VILLAINS-- BUT TO *FIGHT* THEM!

I KNOW YOUR TERRIBLE SECRET! YOU CAN'T FOOL ME ANY LONGER! YOU ARE SPIDER-MAN, AND I...

...I AM SO AFRAID!

A parade of beauty

Peter didn't want a serious relationship after he lost Gwen Stacy. He spent a lot of time with Mary Jane Watson (*see pages 18-19*), but he considered her more of a friend than a girlfriend in those days. Soon enough, he returned to the dating game and started seeing Debra Whitman as well as spending time with girls like Cissy Ironwood and Marcy Kane. Even Amy Powell, a gorgeous blonde, pursued him for a while. But he already knew that there was only one girl for him—Mary Jane.

DEBRA WHITMAN
Debra Whitman had once been married to a man who beat her.

17

MARY JANE

For her first few appearances, Mary Jane's face was always obscured, leaving the readers guessing about her appearance.

O N THE surface, Mary Jane Watson is the complete opposite of Peter Parker. She appears to be a popular, fun-loving young lady who is always looking for a party. She usually has a smile on her face, and seems to be without a care or responsibility in the world. But appearances can be deceiving. Mary Jane was the daughter of Philip and Madeline Watson. Her mother was a drama student, while Philip majored in American literature and wanted to be a writer. The two married as soon as they graduated from college. But as his dreams of becoming a writer faltered, Philip turned on his family, verbally abusing them and blaming them for his inability to concentrate. The relationship continued to deteriorate to the extent that Madeline took their young children, Gayle and Mary Jane, and left Philip.

BROKEN DREAMS

Life did not get any easier for the Watson family. Gayle married her high school sweetheart right after graduation. He planned to be a lawyer, but Gayle became pregnant and gave birth. Unable to cope with the pressures of law school, and with yet another child on the way, Gayle's husband deserted her. Disaster struck again, when Madeline died just before the birth of Gayle's second child. Gayle turned to her sister, hoping for support. But Mary Jane wasn't willing to give up her dreams to help her sister. Instead, she left to stay with her favorite aunt, Anna Watson, who was living in Forest Hills. During her time there, Aunt Anna tried several times to set up Mary Jane on a date with her neighbor's nephew—a certain Peter Parker.

JACKPOT
Peter couldn't contain his shock when he saw how beautiful Mary Jane was. In response, Mary Jane uttered the words that are now part of comic book lore.

Donning a mask
When she was younger, Mary Jane always disguised her true feelings. She played and laughed and pretended that everything was just fine. On the day Philip Watson struck her older sister, Mary Jane did cartwheels to amuse her friends and partied long into the night.

Mary Jane is a natural redhead.

HIGH FASHION
Mary Jane's career as a model has meant that her clothes are always the height of fashion. Even her wedding dress was created by a leading fashion designer (see pages 114-115).

Hold that pose

Having discovered a taste for performing in high school plays, Mary Jane turned to a career first as a dancer and then as an actress. She even had a brief role in a daily soap opera called *Secret Hospital*. However, she had her greatest success as a model. With the money from her modeling, Mary Jane and Peter were able to move into a luxurious apartment. But it was also her modeling work which took her on an ill-fated trip to Latveria (*see pages 150-151*).

The secret

Mary Jane was 13 years old the first time she saw Peter Parker, and she thought he looked cute. She later discovered that he was secretly Spider-Man when she accidentally spotted him sneaking out of his aunt's house. Though her Aunt Anna kept trying to get them together, Mary Jane didn't want anything to do with him. She had no use for a quiet and sensitive boy who hid the truth about himself behind a mask. They eventually met, and began their often-rocky relationship. Many years would pass before Mary Jane revealed that she had always known Peter's greatest secret.

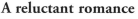

Dangerous occupation

Being Spider-Man's girlfriend and then wife has not been without its dangers. Particularly as some of Spider-Man's most dangerous enemies know who he really is and who his nearest and dearest are! Mary Jane has been attacked by the likes of Tombstone (*see page 112*) and the second incarnation of the Green Goblin (*see pages 132-133*). However, the greatest impact was made by Venom (*see pages 120-121*). When the villain first arrived on the scene, he went straight to Mary Jane and Peter's apartment. Here he confronted the model and asked her about Peter's whereabouts, scaring Mary Jane out of her wits.

BACK TO THE RED AND BLUE
Mary Jane was so scared by Venom's visit that she persuaded Peter to change apartments and to discard his black costume in favor of his more traditional red-and-blue one.

A reluctant romance

Mary Jane had always been attracted to Peter, but often feigned indifference toward him. She admired his sense of responsibility and respected his courage, but hated the fact that he was constantly risking his life as Spider-Man. She truly understood all the sacrifices he had made, but, at first, she was not willing to share her pain.

FATED
Mary Jane did everything in her power to keep Peter at a distance. She flirted with Flash Thompson and dated Harry Osborn, his best friend and roommate. And yet, she was always there when Peter needed a shoulder to cry on. Eventually, fate proved too hard a force to resist, and despite turning Peter down on a number of occasions, she eventually agreed to become his wife.

ORIGIN OF SPIDER-MAN

THE FIRST day of the rest of Peter Parker's life started like any other. Gently tickled awake by his Uncle Ben, Peter was victim of too much studying and too little sleep. Still he managed to put on a smile by the time he joined his aunt and uncle for breakfast as usual. Peter's shyness and scholastic interests had made him a bit of a social outcast at school. But his late night study sessions paid off when his science teacher singled out his work, mentioning that he was practically assured of getting a scholarship when he graduated. Later that day, in an attempt to forget about his failure to fit in at school, Peter visited a science exhibition. During one of the demonstrations, a common house spider was exposed to a massive dose of radiation when it swung into the path of a particle accelerator. The stricken spider landed on Peter's hand and bit him as it died. With his hand burning from the bite, Peter began to feel nauseated and stumbled outside for some fresh air. What he didn't realize was that the spider's irradiated venom had begun to alter his biochemistry. Peter's body was already mutating, gaining the fantastic powers that would transform him into the amazing Spider-Man.

THE FIRST HINTS OF POWER
Still dazed by his unpleasant experience in the science hall, Peter carelessly stepped in front of a speeding car. The driver's horn startled the teenager, causing him to leap to safety. It was a leap that propelled him almost 30 feet up the side of a nearby building. Peter's was astounded to discover that he was able to stick to the wall of the building with his fingertips. While scaling the wall, he also discovered that he was amazingly strong by crushing a steel pipe.

WHAT'S COME OVER ME! I—I'M SCALING THIS WALL JUST AS EASILY AS I CAN WALK!

Peter was shocked when he stuck to the wall of a nearby building.

-- HE SET OUT TO TAKE SHOW BUSINESS BY STORM --

-- AS THE SPIDER-MAN!

In the ring
Peter spotted an opportunity to test his powers when he came across a wrestling challenge. Disguised by a mask, Peter easily defeated the wrestler, Crusher Hogan. A TV producer in the crowd eagerly offered Peter a spot on a show, and the youngster accepted. He even designed a new costume for his TV debut.

From zero to hero
Peter also built a pair of web-shooters and started to practice his act. On the night of his debut performance, Spider-Man wowed the crowds and got a standing ovation. After years of being an unwanted misfit, Peter Parker was now a media darling. Fame and riches were finally within his reach, and over the next few days the amazing Spider-Man became a sensation!

Peter was horrified when the radioactive spider bit him.

BUT HIS EGO SWELLED WITH HIS FIRST TASTE OF FAME AND SUCCESS.

HE ALLOWED A THIEF TO ESCAPE, WHEN IT WOULD HAVE BEEN SO EASY TO STOP HIM, FIGURING IT WASN'T *HIS* PROBLEM!

No business like show business
While he was leaving the show one night, Peter suddenly heard a shout. An elderly security guard was chasing a burglar. Even though the guard ordered Spider-Man to stop the fleeing man, the masked teenager did nothing, and the burglar managed to escape down a high-speed express elevator. The outraged guard immediately turned on Spider-Man, berating him for failing to act. Peter arrogantly replied that he was a star and didn't take orders from anyone. Peter was through being pushed around; he swaggered away and promptly forgot about the incident.

--AND HIS BELOVED UNCLE BEN HAD BEEN SHOT *DEAD!*

WITH TEARS OF RAGE AND LOSS STINGING HIS EYES, HE SWORE HE'D BRING THE MURDERER TO JUSTICE!

TO THE DEPTHS OF DESPAIR
Spider-Man's popularity increased in the weeks that followed, and offers flooded in. Peter felt like he was on top of the world. But it was a world that suddenly crashed in on him when his Uncle Ben was murdered by a burglar.

The spider strikes

When Peter returned home one night after a personal appearance, he was shocked to discover that a burglar had murdered his Uncle Ben. Grief-stricken, Peter donned his costume and made his way to a nearby warehouse where the criminal was hiding. Arriving at the warehouse in no time, Spider-Man found the ruined building surrounded by police. But the officers were powerless—there was plenty of cover for the killer to hide behind, and he could easily pick off the police if they decided to charge. Spider-Man realized that it was only a matter of time before darkness fell and the criminal could escape, so he sprang into action.

AND THEN MY *FISTS* WILL DO THE REST!

Criminal's gun covered in webbing.

A startling realization

Using his webbing to stop the killer from firing his gun, Spider-Man then knocked him unconscious with a single blow. Only then did the stunned teenager get a good look at the burglar's face. It was the unnamed fugitive who ran past him in the studio!

IT'S *HIM!*

ON A-- SPIDER'S WEB!

The burglar who murdered Uncle Ben was the first criminal that Spider-Man apprehended.

RESPONSIBILITY
Seeing the face of the criminal made Peter realize that he could have prevented Uncle Ben's death. His refusal to use his powers to stop the thief in the TV studio had backfired horribly on the teenager, and he had lost one of the few people he really loved.

THAT-- THAT *FACE!* IT'S-- OH NO, IT *CAN'T* BE!

AND, A SHORT DISTANCE AWAY...

MY FAULT--ALL MY FAULT! IF ONLY I HAD STOPPED HIM WHEN I *COULD* HAVE! BUT I *DIDN'T*--AND NOW --UNCLE BEN-- IS DEAD...

With great power...

Peter realized that he must have been given his great powers for a reason. Instead of using them for personal gain, he should have been employing them to protect the innocent and to stop the guilty. Spider-Man would never shirk his duty again. He had finally learned that with great power there also comes great responsibility.

SPIDER-SENSE

H E MAY not know if you've been bad or good, but he can always sense when you're dangerous. Spider-Man possesses many incredible abilities, but his most amazing power must be his uncanny spider-sense. This strange tingling sensation, which originates in the back of his skull, warns him of danger. The danger could be something immediate, like a gun being aimed at him or a punch being thrown at the back of his head. Or it could be something subtle, like a slippery floor or a sandwich that contains tainted meat. While his spider-sense cannot tell Spider-Man the exact nature of a particular threat, it always lets him know when and which way to move in order to avoid the danger.

BUILT-IN RADAR

Spider-Man's spider-sense is like having a personal radar unit. He doesn't have to worry about watching where he's walking or web-swinging because it always guides him away from danger. Loose ceiling tiles or rotted rooftops don't trouble Spider-Man because his spider-sense warns him in plenty of time to avoid them. Even if he were trapped in complete darkness, his spider-sense would prevent him from bumping into anything. And Spidey's spider-sense tingles if someone can see the web-slinger out of costume, warning him that he may be spotted.

Everything's fine

Peter senses a potential danger

The danger is now imminent

GETTING WARMER
Spider-Man can judge the proximity and severity of a threat by the intensity of his tingles. The nearer the danger, the stronger the tingling.

Peter's spider-sense is always on... even when he's asleep!

Though it takes a conscious effort, Spider-Man can ignore his spider-sense.

BE PREPARED
Spider-Man's spider-sense reacts to all threats, even minor ones caused by friends or family members who don't actually want to hurt him.

OH, GREAT! MY WATCH HAS STOPPED! I DON'T KNOW IF I'M LATE OR NOT!

WHOA! MY SPIDER-SENSE IS SIGNALING DANGER! WHAT COULD POSSIBLY--?

UH-OH! A LITTLE BURST OF THE OL' SPIDER-SPEED WILL PREVENT A NASTY IMPACT!

Early warning
Peter Parker depends on his spider-sense to protect him even when he's not in costume. It's so sensitive that it will alert him in time to avoid even a minor mishap, such as a collision with a fellow pedestrian.

> GOOD OL' SPIDER-SENSE! IT HASN'T FAILED ME *YET!* I CAN FEEL THE HOSTILE EMANATIONS CLEAR UP HERE FROM THAT ABANDONED FACTORY BELOW!

Tracking by tingle

Like a geiger counter that somehow reacts to danger, Spider-Man often uses his spider-sense to track down his enemies. He has also developed special spider-tracers that are attuned to his spider-sense and can help him to pinpoint foes who are far away.

> "IT'S SO *SENSITIVE* THAT I OFTEN DON'T EVEN KNOW *WHAT* I'M SENSING!

> SOMETHING ABOUT THAT MAN IS BOTHERING ME, BUT... *WHAT IS IT?!*

DANGER ALL AROUND
Though his spider-sense reacts to every potential danger, Spider-Man doesn't always know the nature of the peril.

> I'LL STOP 'IM FOR YA, ELECTRO!! HEY--! WHA--??

> DIDN'T THINK *ANYONE* WOULD BE DUMB ENOUGH TO TRY TO SNEAK UP BEHIND A FELLA WITH A *SPIDER-SENSE!!*

Eyes in the back of his head

Thanks to his spider-sense, it's practically impossible to sneak up on Spider-Man or to ambush him. Not only can he sense the exact direction of an impending threat, but his spider-sense immediately triggers his amazing spiderlike reflexes to help him avoid injury. He often dodges blows before they are actually thrown.

Over the years, Spidey's spider-sense has gotten him out of trouble many times. Its one weakness, however, is its inability to detect Carnage (see pages 126-7) and Venom (see pages 120-1).

> "NO ONE--INCLUDING MY OWN WIFE--CAN SNEAK UP ON ME, OR AMBUSH ME FROM BEHIND!

It's all instinct

Since his spider-sense instinctively reacts to trouble, Spider-Man depends on it most when he is in a fight, weaving his way through a hail of bullets without a scratch. Over the years, he has come to realize that his reflexes work a lot faster than his mind. Because he can trust his super-quick reflexes completely, Spidey is free to come up with the witty one-liners he spouts to distract his opponents.

WALL-CRAWLING

NOTHING SEEMS TO UNNERVE a bad guy more than being approached by a certain webbed crime-fighter who is crawling up the side of a nearby wall. Though Spider-Man possesses many amazing powers, his ability to cling to any surface is certainly the most unsettling. No matter how friendly our neighborhood web-slinger claims to be, the sight of him scurrying across a ceiling can be very disturbing. The fact that he looks like a monstrous insect whenever he scampers up a building has helped *Daily Bugle* publisher J. Jonah Jameson convince the public that Spider-Man is a menace. Many people hate spiders, and are easily frightened by someone who can hang from their ceilings and cling to their walls.

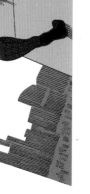

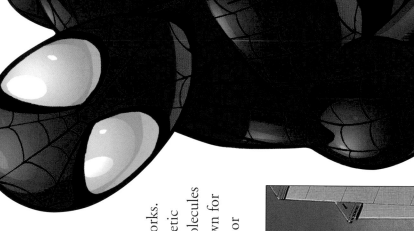

Spider-Man faces down a gunman.

Subject to gravity

Though Spider-Man has the ability to stick to any surface, he cannot defy gravity. That's why he usually crawls up the exterior sides of buildings, instead of walking along the tops. Not only does he present less resistance to the high winds that stalk the upper stories when crawling, but he also makes a smaller target for nervous gunmen.

Spider-Man actively decides which parts of his body are attached to a surface at any given time.

Spidey's lightweight costume and boots are ideal for wall-crawling.

MYSTERIOUS ABILITY

No one knows exactly how Spider-Man's wall-clinging ability works. Peter Parker has often theorized that he has a form of bio-magnetic power that allows him to increase the attraction between the molecules in his body with those of the surfaces he climbs. All that is known for certain is that he can stick to anything. No matter how smooth or slippery a surface may be, Spidey can attach himself. He just has to keep concentrating until he bonds with it. Unlike his spider-sense, the web-head's clinging power is strictly a conscious act. He can never stick to something by accident. He must deliberately press his hand against an object and choose to adhere to it. Of course, Spidey likes to show off as much as the next fellow. He occasionally runs upside down along a ceiling or strides up a wall.

The web-swinger's hands and feet stick to any surface, as if they were locked in place with thousands of tiny suction cups.

SWING AND CLING
Ever wonder why Spider-Man never loses his grip when he's web-swinging around the city? The answer is simple—he uses his clinging ability. He anchors himself to the web-line in his hand, and releases it the instant he reaches for the next one. In this manner, he can safely travel high above the city streets.

Unbreakable

Once Spider-Man has latched on to an object, only he can decide when to release it. No outside force has ever managed to prise him from a surface if he consciously wants to stick to it. Foes with superhuman strength have been known to rip Spidey from walls and ceilings, but that's only because these surfaces have shattered under the strain. Chunks of drywall or pieces of ceiling tile can usually be spotted clinging to Spidey whenever this situation occurs. If someone as strong as the incredible Hulk were to try to pull Spider-Man off a slab of granite, he might accidentally rip off the web-spinner's arms before the rock would splinter. Of course, there is an easy way to separate Spider-Man from an object. All a villain has to do is find a way to knock him out. Once Spidey has lost consciousness, his body will automatically go limp and detach itself from anything it is holding.

Clinging body

Though Spider-Man tends to focus on his hands and feet whenever he's climbing up a wall, every part of his body has the same clinging ability. His back and head can stick to surfaces as easily as his fingers and toes. All he has to do is lean against something and he will stick to it until he decides to free himself.

Not just hanging around

Aside from using his wall-clinging ability to avoid mass transit and impress his fans, Spider-Man has discovered many additional uses for it. He often surreptitiously follows suspected crooks into their hideouts by crawling along the rooftops. He eavesdrops on conversations by clinging to ceilings, and hides under shadowed overhangs. On many occasions, he has held a fleeing thief in place by sticking a finger to the man's back. If the web-head ever decides to retire from crime fighting, he could always become a waiter. With his ability to stick to things, he would never drop a tray of dishes!

CEILING SPY
Since he can travel almost anywhere, Spider-Man never has a problem following a suspect.

Spider-Man can be yanked off a ceiling, but only if the ceiling comes with him!

Spider-Man often takes his strength for granted, which can prove rather disheartening to the average crook.

STRENGTH & AGILITY

SHORTLY AFTER he was bitten by the radioactive spider that gave him his amazing powers (*see pages 20-21*), Peter Parker accidentally crushed a steel pipe as if it were made of paper. He was astonished to discover that he now possessed superhuman strength. Since then, Spider-Man has often told people that he has the proportionate strength of a spider; but he's actually a lot more powerful. While not as strong as the incredible Hulk, the mighty Thor, or the Thing, our friendly neighborhood web-slinger is able to lift almost 10 tons. He can bend a solid iron bar with his bare hands and shatter a concrete wall with a single punch. And in one, spider-powered spring, he has leapt the height of three stories, or the width of a highway.

AMAZING AGILITY

Even more impressive than his spiderlike strength is Spider-Man's amazing speed and agility. When it comes to quick-thinking, death-defying, lightning-swift acrobatic stunts, the wall-crawling wonder is truly without equal. Spider-Man moves with a fluid and casual grace that can't even be equaled by trained superathletes such as Captain America or Daredevil. He leaps from rooftops, somersaults over flagpoles, tumbles off water towers, and balances on top of light poles as he routinely travels across the city in his own unique manner.

WEIGHING THE COMPETITION
While Spider-Man is hardly the strongest costumed hero of all, the combination of his strength, speed, and agility make him a match for almost any foe.

Hercules   Thor   Namor

The Thing

NO PUSHOVER
Many ordinary criminals still insist on taking on Spider-Man in spite of his superior abilities.

Spider of steel
Spider-Man possesses exceptional stamina and can usually recover his full strength after a short rest. Nothing can hold him for too long, and, after a brief respite, he can regain enough strength to shatter even the strongest of chains—you need something pretty strong to tie down this spider!

The stress factor
Average people have been known to lift cars in times of stress. Spider-Man can raise a couple of Cadillacs on a normal day. Add in the excitement of one of his typical battles, and his power level can shoot into uncharted territory. Over the years, the web-slinger has been seen holding up multistory buildings, freeing himself from beneath tons of debris, and flattening cosmically powered aliens.

GOTCHA!
Having crisscrossed thick strands of webbing between buildings to slow a plunging helicopter's momentum, Spider-Man managed to catch the aircraft and prevent it from crashing onto a crowded city street.

So relaxed is Spider-Man as he swings and vaults his way across the city, that it almost looks as if he is showing off.

Even when he's faced by a number of enemies, the wall-crawler's speed means that he can defeat them all without too much effort.

The Hulk

FLASH OF RED AND BLUE
The most nimble of all costumed adventurers, Spider-Man has developed a personal fighting style that no one can match.

DEATH DEFYING
Spider-Man instinctively knows how to adjust his body weight and the position of his limbs. As a result, he can balance himself perfectly on any object, no matter how small or how narrow.

Everywhere at once?
Spider-Man's reflexes operate up to forty times faster than those of a normal person, and he uses them to dazzle much stronger foes. Faced by the Rhino (*see pages 66-67*) or even the Hulk, Spider-Man kicks into high gear, ricocheting off the walls, ceiling, and ground to barrage his opponent with blow after blow. The victim, dazed by the wall-crawler's speed, is left punching thin air.

Spider-Man could never hope to match the strength of the incredible Hulk.

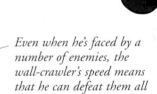

WEB-SLINGING

EVERY SPIDER needs a web, and Spider-Man is no exception. Shortly after he gained his amazing powers, Peter Parker set out to create a web of his own. Peter used his high school's science laboratory after hours and, having studied multipolymer compounds for a few years, he produced an adhesive fluid capable of imitating a spider's silk webbing. To complete the mechanism, Peter then designed and built a pair of web-shooters that snapped on his wrists.

Spidey's web-shooters replace an empty web fluid cartridge automatically.

SO DOES THIS ONE!
I EVEN LOADED THEM
WITH FRESH WET-FLUID
CARTRIDGES, SO I
WON'T HAVE TO WORRY
ABOUT RUNNING LOW
ON WEBBING!

DIFFERENT STROKES

Peter has improved upon his initial design. He now switches between different forms of webbing by the way he taps his trigger. With a short second tap he releases a thin cablelike strand that is perfect for web-swinging. A longer second tap increases the strand's thickness for additional support. If Spidey prolongs the pressure on the trigger, web fluid squirts out in the form of an adhesive liquid which can paste a foe against a wall. A series of brisk taps discharges many thin strands that form a fine spray of webbing, perfect for blinding an opponent.

Belt up

Peter Parker has also designed a special utility belt to carry his spare cartridges of web fluid. The buckle of the belt contains a spider signal which can be projected onto his opponents. Sometimes Peter equips the buckle with a miniature camera.

Spare web-fluid cartridge

CARTRIDGE BELT

The belt can carry 30 cartridges of web-fluid.

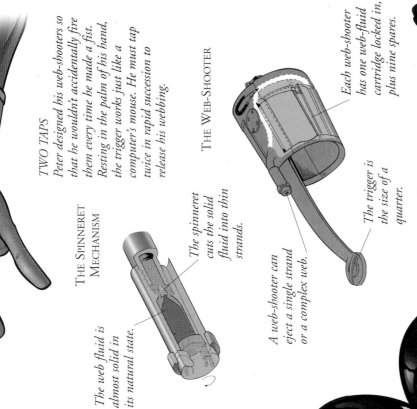

TWO TAPS
Peter designed his web-shooters so that he wouldn't accidentally fire them every time he made a fist. Resting in the palm of his hand, the trigger works just like a computer's mouse. He must tap twice in rapid succession to release his webbing.

THE WEB-SHOOTER

THE SPINNERET MECHANISM

The spinneret cuts the solid fluid into thin strands.

The web fluid is almost solid in its natural state.

Each web-shooter has one web-fluid cartridge locked in, plus nine spares.

The trigger is the size of a quarter.

A web-shooter can eject a single strand or a complex web.

Subcontracting the shooters

Though Peter Parker built the original pair of web-shooters, he now splits up his designs for the various parts and sends them to a number of different machine shops in the New York area. To maintain a degree of secrecy, Peter later assembles all of the pieces himself.

Miles of webbing

The pressure in Spider-Man's web-cartridges is enough to propel a single strand of webbing up to 50 yards, but thicker strands and more complex web patterns can't reach nearly as far. Each of his web-shooters has ten cartridges, and each cartridge contains approximately 1,000 yards of single-strand webbing.

STRANDS OF STRENGTH
Spider-Man's web begins to harden the instant it is exposed to air. Given enough time and sufficient thickness, one strand could even bind the incredible Hulk and hold him prisoner—although it's hard to imagine the Hulk standing still while Spidey applies the necessary webbing!

Reacting almost instantly, Spider-Man can visualize and form a simple item such as a safety net or web-bridge.

ONCE UPON A WEB
After many hours of practice, Spidey has trained himself to use his webbing without conscious thought.

Holding it together

Experience has taught Spider-Man that large objects like a web-trampoline or web-wings tend to lose structural integrity if they extend beyond a diameter of 20 feet. He has also learned that the thicker the webbing, the faster it evaporates.

Fun with webs

The natural strength of Spider-Man's webbing and its ability to harden quickly means it can be formed into a variety of simple shapes and objects. He can easily make web-balls, bats, and bolos, and Spider-Man has also been known to create more complex articles such as rafts, hang-gliders, and skis. Spider-Man can even show his artistic side, by molding simple sculptures with his webbing.

OUR THANKS TO JOLLY JONAH JAMESON, WHO VOLUNTEERED TO DEMONSTRATE SPIDEY'S SAFETY-NET WEBBING... AFTER BEING SLIGHTLY SHOVED THROUGH HIS OFFICE WINDOW!

J. Jonah Jameson (see pages 34-35) has had occasion to thank Spidey's webbing more than once.

Flame resistant

Spidey's normal webbing can easily withstand temperatures of 1,000°F. It melts, but it has never caught on fire. If the wall-crawler is preparing to fight someone like the Human Torch, he can pack a webbing which resists temperatures of up to 10,000°F. This type can only be released in strands that are as thick as a clothesline. Its special cartridge can only hold 10 yards of the webbing at a time.

AND NOW, I'LL MAKE A PAIR OF WINGS OUT OF MY WEB FLUID, AND CRASH-DIVE DOWN AND *PULVERIZE* YOU!

"MY WEBBING HAS AN INCREDIBLE TENSILE STRENGTH--

"--AND IT INCREASES IN DIRECT PROPORTION TO THE THICKNESS OF THE STRAND!

COSTUMES

ONE-WAY LENSES
Spidey can see out through his white eyepieces, but no one can see in.

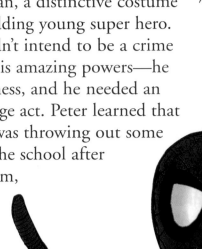

Peter Parker designed his costume so that it would fit beneath his clothes.

I F CLOTHES make the man, a distinctive costume is a definite must for a budding young super hero. Of course, Peter Parker didn't intend to be a crime fighter when he first gained his amazing powers—he wanted to go into show business, and he needed an exciting look to match his stage act. Peter learned that Midtown High's dance class was throwing out some old bodysuits. Slipping into the school after dark, he found one that fit him, took it to the art room, and spent a few hours silk-screening a web pattern on the shirt. He also made a skintight pair of gloves and boots, and with some one-way mirrors he found in the drama class's old prop box, he now had a mask. His first spider-costume was finally ready.

Spider-Man's boots and gloves consist of a thin layer of material so that they do not inhibit his ability to stick to walls.

Spider-Man's bodysuit is composed of a synthetic stretch fabric.

KEEPING UP APPEARANCES

Having the perfect costume is one thing, keeping it is another matter. Peter Parker and his trusty sewing needle have spent many hours repairing the numerous rips and tears his costume has received in battle. Aunt May (*see pages 12-13*) also contributed to Pete's costume woes. She once found his costume behind the bookcase where he had hidden it. Though Peter claimed it was for a practical joke on his friends, she refused to return it. He was forced to buy a Spider-Man suit from a local costume shop. The imitation was so cheap that it began to shrink and came apart during one of his many conflicts!

UNDERARM WEBS
Running from his elbows to his waist, Spidey's underarm webbing is made of flexible nylon netting.

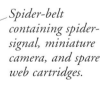

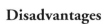

STICKING WITH A CLASSIC
Spider-Man's costume has evolved during the course of his career. The symbol on his chest has changed several times over the years, and the webbing beneath his arms sometimes disappears. The costume has been modified as the wall-crawler has gained additional powers or needed special defenses. And yet, Peter Parker always seems to return to a costume that resembles his original design.

Spider-belt containing spider-signal, miniature camera, and spare web cartridges.

Disadvantages

Beneath his costume's shirt, Spider-Man wears a belt that contains his spider-signal, a miniature camera, and spare web cartridges. He keeps meaning to add a change purse, but has never gotten around to it. The major disadvantage of a skintight costume is that there's no room for Peter's street clothes. He either webs them into a ball attached to his back or he leaves them behind.

THE ALIEN COSTUME

Peter acquired his black costume while fighting on a far-off plant called Battleworld (see pages 108-109). This costume had a lot of advantages over his old one. It had a seemingly endless supply of webbing, and it could change its appearance instantly. It seemed to respond to his thoughts, and would slip over him whenever he wanted to go out web-swinging.

Over the years, the spider on the web-head's costume has assumed many different looks. That's because Peter often changes the symbol when he has to replace his costume shirt.

Peter's alien black costume created "pockets" instantly to store his possessions.

The Amazing Bag-Man

Stranded without clothes after discovering that his black costume was actually an alien symbiote, Peter was at the mercy of the Human Torch... who just couldn't resist a joke at Spidey's expense.

Torn between two costumes

Peter eventually learned that his new black costume was an alien symbiote that wanted to form a permanent attachment to him. He turned it over to the Fantastic Four and went back to his old look. The Black Cat (*see pages 92-93*), however, thought the black costume was sexier. She made a cloth version of it as a gift for Spidey. He used both costumes for many months and didn't get rid of his black one until Venom (*see pages 120-121*) entered his life.

The Spider or the man?

At one point, Peter was so frustrated by the way the public distrusted him that he decided to quit being Spider-Man. He developed a formula that would remove his powers, and even though it hadn't been tested, he drank the liquid. When he eventually came around, Peter discovered that he had grown four extra arms! In desperation, Peter turned to his friend Dr. Curt Connors (*see pages 48-49*) for help.

ARMLESS
With Connors' help, Spider-Man was able to cure himself and lose his extra arms.

VARIOUS LOOKS
From time to time, Peter has been forced to make certain adjustments to his costume. He once donned a steel-plated version (shown right) to battle a heavily armed team of villains known as the New Enforcers, and also designed a special insulated costume for use against Electro.

Spider-Man's armored steel costume was actually a pseudo-metallic composition that Peter created in the labs of Empire State University.

The Reilly factor

Peter Parker retired from costumed crime fighting for a brief time. He turned over his duties as Spider-Man to a friend named Ben Reilly. Reilly designed his own version of Pete's classic costume, with a much larger spider on his chest and a different design on his pants. Plus he redesigned Peter's web-shooters and wrist device.

BEN REILLY AS SPIDER-MAN

SPIDER-MAN'S PARTNERS

OKAY--THAT'S *IT!* NO MORE FUN AND GAMES, FELLA! SOMEONE MIGHT GET *HURT!* NOW, SUPPOSE YOU TELL US WHAT YOU'RE HERE FOR!

GET OUTTA THE WAY, KILL-JOY! GIMME ANOTHER CRACK AT 'IM!

IT'S ABOUT *TIME* SOMEONE ASKED ME!

Needing money when he first gained his amazing powers, Spider-Man tried to join the Fantastic Four. But he left as soon as he realized that they were a nonprofit organization.

SPIDER-MAN IS a friendly neighborhood super hero. He lives in the Marvel Universe, a world which is brimming with superhuman criminals and costumed crime fighters. On any given day, he can run into another masked vigilante, a mythological immortal, or a super-powered mutant. Though a loner by nature, Spidey has teamed up with many different superpowered heroes during the course of his long career. He considers a few of them to be friends, while some are merely acquaintances that fate occasionally throws his way. His relationships with others are more volatile and shift constantly—they can meet as either allies or antagonists, depending on the circumstances.

Captain America's shield

AMAZING ALLIES

Among Spidey's partners is Daredevil, a fearless superathlete whose superhumanly acute senses compensate for the fact that he is completely blind. The web-head has also come across the Fantastic Four, the incredible Hulk, Captain America, the X-Men, and Howard the Duck! And, in the course of these very pages, you'll come across many other allies, including the Prowler, the Punisher, Rocket Racer, Will O' The Wisp, the Black Cat, Silver Sable, and the Scarlet Spider.

STRANGE COMPANION
Dr. Strange and Spidey have often united against menaces on both the supernatural and physical planes.

SPIDER-MAN AND WOLVERINE

Wolverine has claws made from adamantium.

The uncanny X-Men
People born with superhuman abilities, such as the power to read minds or generate vast quantities of ice, are called mutants. A mutant himself, Professor Charles Xavier formed a school to teach these young outcasts from society how to use their special abilities to serve and protect the world. He called this team of mutants the X-Men, and they included Cyclops, the Angel, Beast, Phoenix, Rogue, and Wolverine. Shunned and feared by normal humans, the X-Men share a lot in common with the wall-crawler.

The incredible Hulk

Bruce Banner shares many traits with Peter Parker, but the Hulk couldn't be more different from Spider-Man. The Hulk is a rampaging force of nature who thinks finesse is for sissies. He is easily irritated by Spidey's wisecracks, and has often tried to squash the wall-crawler like a bug.

SPURRED ON BY HIS BURNING HATRED FOR THE HUMAN RACE, THE RACE THAT HAS HOUNDED AND TORMENTED HIM, THE RAMPAGING GREEN FIGURE ATTACKS WITHOUT WARNING.!!

CAPTURE YOU.?? BROTHER, DON'T EVEN WANNA SHARE THE SAME *PLANET* WITH YO

EVEN HERE—DEEP IN MY HIDDEN CAVES, YOU ATTACK ME.! BUT *NO ONE* CAN CAPTURE THE HULK.!

SPIDER-MAN AND CAPTAIN AMERICA

THE AVENGERS
The Avengers are Earth's mightiest heroes, who band together whenever a threat is too great for a single costumed hero. Their membership is constantly changing, but has featured Iron Man, Thor, and Captain America. Spider-Man was invited to join them early in his career, but failed to complete his first assignment. He did, however, become a temporary member a few years later.

SPIDER-MAN AND DRACULA

AMERICA THE BRAVE
Captain America is a highly trained superathlete who thinks Spider-Man's heart is in the right place, but that he lacks the necessary discipline and commitment to become a major costumed hero.

Dracula

Strange situations call for even stranger bedfellows, and Spidey has even found himself working alongside Dracula, the legendary lord of vampires.

SPIDER-MAN AND HOWARD THE DUCK

Here's Howard

On quite a few occasions, Spider-Man has run into Howard the Duck, an abrasive and manipulative little creature who comes from an alternate dimension where ducks rule.

DAILY BUGLE

The Daily Bugle *is housed in an office building which was formerly called the Goodman Building.*

IN LETTERS 30 feet high, the *Daily Bugle* proudly displays its name with a lack of subtlety that can only be matched by the passion of its editorial page and the flamboyance of its publisher, J. Jonah Jameson. The paper itself is a picture-dominated tabloid that goes for the jugular. Its photos are often graphic and shocking, and its stories tend to be sensational and powerful. First published in 1897, this New York newspaper continues to produce several different editions each and every day. The offices of the *Daily Bugle* are currently located on the corner of 39th Street and 2nd Avenue in Manhattan. The building is 46 stories tall, and three of the floors are devoted to the editorial staff of the *Daily Bugle*. Two sub-basement levels house the paper's huge printing presses, and the rest of the building is rented to various other businesses.

PAPER TIGER
When the Bugle *came up for sale, Jonah scraped the money together to purchase the then-struggling paper.*

A lifelong career
Jonah started working for the *Daily Bugle* as a part-time copy boy while he was still in high school. A story he wrote about a soup kitchen riot convinced an editor to start using him as a reporter. He eventually became the paper's editor-in-chief.

No one knows what Jonah's first initial stands for. Rumor has it that it may be "John" or "Jack."

J. JONAH JAMESON

He may appear to be a grouchy, self-centered old skinflint on the outside, but peel away his protective layers and you will discover that the real J. Jonah Jameson is even worse! He can be as petty as he is selfish, and as vindictive as he is self-righteous. The man never tires of hearing his own voice, and he'll gladly give you the opinions he thinks you ought to have. Thanks to Jonah's nose for news, the *Daily Bugle* has become one of the city's most profitable newspapers. Aside from providing New Yorkers with juicy scandals and tantalizing gossip, Jameson has also used his newspaper to crusade for the civil rights of various minority groups, to champion the interests of working people, and to lash out against organized crime.

> OKAY, OKAY! YOU CAN **HAVE** YOUR **LITTLE SECRET**! IT DOESN'T MATTER **HOW** YOU GOT THEM! THE POINT IS, THESE PICTURES WILL MAKE THE NEXT ISSUE OF **NOW** A SELL-OUT! I'LL ISSUE A CHECK TO YOU **IMMEDIATELY!**

> AND REMEMBER, MR. JAMESON, I DON'T WANT MY NAME USED! YOU CAN MERELY GIVE CREDIT TO A **NOW** MAGAZINE STAFF PHOTOGRAPHER!

Peter Parker, freelance photographer
J. Jonah Jameson didn't hesitate to buy photos from the teenage Peter Parker, especially since Parker seemed to have a special talent for catching Spider-Man in action. Peter's first pictures appeared in *Now* Magazine, one of Jameson's other publications, but Jonah soon began to feature his work in the *Daily Bugle*. Despite Peter's consistent success in getting photos of Spider-Man, Jonah has never found out the young man's secret.

Ever since his wife died at the hands of a masked gunman, Jameson has hated all criminals and he distrusts anyone who wears a mask.

Jonah's lament

Jameson's first wife was killed by a masked gunman. Now he distrusts anyone who wears a mask, especially Spider-Man. But though he publicly denounces the wall-crawler, Jameson has come to realize that his own motives aren't as pure as he claims.

Jonah regularly uses the Bugle to vent his dislike of Spider-Man.

SPIDER-MAN REPRESENTS EVERYTHING THAT I'M **NOT**! HE'S BRAVE, POWERFUL AND UNSELFISH! THE TRUTH IS, I **ENVY** HIM! I, J. JONAH JAMESON--MILLIONAIRE, MAN OF THE WORLD, CIVIC LEADER--I'D GIVE EVERYTHING I OWN TO BE THE MAN THAT **HE** IS!

BUT I CAN **NEVER** CLIMB TO HIS LEVEL! SO ALL THAT REMAINS FOR ME IS-- TO TRY TO TEAR HIM DOWN-- BECAUSE, HEAVEN HELP ME-- I'M **JEALOUS** OF HIM!

IT WAS ALL A PLOT BY SPIDER-MAN TO STEAL THE SPOTLIGHT FROM MY SON! I ACCUSE SPIDER-MAN HIM-**SELF** OF SABOTAGING THE CAPSULE SO THAT THE GUIDANCE UNIT WOULD FALL OFF!

SPIDER-MAN UNLAWFULLY BROKE INTO A MILITARY BASE AND COMMAN-DEERED A PLANE BY FORCE!

THEN, BY MEANS OF A GRAND-STAND PLAY, HE TRIED TO MAKE A HERO OF HIMSELF, BUT HE CAUSED AN IMPORTANT MISSILE TEST TO FAIL AND SET OUR SPACE PROGRAM BACK BY MANY WEEKS! I REPEAT--SPIDER-MAN IS A **MENACE** TO AMERICA!

Stealing the spotlight

When Spider-Man first started crime fighting, Jameson believed that he was only trying to publicize his act as a TV entertainer. Jameson became even more outraged when Spider-Man "interfered" with a NASA mission that was being flown by the publisher's own son (*see page 69*). Spider-Man saved Jonah's son, but Jonah still denounced the act as a stunt.

ONLY A FREELANCER
Peter Parker spends so much time at the Daily Bugle's *offices that Jameson often threatens to charge him rent! Peter gets a special pleasure out of selling pictures to the* Daily Bugle, *and knowing that J. Jonah Jameson is actually paying Spider-Man.*

WHERE'S PARKER?!

OH! SHE'S WITH ANOTHER FELLA!!

HELLO, PETER! I... I'M GLAD TO SEE YOU!

I'D LIKE YOU TO MEET A FRIEND OF MINE!

Lance Bannon

A professional photographer who was very serious about his craft, Lance often competed with Peter for freelance assignments. Though the two photographers began as rivals, they eventually became friends. However, Lance's life was tragically cut short when he was murdered while covering a story.

LANCE BANNON

HEARTBREAK AHEAD
Betty Brant was one of Peter's first girlfriends. A few years older than Peter, she worked at the Daily Bugle *as Jameson's secretary. However, a rival for her affections appeared when Ned Leeds arrived on the scene. Betty began to date Ned, hoping to make Peter jealous, but his duties as Spider-Man kept him from pursuing Betty, and she ended up marrying Ned.*

Joe always tries to remain objective about Spider-Man, and he goes out of his way to help Parker.

Joe "Robbie" Robertson

Born in Harlem, Joe Robertson is a graduate of the Columbia School of Journalism. Jameson hired Robertson as the city editor on the *Daily Bugle*. In contrast to his boss, Joe is a soft-spoken man who is usually the voice of compassion and reason—he often functions as Jameson's conscience.

JOE "ROBBIE" ROBERTSON

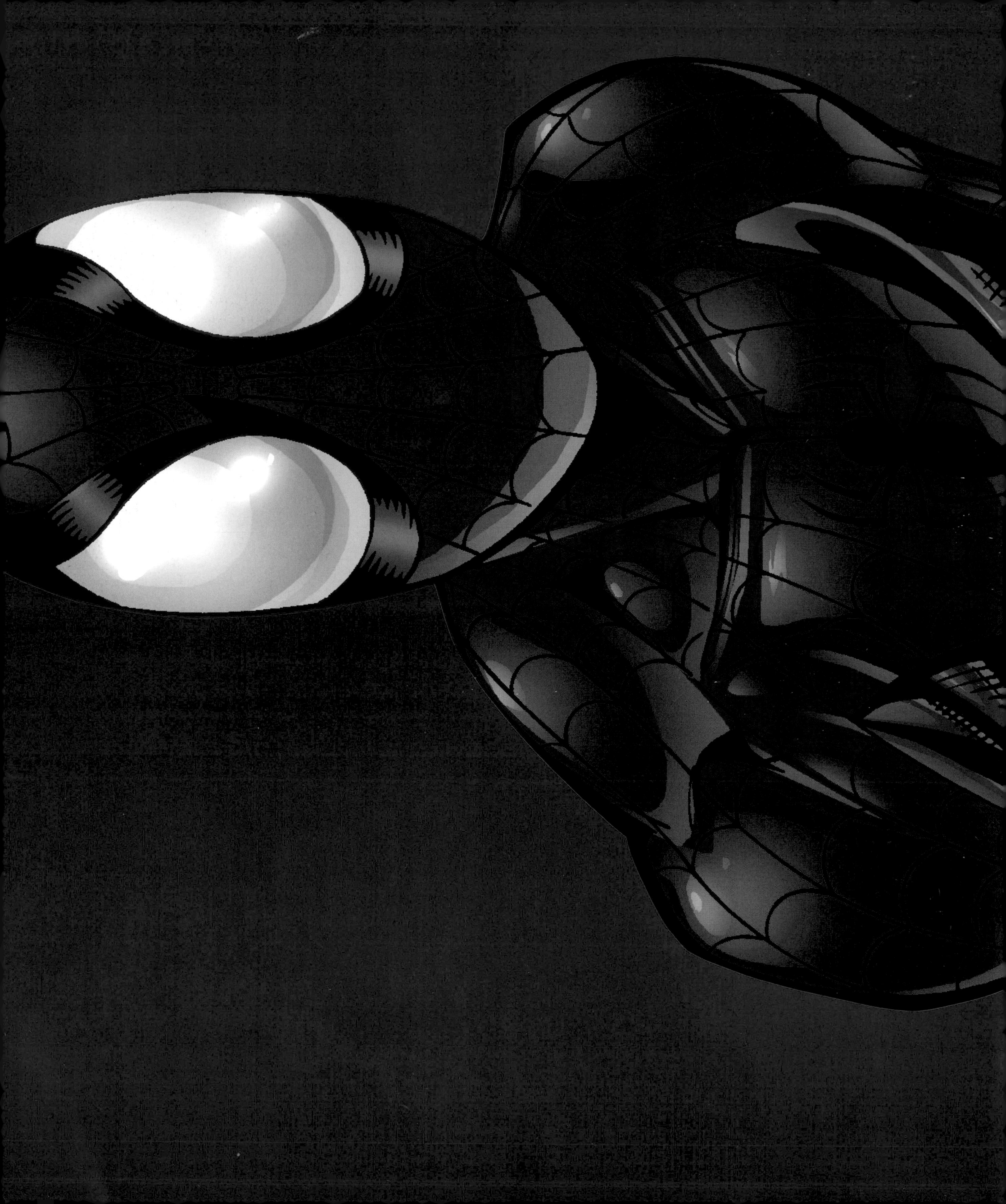

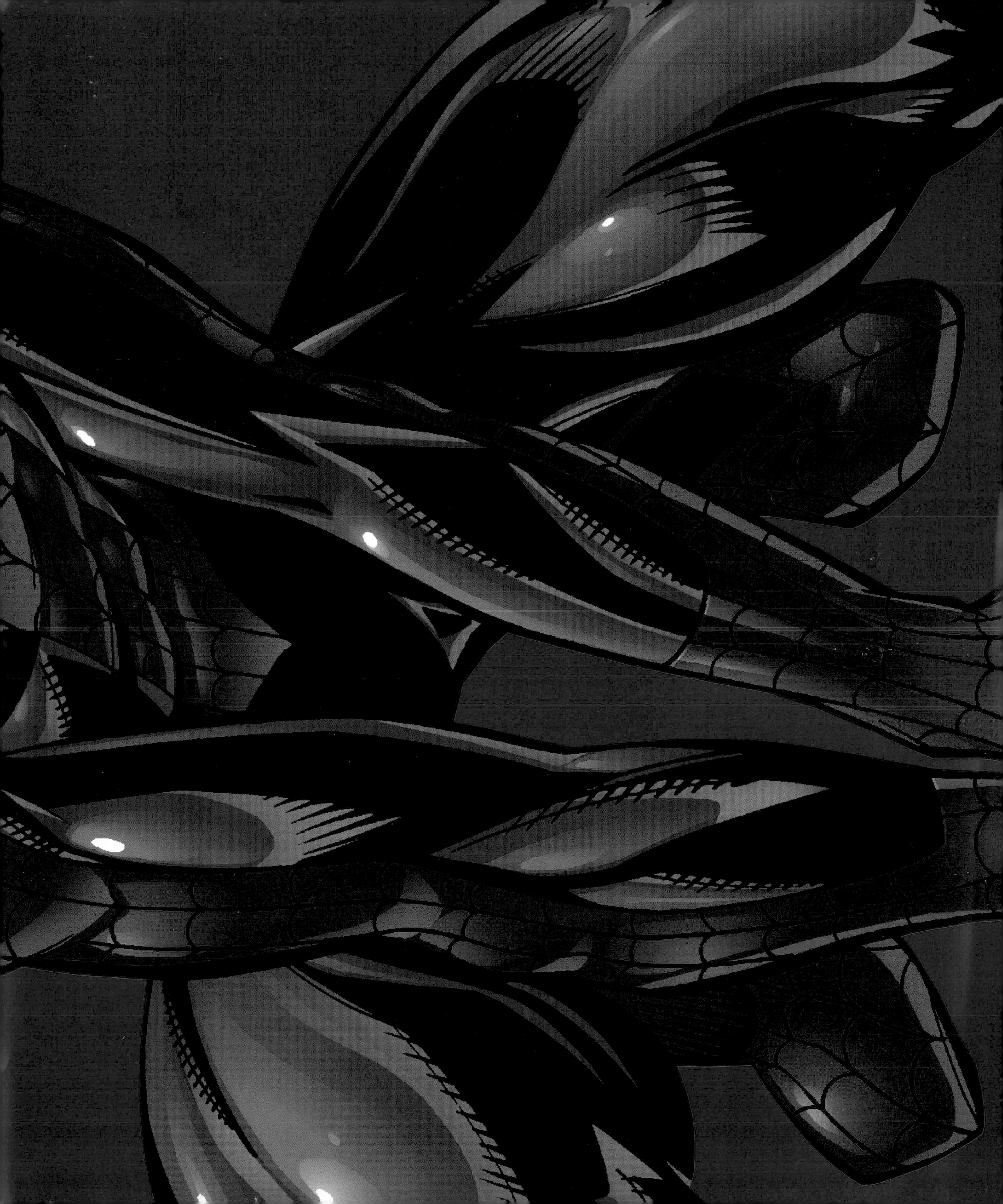

SPIDER-MAN IN THE '60S

SPIDER-MAN was created by writer/editor Stan Lee and artist/co-plotter Steve Ditko. According to comic book legend, Stan first discussed his ideas with artist/creator Jack "King" Kirby. Jack, who had already co-created the Fantastic Four with Stan, designed a character and may have even drawn the first few pages of a story. But Stan thought Jack's version looked too heroic and handsome, and so he turned to Steve Ditko. This collaboration between Stan and Steve produced the version of Peter Parker and Spider-Man that we all know and love today.

Over the course of 38 issues and two giant-sized annuals, Stan and Steve established the tone and laid the foundation for our friendly

Amazing Spider-Man #39 (August 1966)
Norman Osborn is revealed to be the Green Goblin
(Cover art by John Romita)

neighborhood web-slinger. They created enduring characters like Aunt May, J. Jonah Jameson, Flash Thompson, Doctor Octopus, Mysterio, and the Green Goblin. Aside from drawing the stories, Steve's hand can be seen in the intricate plots, the *film noir* settings, and the intriguing villains that popped into the series. The characterization and dialogue, however, are pure Stan, who has been said to share certain personality traits with Peter Parker, Aunt May, and even J. Jonah Jameson.

After Ditko left the series, the art and co-plotting were turned over to another legendary illustrator. John Romita is one of the most respected draftsmen and storytellers in the comic book industry. His artwork brought a new elegance to the series, and his plots were more straightforward. With his help, characters such as Mary Jane Watson, the Kingpin, and the Prowler were introduced.

Amazing Fantasy #15 (August 1963)
First appearance of Spider-Man
(Cover art by Jack Kirby and Steve Ditko)

THE SIXTIES

1963

Amazing Spider-Man
#1 (March 1963)
First appearance of JJJ

1964

Amazing Spider-Man
#14 (July 1964)
*Green Goblin
first appears*

1965

Amazing Spider-Man
#28 (Sept. 1965)
Peter leaves high school

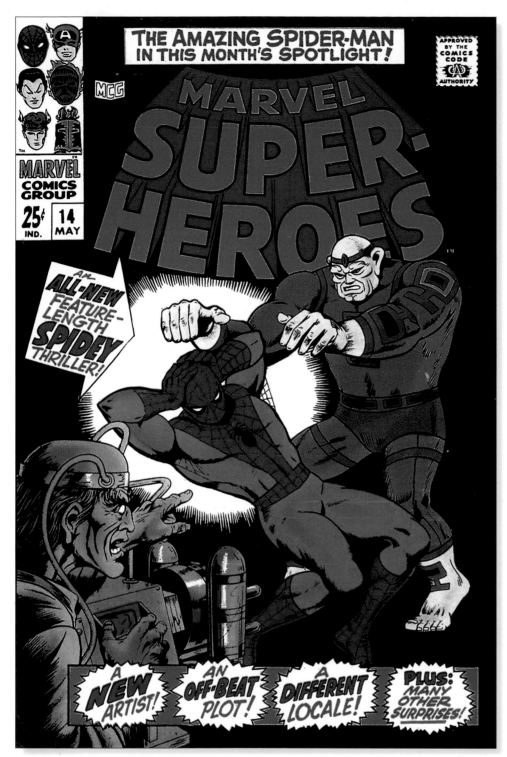

Amazing Spider-Man Annual #3 (Nov. 1966)
Spider-Man fights the incredible Hulk
(Cover art by John Romita and Mike Esposito)

Marvel Super-Heroes #14 (May 1968)
First time Spider-Man featured in another comic
(Cover art by Ross Andru and Bill Everett)

1967

Amazing Spider-Man
#50 (July 1967)
Kingpin' appears

1968

Amazing Spider-Man Annual
#5 (Nov. 1968)
First appearance of Peter's parents

1969

Amazing Spider-Man
#78 (Nov. 1969)
The Prowler appears

THE CHAMELEON

THE CHAMELEON has worn thousands of different faces and assumed countless false identities. He speaks dozens of languages, each with the pronunciation and subtlety of a native. He is a master of disguise, a brilliant actor, and a genius at creating lifelike masks. Thanks to years of practice and his own innate talents, the Chameleon can mimic any individual after only a brief observation. He can alter the pitch of his voice, change the cadence of his words, and assume the stance and mannerisms of any person he chooses. His portrayals are so faithful that the Chameleon routinely fools even close friends and family of his target. A former international superspy, the Chameleon now specializes in industrial espionage and various criminal activities.

During his career, the Chameleon has impersonated businessmen, government officials, and crime lords for prolonged periods.

BORN WITHOUT NAME

The son of an exiled Russian aristocrat and a young servant girl, Dmitri Smerdyakov was never loved as a child. His father hated the sight of him, and his mother considered him an embarrassment. Only Sergei, his older half-brother, deigned grudgingly to acknowledge him. Obsessed with pleasing Sergei, Dmitri often put on little shows for him, acting out the various parts. Dmitri also began impersonating his classmates and neighbors, copying their physical idiosyncrasies with uncanny skill. He learned how to use makeup to modify his appearance and eventually began to create realistic facial masks and disguises.

MAN OF MANY TRICKS
As well as his masks, the Chameleon uses many gadgets to foil the forces of law and order, including smoke bombs.

Jonah in chains

After years of specializing in espionage, the Chameleon decided that it was time to turn toward more profitable endeavors. Attempting to displace the Kingpin (*see pages 70-71*), he formed an alliance with Hammerhead (*see page 80*) and they launched a street war against Wilson Fisk. The Chameleon also kidnapped and began to impersonate J. Jonah Jameson (*see pages 34-35*). He planned to use the power of the *Daily Bugle* to publicize Fisk's misdeeds and to force the authorities to mobilize against him. But when Peter's spider-sense began to tingle whenever Jonah was near, he suspected treachery. Spider-Man exposed the Chameleon and rescued the vitriolic publisher.

MASKS
The Chameleon's masks are made from a synthetic material that looks and feels like human skin.

BENEATH THE MASK
The Chameleon's base mask hides his true identity, and it is designed so that other masks can be attached quickly and securely. It also allows his upper masks to exhibit a full range of expressions.

To the highest bidder

The Chameleon now works as an industrial spy, stealing and selling commercial secrets to the highest bidder. When Spider-Man and the Chameleon first met, the former spy had just stolen secret plans and was planning to offer them to Communist countries for an immense profit. Recognizing that Spider-Man was desperate for money and would do anything, the Chameleon realized that the wall-crawler would make a perfect fall guy for the villain's crimes. Sending a message that only Spidey's special senses would detect, the Chameleon lured the unsuspecting Spidey into his trap.

SELF-LOATHING
Raised to hate the sight of his own face, the Chameleon rarely removes his base mask, preferring to keep it on, even in the company of his own half-brother!

First defeat

After luring Spider-Man into his trap, the Chameleon disguised himself as the web-spinner and tried to frame him for theft. But the wall-crawler managed to clear his name by capturing and exposing the Chameleon. Desperate for revenge, Dmitri called on the services of his half-brother Sergei Kravinov. Now known as Kraven the Hunter (*see pages 56-57*), Sergei joined Dmitri's war against Spider-Man.

STRAINED RELATIONS
Relations between Dmitri and his half-brother had never been close. Sergei had been angry about his father's relationship with a servant, which resulted in the birth of Dmitri. Nevertheless, the two criminals decided to form a team against Spider-Man.

Just between brothers

Though he secretly believed that Sergei was selfish and egotistical, the Chameleon had always wanted to be accepted and respected by his half-brother. Kraven may have possessed greater strength and prowess, but the Chameleon was constantly trying to prove that he was the deadlier brother. He and Sergei often competed for the honor of killing Spider-Man, and the Chameleon was obsessed with winning this contest.

The Chameleon tells his half-brother about his plans to defeat Spider-Man.

KRAVEN THE HUNTER

THE VULTURE

LIKE HIS NAMESAKE, the Vulture is a pitiless predator. This villain, whose real name is Adrian Toomes, preys upon the rich, the powerful, and the unwary. Using an electromagnetic harness of his own invention to fly, he strikes on swift and silent wings. He is a ferocious fighter who attacks without mercy, hunting to feed a ravenous appetite for wealth, power, and revenge.

The Vulture is a bitter man, with an insatiable hunger for vengeance.

BETRAYAL AND REVENGE

Adrian Toomes is an engineer and inventor who started an electronics firm with his best friend Gregory Bestman. With Bestman handling the administrative side of the business, Toomes concentrated solely on his inventions. He dreamed of building an electromagnetically powered body harness that could enable an individual to fly. But Bestman was secretly plotting against Toomes and stealing his share of the profits. Soon, Bestman gained total control of the company and fired the inventor. Yet Toomes continued to work on the harness. Once the device was complete he took his revenge by using it to terrorize his old partner and to steal from his former company. Toomes was intoxicated with the sense of power and freedom, and he decided to pursue a criminal career, calling himself the Vulture. As he gained confidence in his ability to fly, his crimes grew more daring, and he often issued challenges to the police to try and capture him.

PRECISION FLYING
The Vulture maneuvers his wings with practiced precision. He can fly through narrow openings such as doorways and windows, and can squeeze up enclosed stairwells or into cramped tunnels.

The Vulture's flying harness is hidden beneath his costume.

WINGS OF VENGEANCE
The Vulture was determined to get revenge on Gregory Bestman. Even when Spider-Man exposed Bestman as a crook, the Vulture wasn't satisfied. He eventually murdered his former partner.

NOT NOTICING THE POWERFUL FIGURE ON THE ROOF TOP, *THE VULTURE* SWEEPS PAST...

THEY'LL *NEVER* FIGURE OUT HOW I'M GOING TO STEAL THOSE DIAMONDS!

I'VE GOT EVERYONE COMPLETELY BAFFLED! NO ONE HAS YET DISCOVERED HOW I MANAGE TO *FLY* WITH THESE ARTIFICIAL WINGS!

WHAT LUCK!... IT'S *THE VULTURE!*

First blood

Peter Parker began his career as a freelance photographer after realizing that J. Jonah Jameson would pay big money for an exclusive photo of the Vulture. Peter borrowed Aunt May's camera and started prowling the rooftops as Spider-Man. Spidey managed to snap a few pictures of the Vulture, but was defeated in their first battle. So Peter Parker used his scientific background to make a device that took away the Vulture's ability to fly. Outraged by this public humiliation, the Vulture swore vengeance on Spider-Man.

HIGH AND FAST
The Vulture can fly at a top speed of nearly 93 mph. He can glide for long distances and can reach a maximum altitude of nearly 11,500 feet.

It's personal

Adrian Toomes once took refuge in a nursing home to hide from the police. Here he became good friends with Nathan Lubensky, a man who was dating May Parker at the time. Spider-Man forced Adrian to flee the home, only for him to return and unintentionally cause Nathan's death. Months later, Adrian began to stalk May Parker and eventually kidnapped her. But Spider-Man was surprised to discover that Adrian did not intend to hurt May. He only wanted to beg her forgiveness for accidentally killing Nathan.

FOUNTAIN OF YOUTH
The special harness that the Vulture wears somehow increases his physical strength and endurance. He can engage in acrobatic aerial battles for hours without tiring.

A man reborn!

At one point Toomes was convinced that he was dying from cancer. In an attempt to save his own life, he stole a device called the Juvenator, which was designed to transfer the life energy from one source to another. Choosing Spider-Man as his first victim, the Vulture drained the wall-crawler's vitality, charging himself with Spider-Man's energy. Luckily, the effects were only temporary. Spider-Man regained his strength and defeated Toomes. Even so, the Vulture appears to be stronger than before and his cancer has gone into remission.

MAN, THIS IS THE GREATEST! BLACKIE DRAGO IS GONNA MAKE THE *OLD* VULTURE LOOK LIKE A TWO-BIT *PIKER!*

IT'S GETTIN' SO THAT I CAN DO WHATEVER I *WANT* TO... WITHOUT EVEN *THINKIN'* ABOUT IT!

BLACKIE DRAGO

Blackie Drago was a career criminal who once shared a prison cell with Adrian Toomes. Pretending to befriend Toomes, Drago secretly betrayed him, just as Toomes' former partner had once done. Drago arranged an accident in the prison machine shop in which Toomes suffered severe injuries. Afraid that he would die before he could get his revenge on Spider-Man, Toomes told Drago where he had hidden his Vulture costume and flying harness. Drago escaped from prison, found the outfit and harness, and became the new Vulture. But he wasn't as skilled as the original, and was soon defeated by Spider-Man. Meanwhile, Toomes managed to recover from his wounds. Challenging Drago to battle, Toomes proved that he was the true Vulture.

DOUBLE TROUBLE
As if one Vulture weren't enough, Spider-Man was forced to battle two of them!

DOCTOR OCTOPUS

THIS CONTRAPTION, AS YOU CALL IT, ENABLES ME TO WORK *SAFELY* WITH CHEMICALS WHICH ARE FAR TOO *DANGEROUS* TO TOUCH WITHOUT PROTECTION!

AS A YOUNG BOY, Otto Octavius was a shy and sensitive bookworm. A hardworking student, he didn't seem the type to grow up to become one of the world's most dangerous men. Otto's mother, Mary Lavinia Octavius, had high hopes for her son and didn't want Otto to become a manual laborer like his father. To please her, Otto decided to become a scientist, specializing in the field of nuclear research. His mother was thrilled when Otto graduated from college, since it meant that he would never have to dirty his hands like a common workingman. Otto Octavius threw himself into his career, often working 24 hours a day. He eventually became one of the nation's leading scientists.

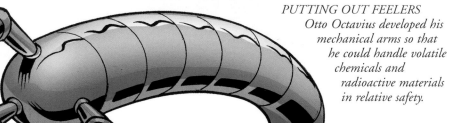

PUTTING OUT FEELERS
Otto Octavius developed his mechanical arms so that he could handle volatile chemicals and radioactive materials in relative safety.

Each pincer can grip with enough force to crush a block of concrete!

ARMS AND THE MAN

As his fame grew, Otto became arrogant, condescending, and self-absorbed. He invented a special mechanical harness that allowed him to perform dangerous experiments at a distance and also discouraged his coworkers from getting too close. However, during a freak laboratory accident, Otto Octavius was somehow physically and mentally bonded with his mechanical arms—he had been turned into Doctor Octopus. Since then, he has fought super heroes such as Daredevil and the Fantastic Four. But Doctor Octopus is particularly obsessed with destroying Spider-Man and believes that he will never know peace until he kills the web-slinger.

His tentacles are about six feet long, but can extend to 25 feet.

OTTO IS TOO *SENSITIVE*, TOO *REFINED* TO USE HIS FISTS! HE'S A *THINKER*! THINKERS USE THEIR *BRAINS*... NOT THEIR *HANDS*!

BUT, *MA!* THE KID'S *WIMP*!

MOTHER WAS *RIGHT!* I NEVER SHOULD HAVE MARRIED A *COMMON WORKMAN!*

Oh, mama!
Throughout his childhood, Otto was sheltered and pampered by his mother. However, his father, Torbert Octavius, was frustrated by the boy's inability to stand up for himself.

Driven to distraction

During an argument with her son, Mary Lavinia Octavius died of a heart attack. Otto was racked with guilt and stumbled through the following weeks as if in a daze. It was in this distracted state that he caused an accident at the Atomic Research Center where he worked. Caught in the resulting explosion, his body was exposed to radiation, which transformed him into Doctor Octopus.

MENTAL CONTROL
After his accident, Doctor Octopus was misdiagnosed with brain damage. In reality, his brain was creating new neuro-pathways so that he could mentally control his metal arms.

My enemy, my stepuncle

While hiding out from the police, Otto rented a room from May Parker, who never realized that he was an escaped criminal. He was forced to leave, however, after a battle with Spider-Man. Later, Otto learned that May was due to receive a large inheritance, namely one of the world's most sophisticated nuclear breeding reactors. With this, Otto could produce his own nuclear arsenal! In order to get his hands on the reactor, Octopus asked May to marry him.

MAN AND MACHINE
So strong is the bond with his tentacles that Doctor Octopus can control them even when they have been separated from his body.

Spider-man arrived just in time to disrupt the wedding between Aunt May and Doctor Octopus.

The female Ock

Carolyn Trainer is a brilliant scientist who specializes in the study of virtual reality. She is also a big fan of Otto Octavius and was outraged when Doctor Octopus was first jailed like a common criminal. For a brief time, she even filled in for him when he was incapacitated, adapting his tentacles for her own use. Carolyn voluntarily returned the tentacles as soon as the real Doc Ock was ready to renew his criminal career.

Kid Ock

Ollie Osnick also admired Doc Ock. He built his own set of mechanical arms and tried to team up with his hero against Spider-Man. But when he was nearly killed by Doctor Octopus, Ollie modified his tentacles and began to imitate Spider-Man instead.

> "STILL, I WONDER WHAT I WOULD HAVE DONE IF I HAD KNOWN THAT THEY WERE GOING TO TEST AN EXPERIMENTAL NUCLEAR DEVICE THAT MORNING—"
>
> "—IF I HAD KNOWN THAT MY BODY WOULD BE BOMBARDED BY THE SEARING RAYS OF SOME CRAZY MUTANT RADIATION..."

Not such sweet dreams

Unwittingly caught by the force of a nuclear test blast at the military base, Marko was exposed to high levels of radiation. After the explosion, he discovered that the molecules in his body had somehow become inextricably bonded with the radioactive sand. Baker discovered that his body had taken on the properties of sand—he had become the Sandman!

> MY HAND! IT'S DISSOLVING INTO A PUDDLE OF SAND!?

> "IT DIDN'T TAKE ME LONG TO REALIZE THE TRUTH — THAT THE MOLECULES OF MY BODY HAD FUSED WITH THE RADIO-ACTIVE SAND!"
>
> "I HAD BECOME ...A LIVING SANDMAN!"

THE SANDMAN

POSSESSING THE ability to convert all or part of his body into sand, the Sandman can mold himself into any continuous shape he desires. He can slither across the ground like a huge sand-snake or take on the form of an army tank. The Sandman's mental control over his body is so precise that he can even assume multiple configurations at the same time. His fists can become hammers while his head transforms itself into a rock-hard battering ram. He can disguise himself as a simple mound of sand or slip beneath a door frame as a moving sand stream. He can also fire his sand particles at high speed so that they strike like a shower of hailstones. The Sandman is actually a career criminal whose real name is William Baker.

FLINT MARKO

Baker learned to steal almost before he could walk. He cheated his way through school, and things didn't come together for him until he reached high school and discovered football. He played with brutal intensity and excelled at the sport. However, when Baker started taking money from local gamblers to throw important games his coach realized that he was cheating, and Baker was thrown off the team and expelled from school. He found steady work with a local mobster, but since he didn't want his mother to learn about his criminal activities, he called himself Flint Marko. Marko was eventually arrested and imprisoned, but he somehow managed to escape. Hunted by the police, he headed south, where he discovered a seemingly deserted military testing site and figured he could hide there. However, Marko didn't realize that the site had been deliberately abandoned so that the military could test a new nuclear weapon.

There's no limit to how far the Sandman can stretch himself... as long as his sand particles remain in contact with each other.

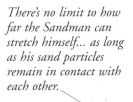

As the first super hero the Sandman ever battled, Spider-Man has a special place in his heart.

BUT *I* CAN HURT *YOU,* PAL! ALL I DO IS *HARDEN* ANY PART OF ME THAT I WANT TO...LIKE *THIS!*

UGH! YOUR JAW IS LIKE *IRON!*

THINK I'M *KIDDIN',* HUH? OKAY, LET'S SEE YOU HOLD ONTO ME *NOW!!*

HE..HE'S SLIPPING THROUGH MY FINGERS...JUST LIKE SOFT SAND!

SEE WHY I'M CALLED THE *SANDMAN?!!*

WELL, I *AIN'T* IMPRESSED-- --AN' I GOT A TRICK OF MY *OWN!*

A Sandman of many talents

Thinking that Baker was just an ordinary criminal, Spider-Man was greatly surprised by the stunts the Sandman could pull when the two first met. Slipping easily out of Spidey's grasp, he turned his jaw rock-hard to deflect the wall-crawler's punch and was able to pin Spider-Man to the floor under a torrent of sand. But Spidey had the last laugh. He tricked the Sandman into dispersing himself and then sucked up the grains of sand in an industrial vacuum cleaner.

Here's mud in your eye

During a battle with Hydro-Man (*see page 106*), Sandman somehow became merged with his watery counterpart to form a giant mudlike monster. Spider-Man defeated this mud monster, and the two criminals were thought to be dead, until the mud separated months later. The Sandman was so traumatized by the experience that he gave up his life of crime.

MIND OVER SAND
The Sandman has always managed to reassemble himself, even when parts of him have been scattered. He can draw up regular sand to make himself bigger, or to replace sand that has been lost in battle. The Sandman's mind continues to be in control of his body at all times, even when his head has been turned into sand or scattered by an enemy's fist.

The Sandman can attack an enemy in many different ways.

Fond farewell?

After turning his back on crime, the Sandman took a job with Silver Sable (*see page 110*) and worked alongside Spider-Man as a team! Then, when the Sandman was poisoned by a bite from Venom (*see pages 120-121*), he blamed Spider-Man for what happened and turned on the wall-crawler. But as his body fell apart, the Sandman repented and gave Spider-Man a final message to deliver to his mother.

THE LIZARD

DOCTOR CONNORS was a peaceful man who loved his family. He lost his arm while serving as an army surgeon during a war, and, as a result, he gave up surgery and started to study reptiles. Realizing that some reptiles can grow a replacement if they lose a leg or any other appendage, Connors was determined to learn their secret and apply it to humans. After years of painstaking research, Connors believed that he had finally isolated the chemical mechanism that gives reptiles the power to regenerate missing limbs. Ignoring his wife's desperate pleas, Connors used himself as a guinea pig and drank his experimental serum.

Connors believed that he had developed a serum that could grow back missing limbs, and he tested the drug on himself.

Best intentions
The doctor's missing arm grew back within minutes of his drinking the serum, and, for a brief time, Doctor Connors thought that he had revolutionized modern medicine. But then reptilian green scales started to spread over his body, and he sprouted a lizardlike tail. Like a latter-day Jekyll and Hyde, Curtis Connors became the Lizard.

MAN INTO MONSTER

This ill-conceived step turned the mild-mannered doctor into the bloodthirsty villain of the Florida Everglades—the Lizard. Even in his reptilian guise Connors walks like a man, but he is now a ruthless beast who possesses incredible strength and inhuman powers. As the Lizard, he has only one desire—to cleanse the world of mammals. Every warm-blooded animal, including humans, must be destroyed so that reptiles can resume their place as the planet's rulers.

The Lizard's claws can slash through concrete.

The Lizard's tail is six feet long and possesses immense physical strength.

WIFE AND CHILD Desperate for his family to share in his new-found power, the Lizard has tried to transform his wife and child, Martha and Billy Connors, into reptiles!

An army of reptiles!
The Lizard can telepathically control any reptile within a one mile radius. Alligators, lizards, and snakes heed his call and obey his simple commands. On many occasions, he has ordered these creatures to stand guard for him or to attack his enemies.

An antidote!
Employing his scientific expertise, Peter Parker was able to find an antidote for Connors' serum. But the cure proved to be temporary, and Doctor Connors eventually reverted back to the green, scaly super-villain. It required another dose of the antidote to make him human again.

AND THEN, BEFORE THE STARTLED EYES OF SPIDER-MAN... IN THE ANCIENT, CRUMBLING, HALF-HIDDEN FORTRESS, A FANTASTIC CHANGE TAKES PLACE...

I-I'M *HUMAN* AGAIN!

A MINDLESS MONSTER
The longer Connors remains the Lizard, the more his abilities to talk and think gradually slip away, and his hunger for violence and destruction grows.

QUICK ON HIS FEET
The Lizard's quick reflexes make him almost as fast as Spider-Man. He can whip his enormous tail at speeds of up to 70 mph, and his top running speed is close to 45 mph.

REPTILE POWER
The Lizard is incredibly strong and he can lift approximately 12 tons. His leg muscles are so powerful that he can leap nearly 12 feet high and cover an average distance of 18 feet with each bound. Thanks to his ability to regenerate, he can fight without fear of fatigue, knowing that his stamina gives him the ability to wear down almost any opponent.

I HAVE ONLY *ONE* PURPOSE... ONLY *ONE* PLAN...

ONLY ONE *DESIRE* THAT WILL NEVER *DIE!*

I MUST CRUSH SPIDER-MAN!

Wall-crawler
The Lizard's hands and feet are covered with scores of tiny claws that create adhesive pads, like those of a gecko. They enable him to scale sheer surfaces.

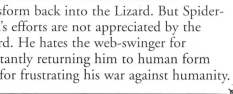

My friend, my enemy
Over the years, Spider-Man has come to rely on Doctor Connors for scientific help. The two have become friends, even though extreme stress can cause Connors to transform back into the Lizard. But Spider-Man's efforts are not appreciated by the Lizard. He hates the web-swinger for constantly returning him to human form and for frustrating his war against humanity.

ELECTRO

"BUT I DIDN'T CARE WHAT ANYBODY THOUGHT OF ME--AND THEN, IT HAPPENED! A MILLION TO ONE CHANCE! I WAS WORKING ALONE ON A POLE, WHEN LIGHTNING STRUCK!"

Max was turned into Electro when a bolt of lightning struck him.

A HUMAN dynamo who controls one of the earth's greatest forms of energy, Max Dillon, a.k.a. Electro, is the master of electricity. His body is a living generator that instinctively knows when to recharge itself. It can produce almost 1,000 volts of electricity per minute, up to a maximum capacity of 100,000 volts. Once Electro reaches his limit, he stops generating energy until he needs more. But though he wears a flashy costume and wields a power that should make him virtually invincible, Electro has always had a bit of an inferiority complex.

MAX DILLON

Max's family was constantly on the move because his father had trouble keeping a steady job. Jonathan Dillon was an accountant who was cursed with an explosive temper. He blamed his wife and child for his own failings, and he deserted them before Max was nine years old. Once her husband moved out, Anita Dillon focused all her attention on young Max. She told him that he was all she had left, and she became obsessed with keeping him safe from disappointment. When Max informed her that he wanted to be an electrical engineer, she convinced him that he didn't have the intelligence for such a career. In the end, he settled for a job as a lineman with the electric company. One day, Max was struck by lightning while holding a pair of damaged electric lines. The accident somehow turned him into Electro. Buoyed by his new powers, Max decided to take the first real risk of his life. He would try to make his fortune the old-fashioned way—by assuming a costumed identity and stealing it.

"I SHOULD HAVE BEEN KILLED INSTANTLY, BUT BY A FANTASTIC FREAK OF FATE -- DUE TO THE WAY I HAD BEEN GRASPING THE ELECTRIC WIRES -- THE TWO BOLTS OF CURRENT CANCELLED EACH OTHER, AND..."

"I-I'M STILL ALIVE!"

"IN FACT, I FEEL BETTER -- STRONGER -- THAN EVER!"

Max couldn't believe that he survived the lightning bolt.

"I'M NO FOOL! I INSTANTLY REALIZED THE ACCIDENT HAD CHARGED MY BODY WITH ELECTRICITY! I RACED HOME AND BEGAN TO EXPERIMENT-- TO SEE HOW POWERFUL I REALLY WAS..."

"IT'S UNBELIEVABLE! MY BODY KEEPS RECHARGING ITSELF! I'M LIKE A LIVING ELECTRICAL GENERATOR!!"

Electro's electrical discharges travel at the speed of lightning, approximately 1,000 feet per second.

Since the electricity coursing through his body augments his strength, Electro is able to lift over 450 pounds.

Transformation

Raised by an overprotective mother, Max Dillon gained new confidence as well as power on the day a fluke lightning bolt transformed him into Electro. He immediately began to experiment with his new abilities and soon learned that he could discharge blasts of electricity which could be used as weapons.

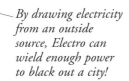

By drawing electricity from an outside source, Electro can wield enough power to black out a city!

Keeping off his toes

The best way to defeat Electro is to stay in the air. His electrostatic blasts can only injure you if you're grounded or if you're in contact with metal.

The maximum effective range of Electro's blasts is approximately 100 feet.

IT'S ALL A MATTER OF CONTROL
Electro can consciously control the amount of electricity he discharges, unleashing anything from a single volt to his full 100,000-volt reserve. On rare occasions, he has become a transformer, drawing power from an outside source and channeling it through his body.

Charging up

Electro can employ his energy in many different ways. He can discharge electricity from his fingertips in the form of lightninglike bolts of energy, or he can send an electrical jolt traveling along the ground or a conductive metal. He is also capable of generating a highly charged electrical field to shield himself from harm. By creating and riding upon a wave of electrical energy, Electro can even propel himself through the air.

YOU WERE LUCKY, THAT'S ALL—YOUR ACCURSED SPIDER-LUCK!

GEE, I WASN'T EVEN AWARE OF *THAT* POWER!

LAUGH ALL YOU WANT, WALL-CRAWLER! I'VE BEEN ADDING TO *MY* POWER ALL NIGHT LONG!

SEARING BOLTS OF LIGHTNING STRIKE SPIDER-MAN...

Down the drain

Electro once tried to drain all the electrical power out of Manhattan. He attached himself to a special device and began to black out the entire city. The strain ultimately proved too much for him, and he would have died if Spider-Man hadn't disconnected him in time. The massive power surge somehow caused Electro's body to temporarily lose its ability to generate electricity.

However, he finally regained his power by strapping himself into an electric chair and giving himself a near-lethal jolt.

A SHOCKING SURPRISE
When Electro is fully charged, a person can be electrocuted just by touching him—Spider-Man learned this rather painful lesson during their first meeting.

MYSTERIO

QUENTIN BECK dreamed of making movies ever since he was a child. Armed with a battered old movie camera, Quentin built monsters out of clay, starring them in little stop-action films that each lasted a couple of minutes. While still a teenager, Quentin got a job on a low-budget monster thriller. He moved to Hollywood on the money he made and started to look for work as a stuntman and a special effects designer. Though his career proved fairly successful, Quentin wanted more. He grew tired of working behind the scenes, and sought the spotlight as an actor and director. But he didn't have the looks or talent to make it as a star, and he was much too temperamental to be at the helm of a production crew. A casual comment by a friend made him realize that he could attain a different kind of fame by using his talent with special effects to become a super hero. And so Mysterio was born!

Disguising himself as a world-renowned psychiatrist, Mysterio used a specially built room to convince Spider-Man that the wall-crawler was having a nervous breakdown.

TARGET: SPIDER-MAN

Since the *Daily Bugle* had declared Spider-Man a menace, Mysterio knew that the paper would give him lots of publicity if he could capture Spidey. There was only one problem— Spider-Man hadn't broken the law. So Mysterio disguised himself as the wall-crawler and convinced the public that Spidey was on a crime spree. Mysterio then challenged the web-head to meet him, and the two fought to a draw. But the web-slinger suspected that Mysterio was behind the crime spree, so he followed and defeated him. With his dreams of being a super hero ruined by Spider-Man, Mysterio now uses his skills to gain revenge against the wall-crawler.

DON'T LOSE YOUR HEAD
Seeing is never believing when fighting a man who is an expert at creating visual hoaxes. He has even faked his own death on more than one occasion.

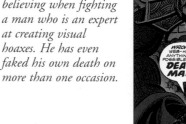

Mysterio's helmet contains a half-hour's supply of air.

"MY HELMET IS BASED ON THE PRINCIPLE OF YOUR EYE PIECES! I CAN SEE *OUT*, BUT NO ONE CAN SEE *IN*!"

"I CREATED A FINE SPRAY MADE OF SPECIALLY TREATED ACID WHICH WAS FOR THE SOLE PURPOSE OF DISSOLVING YOUR WEB IF YOU SHOULD EVER USE IT AGAINST ME!"

"THE BOTTOMS OF MY BOOTS CONTAIN CHEMICAL SMOKE EJECTORS AS WELL AS MAGNETIC PLATE SPRINGS WHICH ENABLE ME TO DUPLICATE YOUR OWN AMAZING LEAPS!"

Mysterio isn't your average criminal. He is a special effects artist who loves his craft and takes it seriously. His costume is testament to that, and it is full of gadgets to help him on his crime sprees. These include a helmet made from two-way glass to disguise his appearance. He also wears special boots that release his chemical smoke, with springs in the heels which enable him to make huge leaps.

Smoke and mirrors

Mysterio's trademark is a trail of smoke, released through nozzles hidden within his gloves and boots. Aside from making him appear more mysterious, it can also be mixed with various toxins, acids, and hallucinogens to disorient, distract, or defeat his opponents. He can even mix in his own powerful chemicals which can dissolve Spidey's webbing!

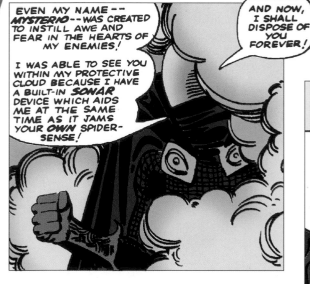

EVEN MY NAME -- *MYSTERIO* -- WAS CREATED TO INSTILL AWE AND FEAR IN THE HEARTS OF MY ENEMIES!

I WAS ABLE TO SEE YOU WITHIN MY PROTECTIVE CLOUD BECAUSE I HAVE A BUILT-IN *SONAR* DEVICE WHICH AIDS ME AT THE SAME TIME AS IT JAMS YOUR *OWN* SPIDER-SENSE!

AND NOW, I SHALL DISPOSE OF YOU FOREVER!

SEEING IN THE DARK
Mysterio doesn't need superpowers—he's got gadgets for everything. He's even got his own form of spider-sense, courtesy of a sonar device which helps him to "see" through his own smoky cloud.

THEN, YIELDING TO A SUDDEN IMPULSE, SPIDER-MAN GRASPS THE "PSYCHIATRIST'S" HAIR, AND GIVES IT A SHARP YANK, REVEALING ...

HOW COULD I HAVE BEEN SO ASLEEP AT THE SWITCH ?? WHY DIDN'T I GUESS SOONER?

IT'S MY OLD ENEMY, *MYSTERIO!* MYSTERIO, THE MASTER OF MYSTIC EFFECTS AND STARTLING ILLUSIONS!

The face of a villain

Lacking the handsome features of a conventional movie star, Mysterio has assumed a number of other identities during the course of his career. He is a master of makeup and disguise who has pretended to be an alien, a psychiatrist, a movie producer, and the director of a nursing home.

THE GREEN GOBLIN

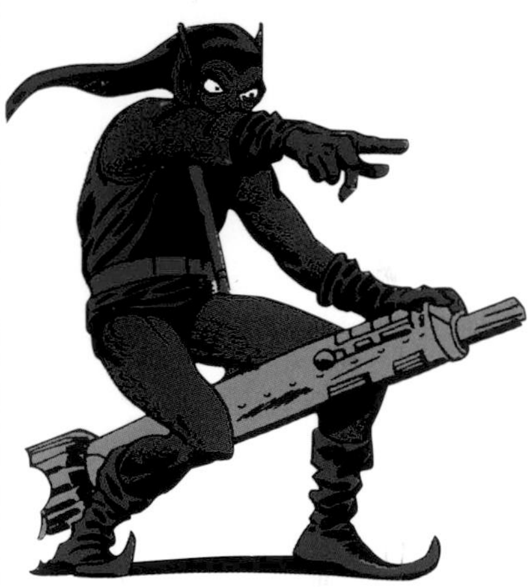

Despite his ridiculous appearance, the Green Goblin became Spider-Man's greatest enemy.

NORMAN OSBORN was just a child when he first became obsessed with acquiring wealth and power. His father was an inventor whose business failed. Claiming that he had been swindled out of his inventions and personal fortune, Amberson Osborn took out his rage on his young son. Norman realized that he couldn't depend on his father for financial security, so he began working after school and saving every cent that he earned. He wouldn't allow himself to become another failure like his father. Norman studied chemistry and electrical engineering in college. He also took a number of courses in business administration. One of his teachers was Professor Mendel Stromm. They became good friends and later formed a business partnership. Since Norman put up the bulk of the financing, they called their company Osborn Chemical.

Trouble in the Laboratory

Norman married his college sweetheart and they had a son, Harry, a few years later. Unfortunately, his wife became ill. After she died, Norman buried himself in his work and rarely had time for young Harry. Norman eventually learned that Stromm had embezzled money from their company. He had his partner arrested and assumed complete control of the company. While going through Stromm's notes, Norman learned of a chemical formula that could increase a person's strength and intelligence. Unaware that Harry had switched a few of his chemicals, Norman tried to recreate the experiment. The solution turned green and exploded.

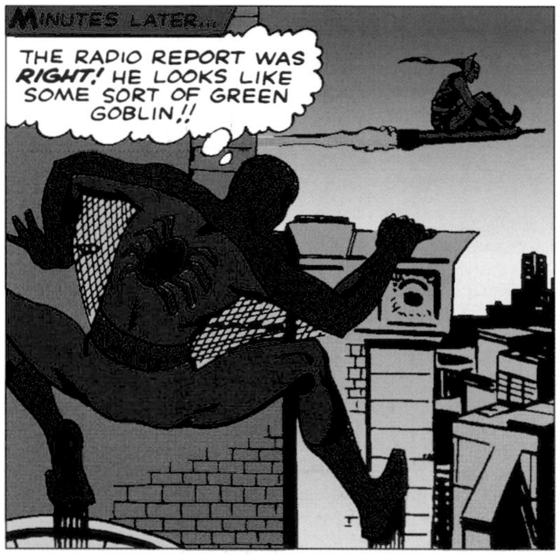
MINUTES LATER...
THE RADIO REPORT WAS RIGHT! HE LOOKS LIKE SOME SORT OF GREEN GOBLIN!!

FLYING BROOMSTICK
The Green Goblin originally traveled on a flying broomstick, which he later discarded in favor of a Goblin Glider.

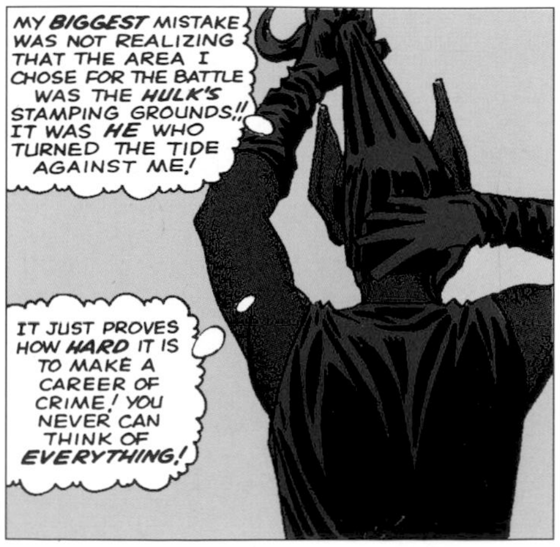
MY BIGGEST MISTAKE WAS NOT REALIZING THAT THE AREA I CHOSE FOR THE BATTLE WAS THE HULK'S STAMPING GROUNDS!! IT WAS HE WHO TURNED THE TIDE AGAINST ME!
IT JUST PROVES HOW HARD IT IS TO MAKE A CAREER OF CRIME! YOU NEVER CAN THINK OF EVERYTHING!

Birth of the Goblin

After he was released from the hospital following the explosion, Norman realized that the formula had worked. He was now stronger and smarter than ever. He didn't know that the explosion had also driven him insane. He decided to increase his personal fortune by turning to crime. He hired and outfitted costumed super-villains like the Scorcher and the Headsman. When these thieves were captured by Spider-Man, Norman decided to take matters into his own hands. He used his company's chemical discoveries to assemble a personal armory and designed a costume for himself. All he needed was the right face to present to the world—he chose the face of the Green Goblin.

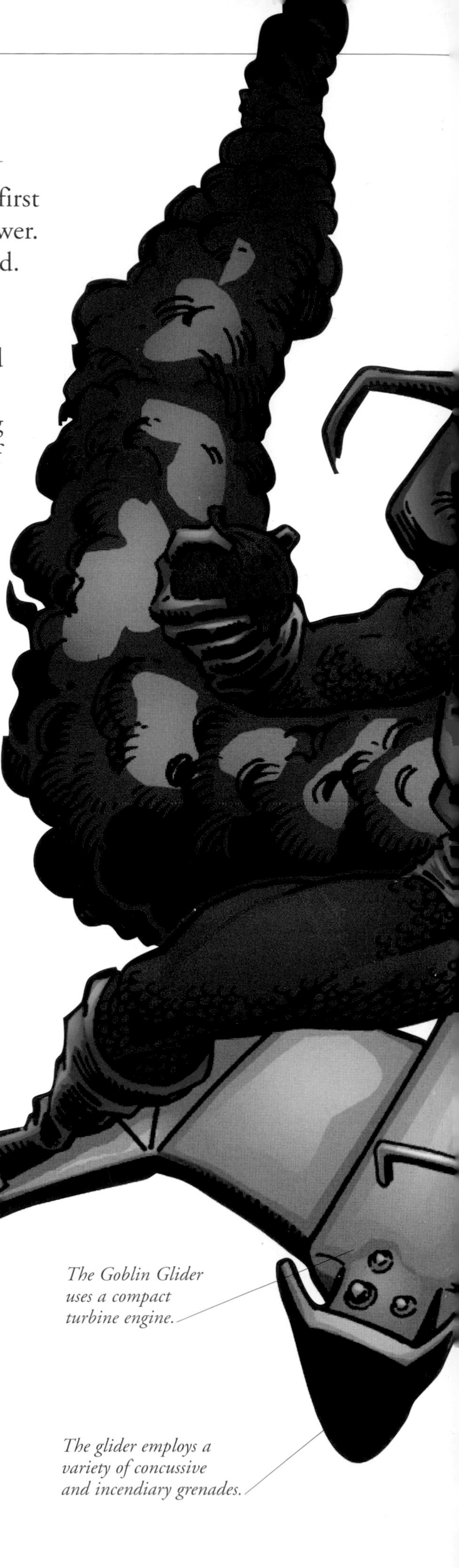
The Goblin Glider uses a compact turbine engine.
The glider employs a variety of concussive and incendiary grenades.

"YOU MUST BE *NUTS,* GOBLIN! I AINT LETTIN' *YOU,* OR ANYONE *ELSE* TAKE OVER MY GANG! NOW HIT THE ROAD, MISTER, WHILE YOU STILL *CAN!*"

"DIG THAT CORNY COSTUME, WILLYA?"

"BUT, UNDER *MY* LEADERSHIP, WE COULD TAKE OVER EVERY RACKET IN THE CITY!"

"HERE, *THIS* WILL STOP YOU FROM-- *BLAST IT!!* IF ONLY YOU'D STAY *STILL* LONG ENOUGH FOR ONE OF MY LITTLE *TRINKETS* TO *HIT* YOU!"

"I DON'T KNOW YOUR REAL IDENTITY, GOBBY, BUT I KNOW *ONE* THING--"

"--YOU SURE *AREN'T* AN EX-BIG-LEAGUE *BASEBALL PITCHER!*"

EQUALS
Although Spider-Man was stronger and faster, the Green Goblin's deadly arsenal and his ruthless cunning made him more than a match for the wisecracking wall-crawler.

From empire to obsession

The Green Goblin planned to become the most powerful ganglord of all by uniting all the independent gangs under his leadership. He wanted to establish a reputation by killing Spider-Man. But every time the Goblin ambushed him, Spidey drove him away. With each new defeat, the Green Goblin became more determined. In time, Osborn became totally obsessed with Spidey and directed all his efforts to finding a way to conquer his web-swinging enemy.

"TAKE A *LOOK,* PARKER-- A *GOOD, LONG* LOOK-- IT'S THE LAST FACE *SPIDER-MAN* WILL EVER SEE--"

"IT'S THE *REAL* FACE OF THE GREEN GOBLIN-- THE FACE OF *NORMAN OSBORN!*"

WHA OOM!

PRIORITIES
Since Norman Osborn seemed more interested in chemicals than in his son's welfare, Harry decided to teach his father a lesson by causing an explosive experiment.

His weapons are held in a "bag of tricks."

"THE GREAT *SPIDER-MAN*-- NOTHING MORE THAN A *CALLOW* YOUTH-- A PATHETIC *STRIPLING!*"

New lease on life

The Green Goblin learned Spider-Man's secret identity by exposing him to a gas that weakened his spider-sense. However, Spidey knocked the Goblin into a mass of live electrical wires. The resultant shock gave Osborn amnesia, wiping out all memory of the Green Goblin.

GAS ATTACK
The Green Goblin equipped his glider with sprayers that could release hallucinogenic and sleep-inducing gases.

The Green Goblin's last stand

The Green Goblin wasn't finished, yet. Norman's evil personality reemerged. He returned to his criminal ways and launched a new attack on Spider-Man. Spidey was at a real disadvantage this time. He now knew that the Green Goblin was his best friend's father, and that Norman couldn't help himself. However, the Green Goblin set up a series of events that resulted in the death of someone very close to Spider-Man. In the battle that followed, the Green Goblin was impaled by his own goblin glider and apparently killed by a trap that he had set for Spider-Man.

The Goblin's boots lock into glider's stirrups and are held in place by electromagnetism.

"YOU... *YOU'RE* NOT MY BOY! WHERE *IS* HARRY? WHO ARE *YOU?*"

"HE DOESN'T *RECOGNIZE* ME! HIS *MEMORY'S* GONE! OR... *IS* IT?"

"IT'S NOT HARD TO FAKE AMNESIA! THE GOBLIN IS CAPABLE OF *ANYTHING!*"

"AND YET..."

KRAVEN THE HUNTER

Thanks to the mutagenic effects of the herbal potion, Kraven could lift almost two tons.

With an intimate knowledge of human and animal physiology, Kraven devised his own fighting style.

SERGEI KRAVINOV was born into a family of Russian aristocrats. Forced into exile during the Russian revolution, Sergei's parents eventually settled in the United Kingdom. But life was hard, and as their finances began to dwindle, Sergei's mother fell into a terrible depression. She committed suicide while Sergei was still a young child. Within a year, his father married a former servant girl, and the young Sergei became furious when he learned that his stepmother was pregnant. He accused his father of betraying his mother's memory and made the life of his half-brother Dmitri miserable. Hating his family situation, Sergei ran away. He traveled throughout Europe, Asia, and Africa, stowing away on cargo ships and trains and using his wit and cunning to survive. Eventually, he found work on a safari, where he discovered that he had a natural talent for hunting.

The horns on Kraven's belt contained various herbs, potions, and toxins that could be used against his prey.

Kraven's strength was sufficient to stop a charging grizzly in its tracks.

INTERNATIONAL CELEBRITY

Over the years, Sergei sharpened his hunting skills and his fame began to spread. A British journalist helped cement his legend by writing articles about the hunter. Not knowing the correct spelling of Sergei's last name, the journalist shortened it to Kraven. During his time in the jungle, Kraven stumbled upon a witch doctor who had created a potion that somehow augmented the hunter's strength and speed. Now Kraven could track and kill jungle animals with ease, and he soon became desperate to find a challenge worthy of his skills. Kraven was then contacted by his half-brother Dmitri, who had also assumed a new name, the Chameleon (*see pages 40-41*). He wanted Kraven's help to fight Spider-Man.

The first hunt
The first meeting between Spider-Man and Kraven did not start off well for the wall-crawler. Surprised by Kraven's speed, Spider-Man then had his shoulder numbed by a devastating punch. But with only one arm working properly, Spidey was still able to defeat Kraven. From that day, Kraven swore to defeat Spider-Man and complete his hunt.

Kraven honed his combat skills by fighting jungle animals. With training, his reflexes became swifter than a darting snake, and he could run faster than a cheetah.

CALYPSO
A jungle witch doctor who specializes in her own form of voodoo, Calypso loved Kraven and constantly encouraged him to destroy Spider-Man.

Employing his own form of martial arts, Kraven could wrestle an enraged bull to its knees, and he had been known to throw a full-grown gorilla from its feet.

The last hunt
Realizing that the best way to beat the spider was to become him, Kraven began his final hunt. He managed to subdue the web-swinger, buried him alive, and then began to impersonate him. In doing so, Kraven was able to "bury" some of his own personal demons. Believing that he had now faced all of life's challenges, Kraven committed suicide. Since then, Kraven's son Alyosha has taken his father's place as the lion-skin-clad hunter.

SINISTER SIX

AFTER SUFFERING three defeats at the hands of Spider-Man, Doctor Octopus realized that he needed help against the web-slinger. He got in touch with every superpowered villain who had battled the wall-crawler. In the end, five other super-criminals heeded Ock's call—the Vulture, Electro, Kraven the Hunter, Mysterio, and the Sandman. However, Doctor Octopus recognized that he would never be able to control these super-villains. They were incapable of working together or functioning as a well-oiled machine. Instead of trying to change this unruly bunch, Doctor Octopus conceived a battle plan that exploited their individual appetites for personal glory. Each member of the Sinister Six would stage a separate battle with Spider-Man at a carefully chosen location. One by one the criminals would fight him until the wall-crawler was finally destroyed.

TEAM SPIRIT
It's one thing to assemble six powerful super-villains, it's quite another to keep them from fighting among themselves. While every member of the Sinister Six had reason to hate Spider-Man, they didn't particularly like each other. No one wanted to appear weak or indecisive in front of his peers. Knowing that it was only a matter of time before the team fell apart, Doctor Octopus proposed his daring plan.

BY INVITATION
Not every super-criminal took up Doc Ock's invitation. Doctor Doom preferred to concentrate his efforts on the Fantastic Four. The Green Goblin refused because he was convinced that he could beat Spidey on his own.

An unexpected complication
As if fighting six of his most powerful enemies weren't bad enough, Spider-Man was forced to face them without his superpowers. On the day before their first appearance, Peter Parker was thinking about how he was partly responsible for the death of his Uncle Ben. Lost in thought, he accidentally tripped and fell off a rooftop. After the fall, Peter realized that his powers had gone and he prepared to live the rest of his life as a normal teenager.

Vulture

Mysterio

Kraven

Electro

Doctor Octopus

Sandman

HANGING
Spider-Man was left clinging on for dear life to a fortunately placed flag pole!

The challenge

While Peter returned to life as a normal teenager, the Sinister Six put their plan into action. Realizing that *Daily Bugle* secretary Betty Brant played an important part in Spider-Man's life, they kidnapped her, along with an innocent bystander—none other than Aunt May. It was then left to the Vulture to deliver the challenge to the offices of the newspaper.

TO FIGHT OR NOT
A distraught Peter was left confused about what to do—without his spider powers he would stand no chance against one super-villain, let alone six of them! But he couldn't leave Betty and Aunt May in the clutches of Doctor Octopus and his team of super-criminals. Bravely, Peter donned his Spider-Man costume and left for building number 4 of the Stark Electric Plant where he met his first adversary, Electro.

RUNNING THE GAUNTLET
During his fight with Electro, Spider-Man instinctively managed to dodge a bolt of electricity. Realizing that his powers had suddenly returned, and suspecting that he only lost them because he was feeling guilty about Uncle Ben, Spider-Man burst into action, defeating Electro before moving on to Kraven, Mysterio, the Sandman, and then the Vulture. This left him with only Doctor Octopus to face.

With his powers restored, Spider-Man easily defeated the Sinister Six.

MY POWERS HAVE *RETURNED* TO ME!! I *HAVEN'T* LOST THEM!! I'M STILL SPIDER-MAN!

BEATEN BUT UNBOWED
The six criminals were all imprisoned after their defeat. Here, they became even more determined to beat Spider-Man. They all managed to escape from prison and to confront Spider-Man again.

A WATERY CLIMAX
Lured into a giant fishbowl, Peter was forced to fight his final battle underwater. Equipped with an air tank and mask, Doctor Octopus tried to drown Spider-Man. But the masked teenager knew that the lives of Aunt May and Betty were at stake, and he refused to give up. Somehow he managed to hold his breath long enough to overpower his tentacled antagonist.

Rotating membership

When the six were free from jail, Doctor Octopus decided to re-form the group. The death of Kraven forced him to find a replacement, and he turned to the Hobgoblin. Since that time, other criminals have joined the Sinister Six, including Venom.

THE SCORPION

Under the eager eyes of Jameson, Mac Gargan underwent the procedures that turned him into a super-villain.

JUST AS real scorpions prey upon spiders, so the Scorpion lives to destroy Spider-Man; and this super-villain certainly has more than enough power for the job. He is twice as strong as his web-slinging foe, and his reflexes are much quicker. The Scorpion even possesses a massive tail that he uses as a deadly weapon, making him Spider-Man's superior in every way. He should be; after all he was specifically created to crush the wall-crawler. Before he became the Scorpion, MacDonald "Mac" Gargan was a down-and-out private detective. His cheap rates attracted the attention of J. Jonah Jameson (*see pages 34-35*). Jameson wanted to find out how Peter Parker managed to take such great photographs of Spider-Man, so he hired Gargan to shadow Parker. Warned by his spider-sense, however, Peter easily avoided his stalker. Gargan reported his failure, only to discover that Jameson had a new plan.

BUILT TO CONQUER

Jameson had become aware of a scientist named Doctor Farley Stillwell who claimed to have found a way to cause mutations in animals. After seeing examples of his work, Jameson made a deal with Stillwell. He wanted Stillwell to produce a man who was more powerful than Spider-Man. Jameson then offered Gargan $10,000 to participate in the dangerous experiment. Subjected to a series of radiological and chemical treatments, Gargan was given the powers of a scorpion, the natural enemy of the spider.

Pardon my tail
Built over a flexible steel framework, the tail is made up of segments, each equipped with an independent motor and power supply. Though it is a formidable weapon, walking around with a six-foot tail isn't easy, and Gargan spent many hours learning how to coordinate his movements. Now that he's mastered this extra appendage, he can use it either as a bludgeon or as a fifth limb.

A SURPRISING DEFEAT
The Scorpion was the first super-foe that Spider-Man had ever encountered who was actually stronger than he was. Spidey was at the peak of his strength when they first met, but even that wasn't enough to save him from a villain whose only purpose was to defeat the wall-crawler.

AND STILL THE INCREDIBLE EXPERIMENT CONTINUES...

THE TALE OF THE TAIL
Doctor Stillwell designed a special bodysuit for Gargan, complete with a mechanical tail. The tail is equipped with a cybernetic link that connects to the base of Gargan's spinal column. This way, he can control it as easily as he controls his arms and legs.

The Scorpion's costume is equipped with powerful pincers on each hand that can rip through Spider-Man's webbing.

The Scorpion's leg muscles are so strong that he can easily leap onto the roof of a single-story building.

Betrayed by Jameson

Fearing lawsuits and public disgrace, Jameson tried to prevent anyone from learning his connection to the Scorpion. The Scorpion was outraged by this betrayal and grew to hate his former employer. He has made many attempts on Jameson's life. Luckily, Spidey has always been there to stop him.

GET HIM, DON'T TAKE ANY CHANCES! LET HIM HAVE IT!

AT EASE, PRUNE-FACE! WHEN I NEED A CHEER-LEADER I'LL LET YOU KNOW!

AS FOR YOU, SCORPY, WE'VE JUST GOT TO RID YOU OF YOUR DEEP-ROOTED HOSTILITY COMPLEX!

GO AHEAD, LOUD MOUTH, HAVE YOUR FUN WHILE YOU CAN...!

The Scorpion can whip his tail at speeds of over 90 mph!

SPRING IN HIS TAIL
By coiling his tail behind him and using it as a spring, the Scorpion can propel himself over 30 feet into the air.

Sting in the tail

The Scorpion hired an underworld arms manufacturer to modify his tail so that it can now fire powerful blasts.

The Scorpion is strong enough to punch his own handholds in concrete.

The Scorpion's battle suit is made of steel mesh and is impervious to small arms fire.

GUILTY CONSCIENCE
Horrified by what he had unleashed, a guilt-ridden Stillwell prepared an antidote that would remove Gargan's powers. However, the repentant scientist was killed before he could deliver the cure.

Mind over muscle

After he was beaten during their first bout, Spider-Man was forced to accept the fact that he could not trade blows with the Scorpion. The wall-crawler had to outthink Gargan as well as outfight him. Spider-Man managed to win his first victory by gluing the Scorpion to the floor with webbing. While he was stuck in place, Spidey used his spider-sense to dodge the Scorpion's blows while delivering dozens of his own.

AN' YOU WON'T BELIEVE WHAT MY NEW TAIL CAN DO!

SORRY, SCORPY--

SPIDER-SLAYERS

THE FIRST Spider-Slayer was designed and built by Professor Spencer Smythe. Smythe was a mild-mannered inventor who was inspired by Jameson's anti-Spidey editorials in the *Daily Bugle*. Believing that Spider-Man was a menace, Smythe created the first Spider-Slayer robot. Peter Parker decided to get even with Jameson by making money photographing the fight between the robot and Spider-Man, so he convinced the publisher to let Smythe demonstrate his invention. However, Peter soon realized that this was a mistake. The robot possessed incredible fighting capabilities and eventually trapped Spider-Man within its steel cables. Fortunately, the quick thinking wall-crawler managed to break into the robot's control panel and free himself before Jameson and Smythe could arrive on the scene.

NEW MODELS, MORE FAILURES

Smythe, humiliated by his failure, went back to the lab and created a new Spider-Slayer with deadlier weapons and more sophisticated sensors. But Jameson and Smythe had an argument as soon as the publisher realized that this model was designed to kill Spider-Man, rather than capture him. The web-head outwitted the new robot by leading it back to Smythe's lab where he caused it to explode. Obsessed with defeating Spider-Man, Smythe kept building newer and more powerful Spider-Slayers. Smythe was ultimately killed by his own inventions when he was exposed to the radioactive materials needed to power his Spider-Slayers.

The first Slayer
The first Spider-Slayer was somewhat crude and clunky, yet it was still a formidable threat to Spider-Man.

The tail of this Spider-Slayer is filled with knockout gas.

ARACHNAPHOBIA
Inspired by various movie monsters, the later robots were designed to terrorize as well as destroy their victims.

This robot's claws are sharp enough to rip through solid steel.

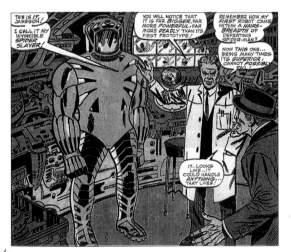

The slayers
Over the years, Smythe improved the designs of his Spider-Slayers, like the Mark II seen here (*left*). However, even these Slayers were no match for the wall-crawler. Spidey quickly defeated each one.

Spider-Slayer Mark III

Despite Jameson's objections, Smythe managed to convince the publisher to finance the Spider-Slayer Mark III, a robot that could shoot its own artificial webbing.

SPIDER-SLAYER MARK III

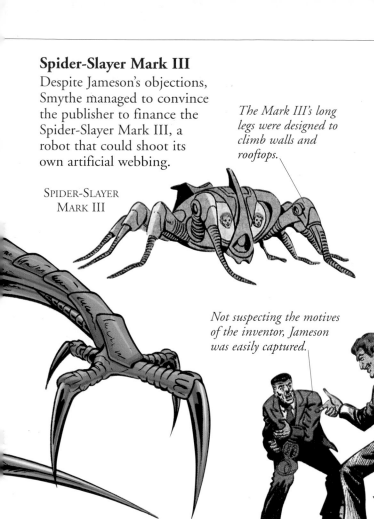

The Mark III's long legs were designed to climb walls and rooftops.

Another failure

Spencer Smythe's Spider-Slayer Mark IV was large enough to house a human driver. Faster, stronger, and deadlier than his previous designs, the Mark IV actually managed to capture Spider-Man. But Spidey freed himself and rigged the Mark IV so that it blew up in Smythe's face.

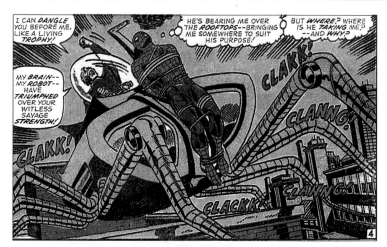

I CAN *DANGLE* YOU BEFORE ME, LIKE A LIVING *TROPHY!*

MY *BRAIN*-- MY *ROBOT*-- HAVE *TRIUMPHED* OVER YOUR *WITLESS* SAVAGE *STRENGTH!*

HE'S BEARING ME OVER THE *ROOFTOPS*--BRINGING ME SOMEWHERE TO SUIT HIS PURPOSE!

BUT *WHERE?* WHERE IS HE *TAKING* ME? --AND *WHY?*

Not suspecting the motives of the inventor, Jameson was easily captured.

AND NOW, BECAUSE OF THE *RADIOACTIVE* MATERIALS I USED TO BUILD YOUR IN-SUFFERABLE SLAYERS, I'M *DYING!*

YES, I'M DYING... AND AFTER I'VE LURED SPIDER-MAN HERE-- YOU, TOO, SHALL DIE AS WELL!

WHAT? I DIDN'T KNOW! HOW COULD I?

AT LEAST ON MY DEATHBED I WILL HAVE ATTAINED MY VENGEANCE!

AS THE COLOR DRAINS FROM JAMESON'S FACE.

Death be not proud

Under the pretence of showing Jameson another design of Spider-Slayer, Smythe kidnapped the publisher and promised to kill him. Smythe had discovered that the radiation he had been exposed to while building the Spider-Slayers was killing him, and he held Jameson responsible.

TO BECOME A SLAYER
Alistair had a number of weapons connected to his spine—he could even fire his own webbing.

The heir apparent

After his father's death, Alistair Smythe began to build his own Spider-Slayers, taking a job with the Kingpin (*see pages 70-71*) to finance his first attempt. Discarding the clunky robots once used by his father, Alistair favored much more sophisticated models. He designed his new Spider-Slayers to inspire terror, and equipped them with razor-sharp claws, venom-coated tails, and pointed fangs.

I HATE ROBOTS.

YUP.

HATE 'EM A LOT!

ALISTAIR SMYTHE

Spidey's spider-sense is one advantage he has over the Spider-Slayers, warning him of their approach.

The ultimate Spider-Slayer

Alistair's robots were repeatedly defeated by Spider-Man. So Smythe had his entire body encased within a special bio-organic shell that protected him from harm and boosted his strength to superhuman levels. In an effort to destroy Spidey, he had physically transformed himself into the ultimate Spider-Slayer. Alistair believed that he was now a match for Spider-Man and attempted to beat him to death. The wall-crawler ultimately survived Smythe's onslaught and finally managed to defeat him.

MASTER PLANNER

SPIDER-MAN HAS always felt guilty about the death of his Uncle Ben. If Spidey had acted responsibly, his uncle would still be alive. Since that day, Spider-Man has done everything he can to make up for his failure. When a band of masked criminals started a major crime wave in New York, the web-swinger didn't realize that he was finally going to get an opportunity to atone for his worst mistake. Then Aunt May suddenly became ill. Peter learned that she was dying and that it was his fault. When a serum that could cure his aunt was finally discovered, it was stolen by the masked gang. Spider-Man scoured the city until he found their secret hideout and their leader, the Master Planner.

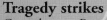

FIRST BATTLE
The Master Planner's men attempted to hijack an armored truck carrying uranium. Using magnetic shoes, they attached themselves to the truck and somehow hurled the wall-crawler from the roof.

The mystery men
A team of strangely garbed thieves who specialized in stealing atomic powered equipment and radioactive materials had descended upon New York City. Working for the Master Planner, their highly advanced weaponry indicated a well-funded organization. Using a helicopter and split-second timing, they were attempting to steal an experimental atomic device when Spider-Man came upon them. Though the web-spinner disabled their getaway vehicle, the crooks still managed to escape with their booty.

With their split-second timing and their advanced weaponry, the Master Planner's gang were more than a match for Spidey.

Tragedy strikes
Once home, Peter quickly forgot about the Master Planner and his men. He was about to begin his college career, and he couldn't wait. He spent the following day registering for courses and buying textbooks. For a brief time it looked like life was finally smiling on him. But then tragedy struck. Aunt May suddenly grew faint and collapsed. She was taken to the hospital, where Peter learned that her condition was critical.

Aunt May collapsed into Peter's arms.

Tainted blood
Aunt May's health continued to decline. To Peter's horror, the doctors discovered that she was dying because a radioactive particle had somehow entered her bloodstream. Peter realized that this particle must have come from him—only a few months earlier she had needed a transfusion and he had donated blood!

HIS FINAL CHAPTER
With the water slowly rising around him, an injured Spider-Man was left trapped beneath tons of fallen steel and rubble after battling the Master Planner.

ISO-36

Peter was desperate to save his aunt, so he stole a sample of her blood from the hospital lab, changed into Spider-Man and sought out the one man who could help him. Doctor Curt Connors, the man who had once been the Lizard (*see pages 48–49*), was eager to aid Spidey. After many experiments, Connors told the wall-crawler about a serum called ISO-36 that might neutralize the radioactive particle in May's blood. Telling Connors to order this wonder drug, Peter pawned everything he had to get the money to pay for it.

STOLEN
Unfortunately for Peter, the Master Planner wanted to study the highly experimental ISO-36 drug. He ordered his men to intercept the delivery and steal the serum. When Spider-Man learned that the serum had been hijacked, he hunted for the location of the Master Planner's hideout.

UNDERWATER BASE
Spider-Man eventually tracked down the masked gang's base to the bottom of a riverbed.

Ock attack

Spider-Man eventually reached the heart of the secret base and entered a large chamber. But before he could reach the vial of ISO-36, Spider-Man realized that he had crawled into a trap. A blast of electricity jolted him from the ceiling and four metal tentacles caught him before he could hit the ground. The Master Planner had finally revealed his true identity. He was Spider-Man's old enemy Doctor Octopus. During the course of their fierce battle, a main support beam was destroyed, the ceiling collapsed, and Spider-Man found himself pinned beneath a mountain of debris.

The Master Planner was actually Doctor Octopus.

His destiny?

While his aunt lay dying and his friend waited for him to deliver the one serum that could save her, Spider-Man lay under tons of twisted steel. The vial of ISO-36 was just beyond his reach. Added to that, a leak had sprung in the ceiling, and the water level was slowly rising around him. He kept trying to free himself, but it was no use. He couldn't budge the massive weight. But he wouldn't give up! Gritting his teeth against the unbearable strain he forced himself upward. Despite the incredible pain, he kept fighting until he finally managed to lift his enormous burden and free himself.

A happy ending

As Spider-Man recovered the ISO-36, the ceiling crumbled and he was swept through the headquarters. Once the waters calmed, he saw that the Master Planner's men stood between him and the only exit. With a desperate fury, he fought his way through them and eventually delivered the serum to the hospital. It was administered to May Parker, and she showed immediate improvement.

REDEMPTION
Though his uncle died because he failed to act responsibly, Peter came through for his aunt when it counted most.

THE RHINO

AS STRONG as the beast whose name he bears, the Rhino is one of Spider-Man's most powerful enemies. He possesses incredible superhuman strength and has been known to lift objects that weigh as much as 80 tons. He is practically impervious to pain and is also very fast for someone of his size and mass. Thanks to his uncanny endurance, he can run for hours at a time without tiring and can achieve a top speed of nearly 100 mph. Nothing can withstand the charge of the Rhino. Concrete buildings crumble before him, trucks are crushed in his path, and cars are left twisted and broken in his destructive wake.

The faster the Rhino charges forward, the more his momentum forces him to run in a straight line.

FACELESS TO FORMIDABLE

The Rhino's real name has never been revealed. All that is known about him is that he was a poor Russian immigrant who worked as a small-time muscle man for professional criminals. He acted as a collection agent for the local loan sharks or was hired whenever a heist required heavy lifting. At one point foreign spies approached him and made him an offer he couldn't refuse. They wanted to create an unstoppable, superhuman agent and chose him because of his muscular physique and his lack of intelligence. Since he needed money to bring his mother and relatives to America, he agreed to their requests. For several months, he underwent a series of chemical and radiation treatments that gave him his powers and turned him into the Rhino.

BEAST FROM THE EAST
Chemical and radiation treatment turned a Russian immigrant into the Rhino.

More than a costume
A team of scientists designed and developed the Rhino's special bodysuit to cover his body, which had been bulked up by the chemical and radiation treatment. The costume is constructed of layers of polymer and, like the hide of a real rhinoceros, is thick, coarse, and highly resistant to damage. It is bulletproof and can even withstand the explosive impact of an antitank missile!

While the Rhino can veer to the right or left once he reaches ramming speed, he cannot make sharp turns or sudden stops.

Target: John Jameson

The Rhino's first assignment was to abduct John Jameson (*see page 69*), the son of J. Jonah Jameson. Since John was an astronaut in the United States space program, the Rhino's bosses intended to sell him to the highest bidder. Spider-Man learned of the Rhino's plan and rushed to John's defense. With his superior speed and agility, Spider-Man dazzled the inexperienced Rhino, who was captured by the police. The Rhino was confined to a prison hospital where he was kept under heavy sedation while awaiting trial.

While earlier versions of his costume were bonded to his skin, the Rhino's present bodysuit can be removed. The horns are made of the same material as the rest of his suit. They are razor-sharp and can easily rip through steel.

Always a professional

While the Rhino truly hates Spider-Man, he never allows himself to be distracted from completing a mission, since he hates to forfeit a fee. The Rhino is also professional enough to realize his own limitations, and he has often sought to ally himself with other powerful villains, including Hydro-Man, Speed Demon, and the Leader.

LOOKS CAN BE DECEPTIVE
During their first encounter, Spider-Man was surprised when he discovered that the Rhino was a lot faster than he looked.

Exposed

With the aid of Dr. Curtis Connors (*see pages 48–49*), Spider-Man once devised a special version of his web fluid which contained acid pellets. This unique webbing melted the Rhino's protective costume and made him far more vulnerable to attack.

THE MOLTEN MAN

GREED RUINED Mark Raxton's life. Raxton was a scientist who couldn't wait to strike it rich. When Professor Spencer Smythe approached him with the idea of creating a liquid metal alloy, Raxton believed his dreams would soon become reality. Raxton couldn't wait to sell the invention, but Smythe thought it needed more testing. The two men argued and began to fight. Raxton lost his balance and the liquid metal spilled all over him. His skin absorbed the alloy, and his body assumed a metallic appearance. Mark Raxton had become the Molten Man.

FATAL MISHAP
As the liquid metal alloy spread over his body, Raxton could feel it seeping into his bloodstream and he immediately feared the worst.

The Molten Man can lift almost 40 tons.

Metallic skin covering slips from any grasp.

LIVING LARGE

Fearing that he might have accidentally poisoned himself, Raxton raced for the nearest hospital. When he stepped into the middle of the street, an irate driver began to berate him for holding up traffic. Raxton responded by punching the man's car. To his surprise, the steel hood buckled beneath his blow. That's when Raxton realized that the accident had given him super-strength. He now possessed enough power to take whatever he wanted.

The only one who stood in his way was Spider-Man. During their first battle, Spidey was shocked to discover that his webbing couldn't stick to the Molten Man's metallic skin. But Spidey was able to whip up a rope of extra-thick webbing, and managed to hog-tie the Molten Man.

Super-strength
With superhuman strength, and fists more powerful than sledgehammers, the Molten Man was more than a match for Spider-Man. But Mark Raxton wasn't a typical mindless thug. He was an educated man whose brain was trained in the scientific method. Each time he battled the web-head, the Molten Man learned from past mistakes. He discovered many new ways of using his powers.

Metallic fingers are sensitive enough to pick the lock on a safe.

Molten power
In his molten state, Raxton can burn anyone who touches him. He can also melt his way through solid steel walls. The Molten Man's skin is so tough that it renders him impervious to pain, and bullets just bounce off him.

A new lease on life
Like the Black Cat and the Prowler, the Molten Man has retired from crime. Raxton became reconciled with his stepsister, Liz Allen, after realizing that she was the only one who had never abandoned him. He even began working for his brother-in-law and helped Liz run Osborn Industries after Harry's death. His relationship with Spider-Man has also changed. They have become friends and occasional allies.

JOHN JAMESON

Space cadet
One of the youngest members of the NASA space program, John Jameson ran into trouble during his first mission. When Spider-Man saved John from certain death, J. Jonah Jameson assumed that it was a publicity stunt to upstage his son and wrote his first editorial denouncing the web-head.

NOT EVERY Jameson hates Spider-Man. J. Jonah Jameson's son John is one of the web-head's biggest supporters. John was a NASA astronaut when he first met Spidey. On a space mission, he contracted an unknown virus that temporarily gave him superhuman strength. At his father's urging, John attempted to capture Spidey. But the wall-crawler managed to nullify the virus and make his escape.

MOONSTONE
John Jameson felt a strange desire to possess a glittering gemstone he spotted on a secret mission to the moon. If only he had realized that the gem would in fact possess him!

THE WEREWOLF'S CURSE

John Jameson made a pendant of a gem he brought back from the Moon. Later, he wore it on the first night of the full moon, and it transformed him into Man-Wolf. Jonah was shocked to discover that this monster was his son. With the help of Dr. Curt Connors, Spider-Man cured John Jameson of this curse.

MAN INTO MONSTER
The light of the full moon somehow triggered a chemical reaction within the gemstone which released an unknown form of radiation. This radiation caused Jameson's body to mutate and take on a wolflike appearance.

His eyes can see in the dark.

Man-Wolf has a highly developed sense of smell.

LIFTING THE CURSE
Jameson found that the gem pendant had fused with his neck. Eventually, Dr. Curt Connors developed a device to sever its ties.

Mindless beast
As the Man-Wolf, John Jameson acted as if he were a real wolf. He had no memory of his actions when he returned to his human form. After he was cured, Jameson left NASA and took a job as chief of security at Ravencroft, a maximum-security institution for the criminally insane. Here, he met the current love of his life, Dr. Ashley Kafka, a brilliant psychologist.

LUPINE
Man-Wolf possesses the agility, speed, stamina, and heightened senses of a true wolf.

Man-Wolf's costume is actually a radiation suit, designed to screen out the moon's rays.

KINGPIN

WILSON FISK came from a poor family, and was a chubby and unpopular child. To protect himself from bullies, he started to train himself in various forms of bodybuilding and personal combat. As his physical strength increased, Fisk realized that he could use it to intimidate the bullies who once threatened him. He quickly organized them into a gang and began to pursue a career in crime. Eventually he came to the attention of Don Rigoletto, a major New York gang lord. Fisk became Don Rigoletto's bodyguard and his most trusted confidant. But when a major rift occurred in Don Rigoletto's mob, Fisk killed his boss, assumed control, and started to build his own criminal empire.

Although Fisk enjoys crushing an enemy in hand-to-hand combat, he always delivers his orders through layers of subordinates. This way the police can never prove that he is responsible for any crime.

FALL AND RISE

Taking the name Kingpin, Fisk ruled the criminal underworld like a medieval warlord. But his position did not make him invincible. At the height of his powers, two organizations joined forces to undermine the Kingpin. The Maggia, an international crime syndicate, and Hydra, a worldwide subversive organization dedicated to global domination, succeeded in destroying Fisk's criminal empire. Barely escaping with his life, Fisk fled to Japan where he used his legitimate spice business to rebuild his wealth. He then proceeded to strike back, undermining the Maggia and inciting gang wars. These created a power vacuum in the underworld that Fisk could step in to fill.

Tough customer
Years of bodybuilding and training have turned Fisk into an expert in Sumo wrestling and other martial arts. However, he is not above using a few weapons of his own when confronted by a difficult adversary. His personal arsenal includes a walking cane which fires a miniature laser beam as well as a concentrated spray of sleeping gas. He occasionally wears a diamond stickpin that also fires sleeping gas.

Spider-Man no more

Frustrated in his attempts to live a normal life, Peter Parker temporarily gave up being Spider-Man and tossed his costume in a nearby trash can. With Spider-Man out of the picture, the Kingpin saw a prime opportunity to cement his control over the New York mobs, and he launched a major crime spree. Peter Parker tried to ignore the crime wave until he stumbled upon a mugging and sprang into action to save an old man who reminded him of his Uncle Ben (*see pages 12-13*). Realizing that he could no longer shirk his responsibilities, Spider-Man came out of retirement to crush the Kingpin's plans.

Vanessa Fisk

Posing as a legitimate businessman, the Kingpin became a prominent member of New York society. He met and married the beautiful Vanessa, who was unaware of his criminal activities. Once she discovered the source of her husband's income, Vanessa insisted that he abandon his life of crime. Desperate to please her, he pretended to go straight, but she soon realized that he was lying to her. She gave Fisk an ultimatum, and he reluctantly agreed to retire from crime in order to save his marriage. The two moved to Japan until a gang war in the US forced Fisk to return and reassume the leadership of his organization.

WHO IS HE?
When the Kingpin finally confronted his massive rival, the Schemer revealed his true identity...

TRUE IDENTITY
The Schemer proved to be none other than Fisk's own son!

Son of the mobster

The only son of Wilson and Vanessa, Richard Fisk grew up believing his father was a good and honest man. It wasn't until Richard reached college that he realized his father was more than he appeared. After his graduation, Richard informed his parents that he intended to travel through Europe. A few months later they received word that Richard, upset by his father's activities, had apparently died in a skiing accident.

THE ROSE

THE ROSE
One of the Kingpin's underlings, the Rose serves in middle management in Fisk's organization. He specializes in gambling and hijacking. Fisk's son took on the role of the first Rose, but others have since adopted this masked identity.

The Schemer

When the Kingpin was temporarily driven into hiding by Spider-Man, a new crime lord appeared on the scene. Calling himself the Schemer, he attempted to take Fisk's place as the new king of crime. He used guerrillalike tactics, raiding the Kingpin's gambling parlors and ruthlessly attacking anyone who remained loyal to Fisk. The Kingpin declared war on the Schemer, and Spider-Man was soon caught between the warring mobsters. The Kingpin was shocked when he discovered that his new enemy was actually the beloved son who he had believed was dead.

Anxious to impress his girlfriend, Hobie planned to use his Prowler identity to gain instant notoriety.

THE PROWLER

STUCK IN a dead-end job as a window washer, Hobie Brown felt like life was passing him by. Everything good seemed to happen to other people. Hobie really wanted to be an inventor, but he was afraid to take a chance. His girlfriend, Mindy, convinced him to stop feeling sorry for himself, so Hobie designed some new safety devices and took them to his boss. But his boss had no interest in funding the inventions. Realizing that he had to move on, Hobie quit his job and began to modify some of his equipment. He transformed a gadget that was originally designed to spray cleaning fluid into a device that fired gas pellets and small explosives. He converted special gloves into steel-tipped gauntlets, and fabricated a mask, costume, and cape. Hobie had decided to embark on a new career —he had become the Prowler.

Hobie wears a special air filter under his mask so that he doesn't breathe in his own gas.

A SLIGHT MISCALCULATION

As he put the finishing touches on his new costumed identity, Hobie was torn by indecision. Would the Prowler be a hero or a villain? Since Hobie was anxious to be noticed, he chose to be both. He planned to steal as the Prowler, and later play the hero by returning the stolen goods as Hobie Brown. He hoped the resulting publicity would make him famous and attract investors for his inventions. Unfortunately, Hobie's plan didn't include Spider-Man. The Prowler managed to fight the wall-crawler to a standstill during their first encounter, but Spidey easily overpowered Hobie during their next fight. Upon hearing Hobie's story, Spider-Man took pity on him and let him go free. The Prowler and Spidey have been friends ever since.

TARGET: THE DAILY BUGLE
As his first target, the Prowler chose to rob the Daily Bugle, unaware that a certain web-head secretly worked for the newspaper.

His boots contain shock-absorbent foam rubber and compressed air to cushion him when he makes high leaps.

Hobie Brown is skilled in hand-to-hand combat and possesses a green belt in tae kwon do.

YOU'RE *FAST*, WALL-CRAWLER --BUT IT WON'T TAKE ME LONG TO GET THE *RANGE*.

THIS IS *TOO MUCH!* JUST A FEW *DAYS* AGO IT WAS *ICEMAN* WHO ATTACKED ME WITHOUT WARNING*--AND NOW, THE *PROWLER!*

IT'S AS THOUGH *FATE* ITSELF IS CONSPIRING TO KEEP ME FROM *GWEN*.

BUT I WON'T LET *ANYTHING* KEEP US APART. I *WON'T!*

GIVE UP, SPIDER-MAN. I'M NOT OUT TO *INJURE* YOU.

ZASK!

A SPIDER HUNT
When Spider-Man was accused of murdering George Stacy (see pages 82-83), Hobie tried to bring the web-slinger to justice. During their battle, the Prowler fell down an elevator shaft and was saved by Spider-Man. This selfless act convinced Hobie that the wall-crawler wasn't a murderer.

MAYBE *THIS'LL* TEACH YOU THAT YOU'RE NOT THE *ONLY* CAT WHO CAN COME UP WITH A *SURPRISE!*

FOOH!

DIDN'T *EXPECT* ME TO HAVE *GAS PELLETS* IN MY *BOOT*, HUH?

THE GAME
Though he hates the thought of risking his life, Hobie always ends up donning his Prowler costume for one more challenge. He recently tried to earn a million-dollar prize by participating as the Prowler in a super-powered gladiator contest known as the Great Game. Unfortunately, he was seriously injured during his bout, and it is unknown if he will ever prowl again.

NO ONE'S PINNIN' A *MURDER* RAP ON ME! NO ONE!

AN AIR BLAST LIKE *THIS* CAN STOP ANY-THING!

SHOOSH!

Fighting boots
Among the Prowler's useful gadgets are his boots, which are equipped with pneumatic cartridges. These cartridges can shoot blasts of tear gas, mace, or compressed air at an unwitting attacker.

All in the wrist
The Prowler's wrist blasters fire steel darts, magnesium flares, small explosives, mace, hallucinogenic liquids, or various forms of gas.

The Prowler's cape contains pneumatic filaments that expand to give it a rigid structure. He can then use the cape to glide over short distances.

A friend in need
Though Hobie has never learned Spider-Man's true identity, he once saved it. While Peter Parker was delirious with fever, he revealed his secret to his friends. As soon as he recovered, Peter realized that only one person could help him, and disguising himself, he asked Hobie for a favor. Later that day, Hobie masqueraded as Spider-Man while Peter was with his friends.

ALL I WANT YOU TO DO IS WEAR MY *SPIDEY SUIT* TONIGHT--- AND SHOW UP AT A CERTAIN PLACE-- AT A CERTAIN *TIME!*

I NEVER FIGGERED *YOU* TO FRAME A GUY!

IT'S *NOT* A FRAME! *TRUST* ME!

OKAY, I'LL *DO* IT! I GUESS I *OWE* YA THAT MUCH!*

AND *NO* QUESTIONS ASKED?

NO QUESTIONS ASKED!

*HE OWES IT FROM *SPIDEY* #79, GIVE OR TAKE A FEW ISSUES! ---STAN.

73

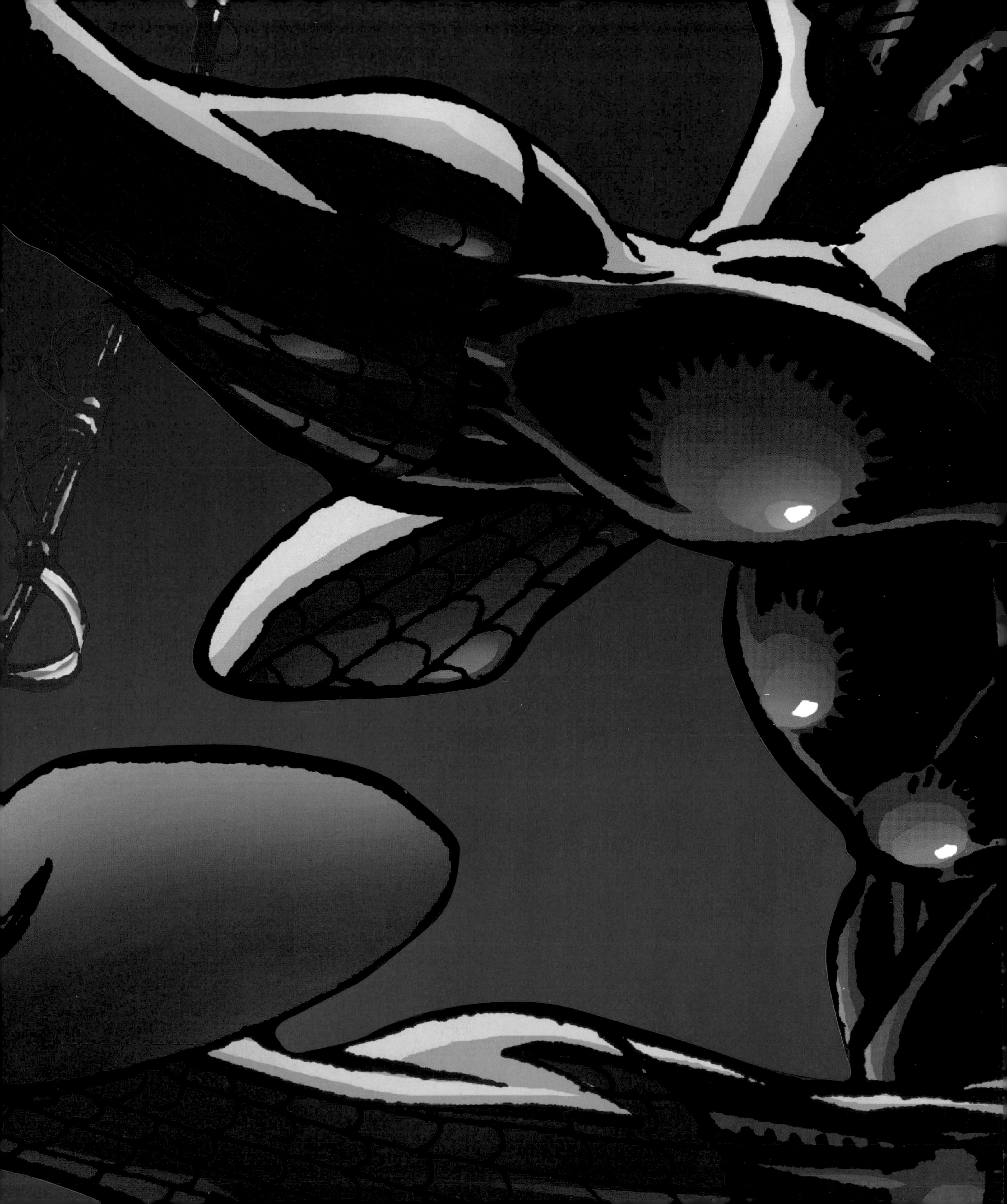

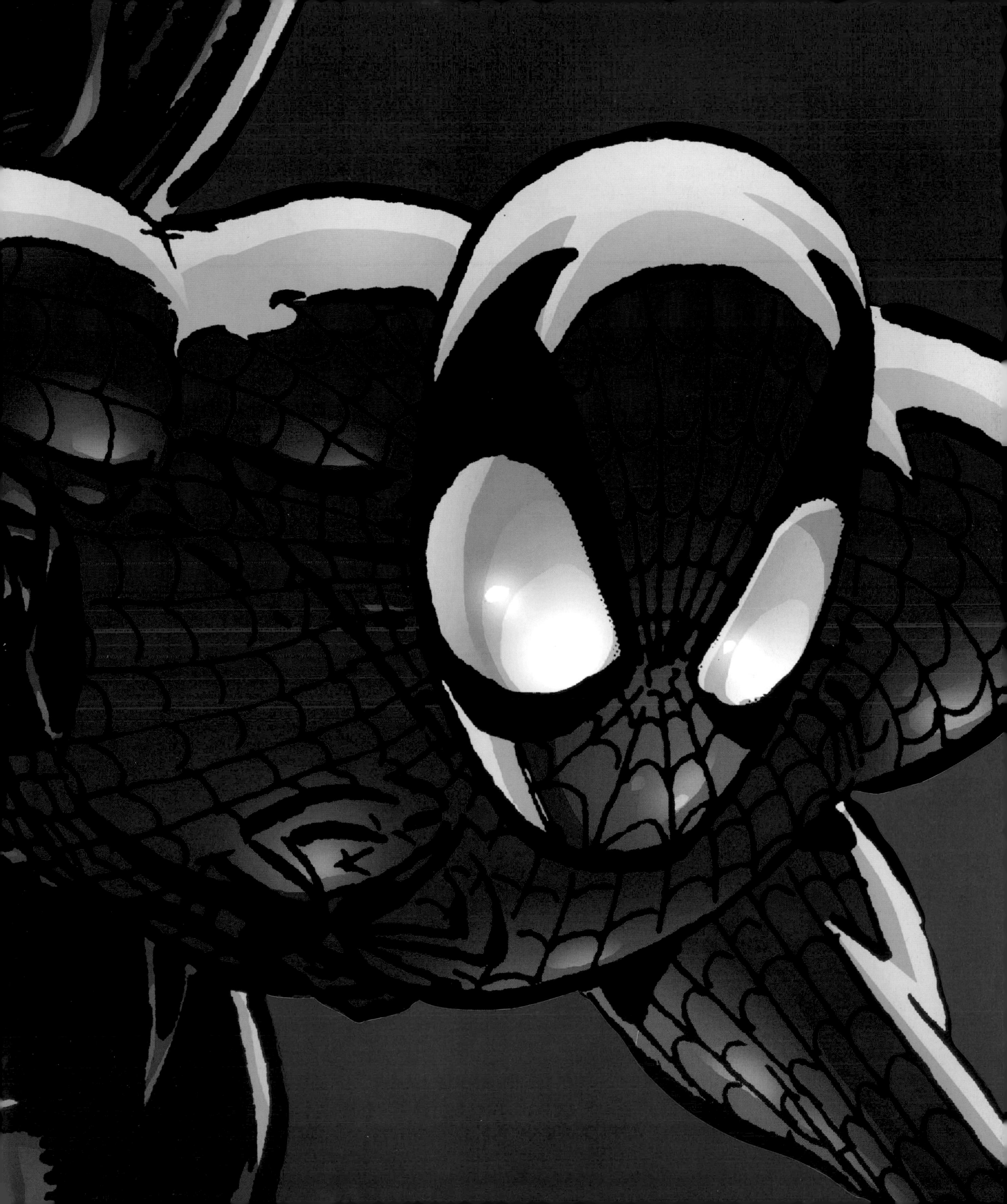

SPIDER-MAN IN THE '70S

STAN LEE and John Romita began the 1970s with a bang, by killing off a major supporting character, Captain George Stacy. Not content with stopping there, Stan Lee wanted to write a story that warned of the dangers of illicit drugs. Unfortunately, the America Comics Code Authority forbid any mention of drug abuse, so Stan was forced to remove the Code's Seal of Approval from *Amazing Spider-Man* #96 and 97.

Roy Thomas, who would later succeed Stan as Marvel's editor-in-chief, briefly filled in as the writer for *Amazing Spider-Man* and introduced Morbius, the living vampire. Comic book legends such as John Buscema and Gil Kane began to help with the art chores. Gerry Conway was ultimately given the writing assignment and is responsible for one of the most controversial comic book stories of all time—the death of Gwen Stacy. He was eventually joined by artist Ross Andru. Characters such as Hammerhead, the Man-Wolf, the Punisher, and the Jackal made their first appearance during Gerry's memorable run.

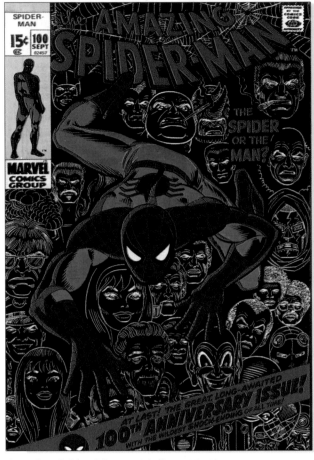

Amazing Spider-Man #100 (Sept. 1971)
Peter tried to renounce his powers and grew four extra arms (Cover art by John Romita and Frank Giacoia)

Amazing Spider-Man #86 (July 1970)
First appearance of the Black Widow (Cover art by John Romita)

As Spider-Man's popularity increased, Marvel introduced more titles devoted to the web-head, including *Giant-Size Super-Heroes* and *Peter Parker, The Spectacular Spider-Man*. A growing army of creators was needed to produce all this material. It included writers Archie Goodwin, Chris Claremont, Bill Mantlo, Len Wein, and Marv Wolfman, and artists such as John Byrne, Sal Buscema, and Jim Mooney.

THE SEVENTIES

1971

Amazing Spider-Man #95 (April 1971)
Spidey goes to London

1972

Marvel Team-Up #1 (March 1972)
First in a new series

1974

Amazing Spider-Man #129 (Feb. 1974)
Arrival of the Punisher

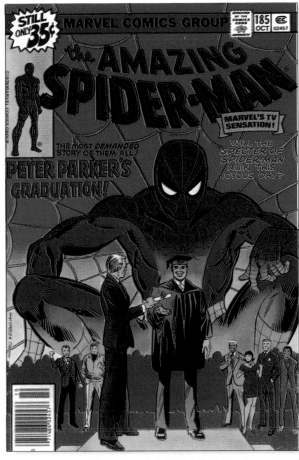

Amazing Spider-Man #185 (Oct. 1978)
Peter "fails" to graduate from college
(Cover art by John Romita and Sal Buscema)

Amazing Spider-Man #121 (June 1973)
The death of Gwen Stacy
(Cover art by John Romita)

1975

Amazing Spider-Man
#150 (Nov. 1975)
Special 150th issue

1976

Peter Parker: The Spectacular
Spider-Man #1 (Dec. 1976)
First in a new series

1979

Amazing Spider-Man #196
(Sept. 1979)
Peter believes Aunt May is dead

MORBIUS

MORBIUS HAS been cursed to a life of stomach-churning horror. He thirsts for human blood and will die unless his monstrous appetite is satisfied. Before he acquired the characteristics of a vampire, Doctor Michael Morbius was a Nobel Prize-winning biochemist from a

small European country. He learned that he was dying from a rare disease that was consuming his blood cells. With the aid of his friend Emil Nikos, he attempted to find

a cure. Together, they produced an experimental formula derived from the DNA of vampire bats. They also tried to stimulate the creation of more blood cells in Morbius' system by subjecting him to electrical shock treatments. The process saved his life, but at a terrible cost.

UNEXPECTED SIDE EFFECTS

The electric shock treatments somehow caused the bat formula to mutate within the body of Dr. Michael Morbius. The quiet and unassuming scientist was suddenly transformed into a creature that resembled a supernatural vampire. His skin lost all color, assuming a deathly white tint, his teeth grew into scalpel-sharp fangs, and he now had an animalistic and uncontrollable lust for human blood. He also possessed superhuman strength. Unable to control himself, Morbius attacked and killed his friend Nikos. As he was about to feed on him, Morbius was suddenly horrified by what he had become. He ran from the dead body, and has been running ever since.

A cure at any price?
Desperate to find a cure for his blood disease, Morbius was willing to take any risk or pay any price. But the process transformed him and doomed him to a life of never-ending horror.

Morbius has a strong aversion to direct sunlight.

The winglike projections on the arms of his costume allow Morbius to glide on strong air currents.

Morbius can transform his victims into vampires like himself.

TORMENT
Morbius has been torn by a sincere desire to end his nightmarish existence and his hunger for life. He has tried to commit suicide on many occasions, but he cannot.

Morbius must ingest fresh blood to survive. He drinks it to replenish the blood cells that are being consumed by his disease.

Vigilante vampire

Realizing that he might never be free of his bloodlust, Morbius attempted to use his power to help people. Instead of choosing his victims at random, he choose to protect the innocent and only feed on the guilty. He stalked street predators, murderers, and other monsters, dispensing his unique form of justice.

--A WORLD RIPE TO BECOME THE PREY OF-- MORBIUS!

BLOOD HUNT
Aside from Spider-Man, Morbius has also battled the Human Torch, the uncanny X-Men, the Lizard, and the Man-Wolf.

Blood thirst

Morbius and Spider-Man have both fought together and worked as a team. On one occasion, Morbius even aided Spider-Man against Carnage. However, Morbius cannot escape his thirst, and he still hungers for the web-swinger's radioactive blood.

--THE CONFRONTATION HE WANTS!

BWAM!

AND HE'LL PROBABLY SHRUG THIS OFF LIKE ALL MY OTHER BLOWS TONIGHT!

MORBIUS MAY HAVE GOTTEN HIS POWERS THROUGH SCIENCE INSTEAD OF THE SUPERNATURAL--

--BUT HE'S MORE DANGEROUS THAN ANY MONSTER HAMMER FILMS EVER SPRUNG ON THE PUBLIC!

NEVER FORGET
Though he truly sympathizes with the cursed scientist, Spider-Man never forgets that Morbius is a monster who feeds on human blood.

A MAN CURSED WITH A THIRST FOR BLOOD.. AND THE POWER TO SATE IT!

YOU COULD LOOK FOR A CURE, MORBIUS!

IMBECILE! I SOUGHT A CURE FOR MONTHS! BUT THERE IS NO HOPE! I AM DOOMED FOREVER! SO BE IT! IF I MUST SUFFER, SO SHALL YOU!

WELL, THEY SAY MISERY LOVES COMPANY!

BLUE FEUD
Though they have had many brutal encounters, the wall-crawler has kept trying to find a cure for the pseudo-vampire. Morbius eventually became convinced that Spidey's irradiated blood might be able to save him, and has often tried to feast on the web-head.

Pawn of Hydra

Obsessed with obtaining some of Spidey's blood to try to cure him, Morbius stopped at nothing to lure out the wall-crawler. He even kidnapped some of Peter's friends, such as Glory Grant. Morbius also turned to other sources for help. One of these, Dr. Andrea Janson, turned out to be working for Hydra, the terrorist organization. They used Morbius to create a race of vampires and sent them to infiltrate the Kingpin's mob. Spider-Man and the vampire hunter Blade managed to destroy them, but Morbius escaped in the resulting confusion.

WHY IN THE NAME OF GOD ARE YOU DOING THIS? WHY?!

I SEEK SPIDER-MAN, WOMAN!

AND I'M DRIVEN BY TOO MANY DEMONS TO BE GENTLE OR REASONABLE AS I DO IT!

HAMMERHEAD

From image to reality

The last thing the gunman saw before passing out was a poster for a movie called *The Al Capone Mob*. This image had such an influence on the criminal that when he recovered Hammerhead became obsessed with the gangster period.

I N SO MANY WAYS, Hammerhead is a throwback to the gangster movies of the 1920s. He favors clothing and weaponry that are more suited to that period than today. However, beneath his outmoded exterior lurks a criminal mastermind. Hammerhead's real name is unknown even to him. Many years ago, Dr. Jonas Harrow, a surgeon who had lost his medical license for conducting illegal experiments, found a dying gunman in a New York City back alley. Seeing an opportunity to save a man's life and redeem his own reputation, Harrow operated

on the gunman, replacing much of his shattered skull with a special steel alloy. In doing so, Harrow transformed the unnamed thug into Hammerhead.

GANG WAR

Spider-Man first came across Hammerhead when the villain started a gang war with the criminal organization led by Doctor Octopus (*see pages 44-45*). The wall-crawler managed to stop the war before any innocent people were hurt. But still, Hammerhead has returned on many occasions. Aside from Spider-Man and Doctor Octopus, Hammerhead has also warred with Norman Osborn, Silvermane, and the Kingpin (*see pages 70-71*). He recently attempted a takeover of the New York branch of the Maggia, an international criminal organization, but a crime lord known as Don Fortunato defeated him and forced him to swear allegiance. It is very probable, however, that Hammerhead is already plotting to overthrow his new boss.

A head start

Thanks to his steel-plated skull, Hammerhead can easily flatten enemies, smash through walls, and even withstand a spider-powered punch!

Hammerhead's suits are designed to look like gangster clothing of the 1920s, even though they are sometimes lined with Kevlar.

SILVERMANE

YEARS AGO...WHEN IN MY PRIME...I COULD HAVE HUMBLED CAESAR CICERO...AND A DOZEN LIKE HIM... WITH ONE BLOW!

AND SOON...I SHALL BE ABLE TO, DO SO--AGAIN!

NO! DON'T DRINK IT! IT'S A TRICK! WHAT IF HE POISONED YA--?!!

SILENCE, MARKO! THERE ARE NONE WHO CAN OUTSMART SILVERMANE!

YOU'RE... STILL ALIVE! BUT... YOU'RE NOT THE SAME! YOU'RE YOUNGER... STRONGER!!

OF COURSE I AM! THAT WAS THE PURPOSE... THAT WAS THE PLAN!

I GAMBLED EVERY-THING ON BEING RIGHT ABOUT THE TABLET'S SECRET...THE ONLY SECRET THAT COULD SAVE ME--

...THE SECRET OF... THE FOUNTAIN OF YOUTH!

THE QUEST
Silvermane had never enjoyed a normal childhood and feared death, so he devoted vast resources to locating an ancient formula that he believed would rejuvenate him.

NICKNAMED "SILVERMANE" because his hair turned gray while he was still in his forties, the elderly Silvio Manfredi has been a professional criminal for most of his life. By the time he was a teenager, Silvio had already joined the crime syndicate known as the Maggia. Using cunning and ruthlessness, Silvio rose through the ranks until he became head of his own crime family. He eventually branched out and formed an alliance with Hydra, a worldwide organization dedicated to global domination. Using his new contacts, Silvermane formed an international crime ring that was devoted to the manufacturing and trafficking of drugs.

THE REWARD
To Silvermane's surprise, the ancient formula worked, giving him back his youth for a brief period.

THE FOUNTAIN OF YOUTH

As Silvermane grew older he became obsessed with finding the secret to immortality. He eventually learned of an ancient stone tablet inscribed with a formula that could allegedly restore his youth. Once he obtained the tablet, he kidnapped Dr. Curt Connors (*see pages 48-49*) and forced him to prepare the serum Spider-Man learned of Silvermane's plan and rescued Connors, but couldn't prevent the ancient crime lord from drinking the potion and regaining some of his lost vitality. The effects eventually wore off, and Silvermane reverted to his original age.

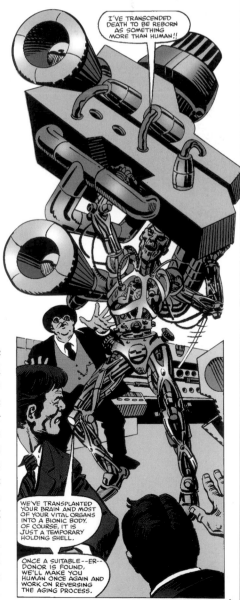

I'VE TRANSCENDED DEATH TO BE REBORN AS SOMETHING MORE THAN HUMAN!!

WE'VE TRANSPLANTED YOUR BRAIN AND MOST OF YOUR VITAL ORGANS INTO A BIONIC BODY. OF COURSE, IT IS JUST A TEMPORARY HOLDING SHELL.

ONCE A SUITABLE--ER--DONOR IS FOUND, WE'LL MAKE YOU HUMAN ONCE AGAIN AND WORK ON REVERSING THE AGING PROCESS.

A new lease on life
The vigilantes called Cloak and Dagger (*see pages 104-105*) despised Silvermane for his organization's role in their creation, and they tried to assassinate him. But his life was saved when his brain was transplanted into a robotic body. Silvermane is now an android who possesses amazing powers, yet his mind is still his greatest weapon. He was behind the criminal alliance that undermined the Kingpin (*see pages 70-71*).

DEATH OF THE STACYS

GWEN STACY was the first woman who truly captured the heart of Peter Parker. He fell deeply in love with her and was convinced that they would spend the rest of their lives together. Gwen lived with her widowed father, George Stacy, a retired New York City police captain. He liked Peter and approved of the relationship. George also seemed to have a grudging respect for Spider-Man, and he wanted to learn more about the masked crime fighter. He and his good friend Joe Robertson often met to discuss the wall-crawler, in an attempt to uncover Spider-Man's secret identity. Meanwhile, Peter and Gwen continued to grow closer, but tragedy was on the horizon.

SWINGING WILD
Doctor Octopus panicked when Spider-Man's special web-fluid destroyed his ability to control his tentacles.

No control
Spider-Man was nearly overwhelmed by the new and powerful Doctor Octopus. Fleeing to his college laboratory, Peter designed a new weapon to use against his enemy—a special web-fluid which would sever Ock's mental control over his tentacles. However, little did Spidey know what disastrous consequences this new weapon would bring.

THE FATAL FLUID

The return of Doctor Octopus to New York pushed Spider-Man to the limit. Somehow, the Doc had become more powerful than ever. But Spidey had one more trick up his sleeve. The wall-crawler managed to corner Doctor Octopus on a rooftop, while on the street below George

Stacy arrived in time to watch as the two started to battle. During the course of their fight, Spider-Man sprayed Ock with a special web-fluid. The metal tentacles immediately went wild, knocking over a nearby chimney. As Spider-Man grappled with Doctor Octopus, George Stacy saw that a small boy was about to be hit by the falling debris. Without thinking of his own safety, George rushed forward. He pushed the child clear of danger, but was buried beneath tons of masonry.

NOBLE SACRIFICE
Acting instinctively, George Stacy threw himself at the child when he realized that the falling bricks would crush the youngster. He managed to reach the child in time, but paid the ultimate price for his courage.

Last request
Horrified at what had happened, Spider-Man pulled his girlfriend's father from the rubble. George Stacy knew that he was dying and revealed that he had deduced Spider-Man's secret identity. As he died in Peter's arms, he begged Peter to watch over Gwen and to take care of her. Blaming his special web-fluid for causing the death of George Stacy, Spider-Man was filled with remorse.

Spider-Man was unable to save the woman he loved from the vengeance of the Green Goblin.

ALTERNATIVE TARGET
Since the Green Goblin knew Spidey's real identity, he took Peter's girlfriend.

Over the edge
Several years after George Stacy's death, trouble started to brew again for Peter's friends. Harry Osborn (*see pages 14-15*) had started taking drugs, and the stress of dealing with this pushed his father, Norman, into insanity. He resumed his role as the Green Goblin (*see pages 54-55*). Norman blamed Peter for his son's condition and set out to get revenge on him by abducting his girlfriend, Gwen Stacy.

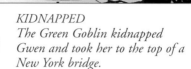

It's quite *simple*, web-spinner...

Your presence in this world has been a source of constant *agony* to me.

I wish you to *leave* it-- permanently.

Or... else... Gwen Stacy *dies!*

KIDNAPPED
The Green Goblin kidnapped Gwen and took her to the top of a New York bridge.

Kidnapped!
When Spider-Man finally showed up at his apartment, the place was in shambles and a jack-o'-lantern, the Green Goblin's trademark weapon, rested on Gwen's purse. Realizing she had been snatched, Spider-Man used his spider-sense (*see pages 22-23*) to track the Green Goblin down to the top of the George Washington Bridge.

She's *doomed*, do you hear me?

Doomed-- and so are *you!*

The night Gwen Stacy died
Gwen lay on top of the bridge, unconscious. Desperate to save her, Spider-Man pulled out all the stops as he battled the Green Goblin. On the verge of defeat, the Goblin hurled Gwen from the bridge. Spider-Man quickly shot out a web-line that caught the falling Gwen by the leg. When he pulled her up, he was horrified to discover that she was already dead. Desperate for revenge, Spider-Man set out to hunt down the Green Goblin and end his career once and for all.

DID IT!

SPIDER MAN

SLEEPLESS NIGHTS
Spider-Man has tortured himself on many a sleepless night replaying the horror in his head. Was Gwen dead when the webbing caught her? Or did the web-line accidentally snap her neck? Did Peter Parker kill his own girlfriend?

YAAAAAAH!

CHUNK!

Killed by his own glider
As much as he hated the Green Goblin after Gwen's death, Spider-Man realized that he couldn't take the life of another human being. He was about to take his enemy captive when Osborn mentally ordered his glider to impale Spider-Man. Warned by spider-sense, the web-head ducked at the last moment. The glider impaled the Green Goblin, killing him instantly—or so it seemed...

THE PUNISHER

THE MAN who became the Punisher had intended to be a priest when he grew up. However, Frank Castiglione began to question his vocation when he realized that he had a problem with granting forgiveness to people who broke the commandments.

Shortly after he dropped out of the seminary, Frank met Maria Falconio. They fell in love and were married. Since the priesthood was no longer an option, Frank enlisted in the Marines. He served numerous tours in war zones, and shortened his name to Castle. Frank underwent SEAL (sea, air, and land) and UDT (underwater demolition team) training. He rose to the rank of captain, nicknamed the Punisher because he was so relentless against the enemy. Then a tragic family outing changed his life forever...

REVENGE ISN'T SWEET

The brutal murder of his family made Frank decide to put his military training to good use. He concentrated on punishing criminals who were beyond the reach of the law. Frank eventually learned the identity of the gang who murdered his family. He hunted them down and eliminated them all—before dedicating his life to punishing the entire criminal underworld. Though he uses lethal force against the guilty, the Punisher protects innocent people from harm and he never battles the police.

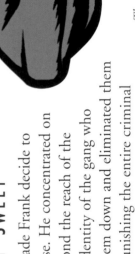

Fatal picnic

While on leave in New York, Frank Castle took his wife and two children to Central Park for a picnic. They accidentally stumbled upon a gangland killing. The mobsters feared being identified and immediately opened fire on the Castles. Frank somehow managed to survive, but his wife and children did not. Traumatized by the incident, Frank Castle vowed to punish the mobsters. He deserted the Marines and outfitted himself for a one-man war on crime.

CODE NAME
After the picnic massacre, Frank Castle revived his old code name and began calling himself the Punisher.

The battle suit is made of reinforced body armor, which is concentrated behind his chest symbol. This chest skull is designed to look like a target to draw fire.

The Punisher employs a wide range of portable weaponry, though he favors an M16 automatic rifle.

His belt contains ammo clips and concussion and tear-gas grenades.

OTHER ENEMIES
In addition to Spider-Man, Frank Castle has also encountered Captain America, the Black Widow, Daredevil, and Cloak and Dagger.

Pistol in holster

AGAINST TOMBSTONE
At one point, the two crimefighters teamed up against one of the most feared hitmen of all, Tombstone (see page 112).

A hero

Before he deserted the Marines to pursue his war on crime, Frank Castle was awarded both the Bronze and Silver Star, and he received four Purple Hearts. He was also scheduled to receive the Presidential Medal of Freedom, but his family was murdered days before the ceremony.

OPPOSING METHODS
Spider-Man and the Punisher hold different views on the best way to protect the innocent.

SHARPSHOOTER
The Punisher is an expert marksman and rarely misses. He knows how to lead a moving target and how to anticipate his opponents.

Frank Castle does not like being the Punisher. He considers himself a soldier in the war on crime. He has chosen this life to punish himself for failing to save his family.

CODE OF HONOR
Like a true Marine, the Punisher follows a strict code of honor. He is neither an assassin nor a sniper. Though he employs lethal force, he confronts his enemies face-to-face and is a man of his word.

Allies or adversaries?

Spider-Man and the Punisher have repeatedly teamed up, but they are not friends. Frank sees the web-head as an idealistic fool who lacks the stomach to use lethal force. Spider-Man thinks the Punisher is a tormented serial killer who uses unacceptable actions to ultimately achieve his own good intentions. Spidey wants to get Frank off the streets. Though they constantly waver between being allies and adversaries, Spider-Man and the Punisher both try to protect the innocent, and circumstances often force them to work together.

Pawn of the Jackal

The Punisher first met Spider-Man after the death of Gwen Stacy (*see pages 82–83*), and after J. Jonah Jameson had publicly accused the web-head of killing Norman Osborn, unaware that Osborn had been the Green Goblin. Working with the Jackal (*see pages 86–87*), whom Frank thought was just another costumed vigilante, the Punisher became convinced that Spidey was a murderer and attempted to bring him to justice. During the course of their battle, Spider-Man managed to prove his innocence, and the Punisher soon realized that the Jackal had lied to him. Though they tried to capture him, the Jackal escaped. Later, a terrorist sniper pretended to be the Punisher. Together, Spidey and Frank learned that the imposter was a man called Jigsaw, who sought revenge on the Punisher for permanently scarring his face.

The claws of the Jackal
The Jackal's gloves and boots are equipped with razor-sharp steel claws. These claws are often coated with poison or hallucinogens, or attached to electrical devices which can shock an enemy into unconsciousness.

THE JACKAL

THE MAN who ultimately became the Jackal was originally a shy and unassuming biology teacher at Empire State University. Professor Miles Warren taught both Peter Parker and Gwen Stacy. Warren found himself quite taken with the beautiful Gwen, though he believed that his feelings were only avuncular in nature. When she was accidentally killed during a battle between Spider-Man and the Green Goblin (*see pages 82-83*), the grief-stricken Warren fell into a deep depression. He suddenly realized that he had actually been in love with Gwen. Warren blamed Spider-Man for Gwen's death, and he vowed vengeance upon the wall-crawler.

THE JACKAL UNMASKED
Kindly old Professor Miles Warren was actually the man behind the Jackal's mask.

The Jackal's original costume was composed of stretch fabric and a latex mask.

GENETIC CHANGE
The Jackal later used his mastery of genetics to mutate his appearance so that he actually looked like a human jackal.

Though the Jackal didn't possess any superhuman abilities when he first appeared, he was skilled in gymnastics and hand-to-hand combat.

FROM MADMAN TO MURDERER

One night, Warren was approached by a mysterious figure named Scrier (*see pages 140-141*), who offered to help Warren with his secret experiment in cloning humans. Since Warren had taken cell samples from all his students, he immediately wanted to try to resurrect Gwen Stacy, but Scrier suggested that he begin with another student. Peter Parker was chosen. Warren's lab assistant eventually learned that he was growing human clones and threatened to expose him. Warren became enraged and killed the man. Unable to accept responsibility for his actions, the mentally unstable Warren convinced himself that some unknown predator had done it, someone who acted like a human jackal.

Bring her back
Though Miles Warren had at first believed that he looked on Gwen as a daughter, he later realized that he was actually in love with her. Cloning Gwen was his way of bringing her back.

"THE NEXT SEVERAL MONTHS WERE QUITE *BUSY* ONES, PARKER. I HAD TO CARE FOR THE *CLONES*, DESIGN MY *JACKAL* EQUIPMENT AND COSTUME, TRAIN MYSELF *ATHLETICALLY*, ALL THE WHILE BEING DRIVEN BY ONE CONSUMING *PASSION*:

His evil twin

To distance himself from the Jackal, Miles Warren designed a costume and some personal weaponry for his other identity. He planned to use the Jackal to get his revenge on Spider-Man. In addition, Professor Warren continued to conduct his cloning experiments. He eventually produced a perfect duplicate of Peter Parker. That's when he suddenly realized that his rival for Gwen's affections was also his greatest enemy. Warren then attempted to recreate Gwen Stacy. He produced a clone with all the girl's memories up to the time that he had taken her cell samples. But she also shared the original Gwen's emotions. She, too, loved Peter Parker and had absolutely no romantic feelings for Warren.

Clone confusion

After being knocked unconscious during a battle with the Jackal, Spider-Man awoke to find himself facing himself. One web-slinger was the real Spider-Man and the other was the Spider-Clone... but who was who?

HUH? WHO THE HECK ARE YOU, FELLA--AND WHERE'S THE *JACKAL?*

HUH? WHO THE HECK ARE *YOU*, FELLA --AND WHERE'S THE *JACKAL?*

HOLD IT RIGHT *THERE*...

I-I DIDN'T *MEAN* NED. I MEANT--

BUT-- ARE YOU *SURE*--THAT YOU'RE--?

BUT...HOW CAN YOU *TELL*...?

"THE OTHER *ME*"? HE'S GONE, GWEN.

OH, I'M THE *REAL* ONE, GWEN. BELIEVE ME.

THE ORIGINAL?
After one of the Spideys was apparently killed in an explosion, the remaining Spider-Man could only assume that he was the original wall-crawler.

--THE HATRED I *FEEL* FOR YOU, BECAUSE OF WHAT YOU *DID* TO THIS POOR, DARLING YOUNG *GIRL?*

DON'T LOOK TO HER FOR *HELP*, SPIDER-MAN. SHE'S *MINE* NOW--AND YOU CAN'T *HURT HER* ANYMORE!

I GAVE HER LIFE-

SIMPLE. I...

UH...

FAR OUT.

A living weapon

The Jackal programmed the Gwen clone with posthypnotic commands and used her as a psychological weapon against the web-swinger. Peter was shocked when he first saw the new Gwen, and could only stare at her in disbelief. Later, the Gwen clone broke free of the Jackal's mental control, and she angrily defied her creator. As the two Spider-Men battled, a bomb the Jackal had planted suddenly exploded. The blast appeared to kill both Professor Warren and one of the Spider-Men—but was the menace of the Jackal over?

Resurrection

Miles Warren appeared to die in the explosion. In actual fact he had cloned himself, and sent his double to die in his place. Entering a genetic accelerator, Miles Warren altered his own DNA. He assumed the characteristics of a true jackal and enhanced his strength, agility, and speed to superhuman levels. He had devised a truly twisted plan to get his revenge on the wall-crawler, a plan that became known as the Clone Saga (*see pages 136-137*).

PLANNING AHEAD
The Jackal is a master manipulator who always plans ahead. He set Hammerhead, Doctor Octopus, and Spider-Man against one another, hoping they would eventually destroy each other.

SOMEDAY I'LL MAKE YOU *PAY* FOR WHAT YOU SAID, PUNK-- SOMEDAY I'LL MAKE YOU *BURN*--YOU AND DOC OCK *BOTH!*

HAMMERHEAD DOESN'T *FORGET* THINGS LIKE THIS--

NOT NOW! NOT *EVER!*

AND THAT'S PRECISELY WHAT I'M *COUNTING* ON, YOU BLUNDERING *BABOON!*

YOU'RE PLAYING RIGHT INTO MY *HANDS*--AND IN THE END, AFTER THE APPROACHING *BATTLE ROYAL*, ONLY THE JACKAL WILL *SURVIVE!*

SHE'S *LEFT...* I'M *ALONE* AGAIN.

FATHER WOULDN'T *LIKE* ME TO SEE PEOPLE HE *HATES*-- JUST LIKE HE WOULDN'T HAVE WANTED PEOPLE TO SEE HIS *COSTUME.*

Harry Osborn became the second Green Goblin after his father died.

OTHER GREEN GOBLINS

HAROLD "HARRY" Osborn was Peter Parker's best friend (*see pages 14-15*). He was also one of Spider-Man's deadliest foes. The son of millionaire industrialist Norman Osborn, Harry had long been a troubled man. His mother died while he was a child, and his father buried himself in his work and was a domineering parent who rarely had time for his son. As a result, Harry grew up feeling inadequate. He both resented his father and would do almost anything to win his approval. Harry attended Standard High School with Gwen Stacy. He had a crush on her, but never found the courage to ask her out. Both Harry and Gwen went to college at New York City's Empire State University, where they met Peter Parker. After a rocky start, Harry began to form a friendship with Peter. Of course, this was before he discovered that his father was the Green Goblin and that Peter was Spider-Man.

WE ARE NOT *"FRIENDS",* PARKER. WE NEVER *HAVE* BEEN.

WE JUST SHARED AN *APARTMENT.* THAT'S ALL.

DO YOU HEAR?

THAT'S ALL!

RIGHT. IF THAT'S THE WAY YOU *WANT* IT... THAT'S FINE WITH *ME!*

The best of enemies
After his father's death, Harry turned against Peter Parker and began plotting his former friend's destruction. He believed that he had a responsibility to avenge his father's death and prove that he was strong enough to be the new Green Goblin.

HARRY'S FAILURES

Peter introduced Harry Osborn to Mary Jane Watson, and the two began to date. But Mary Jane didn't want a serious relationship, and she dumped him as soon as he became too possessive. Frustrated over his failure with Mary Jane and depressed over his relationship with his father, Harry turned to drugs. When Norman Osborn learned that Harry had almost died from an overdose, he blamed Peter Parker and wanted revenge. Norman became the Green Goblin and kidnapped Gwen Stacy, who died in the resulting battle (*see pages 82-83*).

WILD CLAIM
To protect his father's memory, Harry claimed that he was the original Green Goblin, but the police didn't believe him. By becoming the second Green Goblin, Harry intended to continue the family business.

THAT'S *OBVIOUS,* OFFICER.

I'M THE *GREEN GOBLIN!*

--BUT THERE'S NO WAY I'M GOING TO LET YOU *FOLLOW* IN YOUR FATHER'S *FOOTSTEPS!*

YOU NEED PRO-FESSIONAL *HELP,* HARRY--

NO!!

--AND I'M GOING TO SEE THAT YOU *GET* IT!!

Covering up
Still under the influence of the drugs he had been taking, Harry secretly witnessed Spider-Man's final battle with the original Green Goblin. He was present when his father was impaled. Before anyone else arrived, Harry removed the Goblin's mask and costume from his father's body. He made absolutely sure that the police couldn't link the dead industrialist with the Green Goblin.

You need help!
Using clues left in his father's diaries, Harry learned that Peter Parker was the web-head, and became determined to destroy Spider-Man. However, the wall-crawler was equally determined to see that Harry got the help he needed to cure his madness.

BLIND OBSESSION
Unlike his father, Harry Osborn had no interest in gaining wealth or power. He only wanted to kill Spider-Man.

Too young

After Spider-Man defeated the second Green Goblin, Peter Parker couldn't abandon his friend. Even though he knew that Harry planned to reveal his secret identity, he removed Harry's costume before the authorities arrived. When Harry awoke, he confessed to being the original Green Goblin. However, since the police knew that the Goblin had been active for many years, they assumed that Harry was hallucinating and ignored everything he said.

Third Green Goblin

Harry was placed under the care of Dr. Barton Hamilton, who successfully cured him of his insanity. Hamilton even found a way to purge Harry's memories of ever having been the Green Goblin. Then, after learning Harry's secrets, Barton Hamilton became the third Green Goblin. Peter Parker assumed Harry was behind the mask, not realizing that his friend was actually Hamilton's prisoner. Harry finally escaped and confronted Hamilton. The third Green Goblin was eventually killed by a bomb he had intended for Spider-Man.

Pumpkin bomb

WEAPONS
When he began his career as the second Green Goblin, Harry used his father's old equipment. It wasn't until he had assumed the presidency of Osborn Industries that Harry began to upgrade his arsenal.

COSTUME CHANGE
Armed with knowledge of Harry Osborn's secret identity, Hamilton went to Harry's secret hideout, where he discovered the goblin costume that belonged to Harry. The costume also gave him some of the Goblin's powers and weapons.

The Goblin Glider was eventually replaced by a newer model, designed and built by Harry, and later used by Phil Urich.

Living with the cure

Peter never gave up on Harry, and eventually found a way to cure his friend's madness. Harry became the president of his father's company. He met and began to date Liz Allen, one of Peter's high school classmates. They eloped, and Liz eventually gave birth to a child. Their marriage always seemed peaceful and happy on the surface, but the specter of the Osborn legacy continued to haunt them, and eventually led to Harry's death (*see pages 132-133*).

The original Goblin Glider was customized by Harry to improve its speed and performance.

FOURTH GREEN GOBLIN
Phil Urich, a college dropout and the nephew of reporter Ben Urich, became the fourth Green Goblin after stumbling upon Harry's secret hideout.

WILL O' THE WISP

POSSESSING A ghostlike appearance and powers to match, Will O' The Wisp is one of Spider-Man's eeriest allies. Jackson Arvad was a scientist who specialized in electromagnetic research. When faced with the danger of losing his funding, he began to work late into the night, desperate to prove that his research could produce concrete and commercial results. Working without any real rest, Arvad eventually grew careless and caused an unfortunate accident. A gravimetric power surge plunged Arvad into a self-sustaining magnetic field, and somehow caused the molecules in his body to gradually disperse.

TOO MUCH OVERTIME
Arvad was so tired from working late at the lab that he couldn't prevent the accident that turned him into Will O' The Wisp.

FALLING APART

Instead of dying, Arvad learned that he could control his molecules and keep them together. Arvad feared that he would eventually lose this control and contacted Dr. Jonas Harrow, the criminal surgeon who had given Hammerhead (*see page 80*) his powers. While pretending to help Arvad, Harrow planted a device in his skull that forced him to obey Harrow's commands. Under this influence, Arvad committed a number of robberies, and this led to a clash with Spider-Man. With Spidey's aid, however, Arvad managed to free himself from Harrow's control.

Intangibility
By willing himself to assume his minimum density, Will O' The Wisp can become immaterial and pass through solid objects. This process produces a bright, sparkling light.

MAXIMUM DENSITY
Will O' The Wisp can control the subatomic electromagnetic particles that hold his body together. This allows him to alter his density at will. He can make his flesh and muscles as hard as steel and temporarily gain superhuman strength as a result. However, he can only maintain maximum density for about 10 minutes.

MORE GHOST THAN MAN
Will O' the Wisp's voice sounds as cold and distant as his personality, and he hasn't attempted to form any lasting friendships since his transformation. He seems to value vengeance more than justice and has fought Spider-Man nearly as often as he's aided him.

HE'S FASTER THAN EVER! EVEN WITH MY SPIDER-SENSE EARLY-WARNING--

--I WAS JUST BARELY ABLE TO ROLL WITH THAT PUNCH!

BUT WISPY DOESN'T KNOW THAT! HE DOESN'T KNOW I CAN SENSE HIM COMING AROUND FOR ANOTHER SHOT!

A glowing ball
Will O' The Wisp can also fly by becoming lighter than air, and expelling a trail of excess molecules behind him. He usually gives off so much light when he does this that he appears to be an ethereal glowing sphere.

OTHER WORLDLY
Will O' The Wisp can will the molecules of his body to oscillate a short distance from himself, making him look like an unearthly spirit.

WHERE THERE'S A WILL
Will O' The Wisp also has the ability to mesmerize people and make them follow simple commands. He does this by causing his chest emblem to glow bright enough to hypnotize anyone who is gazing at it.

ROCKET RACER

ROBERT FARRELL always had a need for speed. The oldest of seven children, he was a science whiz who often went skateboarding when he wanted privacy. The sport gave him a sense of freedom, and he loved to feel the wind whipping at his face. However, he hung up his board when his father left the family. To help his mother, Robert joined the Air Force after he graduated from high school. He sent most of his money home, and learned how to build and repair jet engines. After he was discharged, Robert planned to get a good job and make life a lot easier for his mother.

NEED FOR CASH

Unfortunately, before Robert could start looking for work, his mother suffered a heart attack. Faced with mounting hospital bills and the need to support his siblings, Robert became desperate for cash. He turned to crime, combining his flair for engines with his love of skateboarding to become the Rocket Racer.

Jet engines give the skateboard fantastic speed.

The Rocket Racer's skateboard is guided by a cybernetic link that is built into his headset.

His gloves fire miniature explosives and can deliver a rocket-powered punch.

Special electromagnetic boot clamps anchor the Rocket Racer to his skateboard.

Money troubles

Spider-Man decided to help the Rocket Racer once he learned about his troubled background. By turning to crime, Robert Farrell had put further financial pressure on his family as they now needed the services of a bail bondsman. After he had served his sentence, Robert thought his days as the Rocket Racer were over, until he learned that Spider-Man had been accused of a crime. While attempting to help the web-swinger, the Rocket Racer met Silver Sable (*see page 110*) and she offered him a job as one of her superpowered mercenaries.

WALL-RIDER
The Rocket Racer can perform the most difficult stunts. He has designed his board with special gyro-wheels that allow him to race up sheer walls and stick to the sides of buildings.

A failure as a crook

After many hours of practice, the Rocket Racer committed his first crime. He stole a briefcase filled with negotiable securities, and was immediately captured by Spider-Man. Then Rocket Racer learned the identity of an embezzler and attempted to blackmail him. When the embezzler tried to kill Robert, Spider-Man intervened and saved the Rocket Racer's life.

MASTER INVENTOR
Robert Farrell is a natural inventor. Thanks to his work with jet engines in the Air Force, he was able to design miniature jet turbines that he attached to his skateboard. His board can reach a top speed of 60 mph, and travel about 75 miles before running out of fuel.

BLACK CAT

NIMBLE
The Black Cat is extremely agile, and she possesses exceptional reflexes. She can execute flips, springs, and somersaults easily.

Desperate to copy her father's criminal career, Felicia Hardy trained as an athlete and a gymnast. She also acquired videos taken of her father to study all his moves.

FELICIA HARDY was only 13 years old when she learned that her father had a secret life. Though Walter Hardy pretended to be a traveling salesman, he was actually a famous cat burglar. When her dad was captured and sentenced to life in prison, Felicia decided to take up where he left off.

She began a physical training program to increase her strength, endurance, and agility. She also studied the martial arts, and acquired skills such as lockpicking and safecracking. After years of preparation, Felicia designed a costume to hide her identity, and went out to seek fun and excitement as the Black Cat.

BAD LUCK

A real black cat is supposed to bring bad luck, and Felicia tried to use that old superstition to her advantage. Before committing a crime, she studied the surrounding area and chose an escape route. She then rigged the location so that convenient accidents stopped anyone who attempted to chase her. Walls collapsed, ropes snapped, and cars suddenly lost control. These carefully planned tricks convinced her enemies that the Black Cat caused bad luck to befall anyone who crossed her path.

CAT'S CABLE
The Black Cat sometimes carries a length of cable that can be used as a swing-line. This cable has two attachments: a grappling hook and a super-adhesive ball that sticks like Spider-Man's web.

The spider-shrine
Spider-Man and the Black Cat crossed paths so often that the feline criminal became attracted to the wall-crawler. She even built a shrine in his honor, filling it with pictures and mementos of the webhead! She also changed her evil ways and started to help Spider-Man battle criminals. Eventually, she succeeded in winning Spider-Man's love, as well as a pardon for her past offenses.

A SURPRISED WEB-SPINNER
Spider-Man was completely taken aback when the Black Cat first announced her love for him. Though he was very attracted to her, he assumed that this was just another trick and that she was only trying to avoid a prison term.

A COSTUMED COUPLE
Once Spider-Man realized that the Black Cat was serious about going straight, he began spending a lot of time with her.

A costumed couple

Realizing that the Black Cat possessed no superpowers of her own, Spider-Man started to fear for her safety and tried to discourage her from joining him against his superhuman enemies. Felicia immediately went on a quest to gain superpowers. Scientists in the employ of an unknown benefactor claimed they could help her if she agreed to work for their boss. She suspected the man was a criminal, but she was so desperate that she agreed to his terms. The scientists somehow gave her the ability to affect probability and to cause improbable things to happen. Machines would explode and guns backfire. She now truly possessed the bad luck powers that she once used to fake with elaborate traps.

I NEVER KNOW WHAT TO EXPECT WHEN YOU'RE AROUND!

DON'T BE MAD! I ONLY WANTED TO HELP! AND, ANYWAY, THINGS *DID* TURN OUT RIGHT!

NOW ARE YOU CONVINCED THAT I WANT TO GO STRAIGHT?

WE HAVE TO TALK MORE ABOUT THAT!

WHY DON'T WE KISS FIRST?

Pawn of the Kingpin

The Black Cat eventually learned that the man behind her new powers was actually the Kingpin. He gave them to her to get revenge on Spider-Man. When the wall-crawler learned about her connection to the Kingpin, he ended his relationship with the Black Cat.

THESE ARE THE MOMENTS FELICIA HARDY LIVES FOR... WHEN SHE SWINGS THROUGH THE CONCRETE CANYONS OF NEW YORK BESIDE HER SPIDER-MAN!

On the prowl

After splitting with Spider-Man, the Black Cat traveled through Europe where she had an affair with a criminal known as the Foreigner, who had been married to Silver Sable (*see page 110*). The Black Cat didn't return to New York until after Peter Parker was married, and she decided to annoy her ex-boyfriend by going out with Flash Thompson (*see pages 14-15*). To her surprise, she fell in love with Flash, and was heartbroken when he stopped seeing her.

UNDER THE MASK
Though she loved Spider-Man, and probably still does, the Black Cat has no interest in the man behind the mask. She doesn't find Peter Parker attractive, and she thinks he lives a boring life.

SO NOW YOU KNOW, CAT. I'VE NEVER REVEALED MY IDENTITY TO ANYONE BEFORE. I'M TELLING YOU NOW BECAUSE I LOVE YOU--

--AND BECAUSE FROM NOW ON WE'RE GONNA SHARE OUR LIVES TOGETHER.

SP-SPIDER...

YES, MY DARLING?

Y-YOUR MASK...

...PLEASE...

...PUT YOUR MASK BACK ON!!!

I LOVE YOU!

AND I LOVE YOU... SPIDER-MAN!

The Cat's Eye

Having completely reformed, the Black Cat recently established her own private security agency. Cat's Eye Investigations provides background checks, bodyguards, and bounty hunters, and specializes in installing burglarproof security systems. One of her employees is a computer whiz named Loop who used to work with her father. He is currently serving time in a minimum-security prison, and he keeps in touch via a computer hidden in his jail cell.

Jessica was injected with an experimental serum of irradiated spider's blood.

SPIDER-WOMAN

MORE THAN one woman has taken on the mantle of Spider-Woman—in total, there have been four (although one of them turned out to be the creation of an evil genius). The first Spider-Woman was the daughter of an American anthropologist and his British wife. When she was a child, Jessica Drew was exposed to radiation which made her seriously ill. Her father's research into spiders showed that a spider had a far greater resistance to radiation than a human. So he injected Jessica with a serum of spider's blood, causing her to fall into a coma. When she awoke, years later, Jessica didn't realize that the serum had given her strange powers. Then, at 17, she accidentally discharged a blast of bioelectricity which almost killed her boyfriend!

DARK DESTINY

Horrified by what she had done, Jessica ran away. She was discovered by agents of Hydra, the terrorist organization, who recognized her unique abilities. They brainwashed her and planned to use her as an assassin, but Jessica had other ideas. Escaping from Hydra, she began her career as a costumed crimefighter. Calling herself Spider-Woman, Jessica moved to San Francisco and became a private detective in her civilian identity.

She's electric
Jessica had the power to generate and project a form of bioelectricity. Her blasts could stun or kill at close range, and reached a maximum distance of 25 feet. She also exuded a high concentration of pheromones that elicited desire in men and fear in women.

END OF HER CAREER
Over the years, Spider-Woman teamed up with such heroes as Spider-Man, Wolverine, the Thing, Captain America, Doctor Strange, and the Avengers. She eventually lost her spiderlike powers, but she continues to work as an investigator and a bounty hunter.

A gift
Spider-Woman's first costume was a gift from Hydra. It was equipped with special glider-wings and powered by harnessing her own bioelectricity.

SPIDER-WOMAN #1

GLIDER WINGS
Jessica's special glider-wings had a network of metal filaments woven into the material.

Jessica's body was immune to all poisons and radiation, and she also possessed superhuman strength.

Jessica had the ability to stick to walls by excreting an unknown adhesive from her palms and soles.

SPIDER-WOMAN #2

Mattie Franklin loves being a costumed hero, and she rarely wears the same costume twice.

Mattie is 5 feet 8 inches tall.

SPIDER-WOMAN #3

The Gathering of Five

The third Spider-Woman actually wanted her powers. Martha "Mattie" Franklin was a 15-year-old runaway. Stealing a mystical object from her father, she took his place in an arcane ceremony called the Gathering of Five. The ceremony promised to bring immortality, knowledge, and power to three of the participants, leaving the other two with death and madness. Mattie was granted the gift of unlimited power, and she has used her newfound super-powers to imitate her idol, the amazing Spider-Man.

AN EXTENDED VISIT
The daughter of an old friend of Marla Jameson, the wife of Jonah (see pages 34–35), Mattie is currently living in New York and staying with the Jamesons.

STOLEN POWER
Mattie can project huge spider-like legs from her back, a power that she somehow obtained from the fourth Spider-Woman.

Mattie can fly through the air and has superhuman strength.

Like Spider-Man, the second Spider-Woman has the proportionate strength of a spider.

Spider-Woman #3
Mattie became the third costumed hero to call herself Spider-Woman. Working closely with Madam Web and Jessica Drew, Mattie has battled super-criminals such as Doctor Octopus, the Rhino, and a fourth Spider-Woman who had been created by Doctor Octopus. Mattie currently attends an all-girls private high school, and she is still an active crimefighter.

SPIDER-WOMAN #2
The second Spider-Woman was given her powers by a secret commission, which was established to create super heroes who would be under government control. Julia Carpenter was its first test subject. They injected her with an experimental formula that eventually transformed her into Spider-Woman.

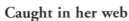

Caught in her web
After her treatment, Julia found that she developed some amazing new powers. She could spin a "psi-web," a web of psychically produced strands which could trap anyone. She could also produce enough psi-energy through her hands and feet to allow her to stick to walls. On top of this, she had superhuman strength and was able to lift 10 tons, as well as enhanced speed and incredible agility and reflexes.

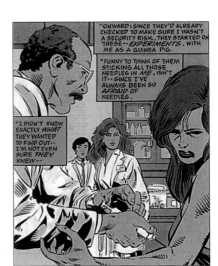

BETRAYED
Julia Carpenter assumed that she could trust the government and meekly allowed the commission's scientists to inject her with an experimental formula.

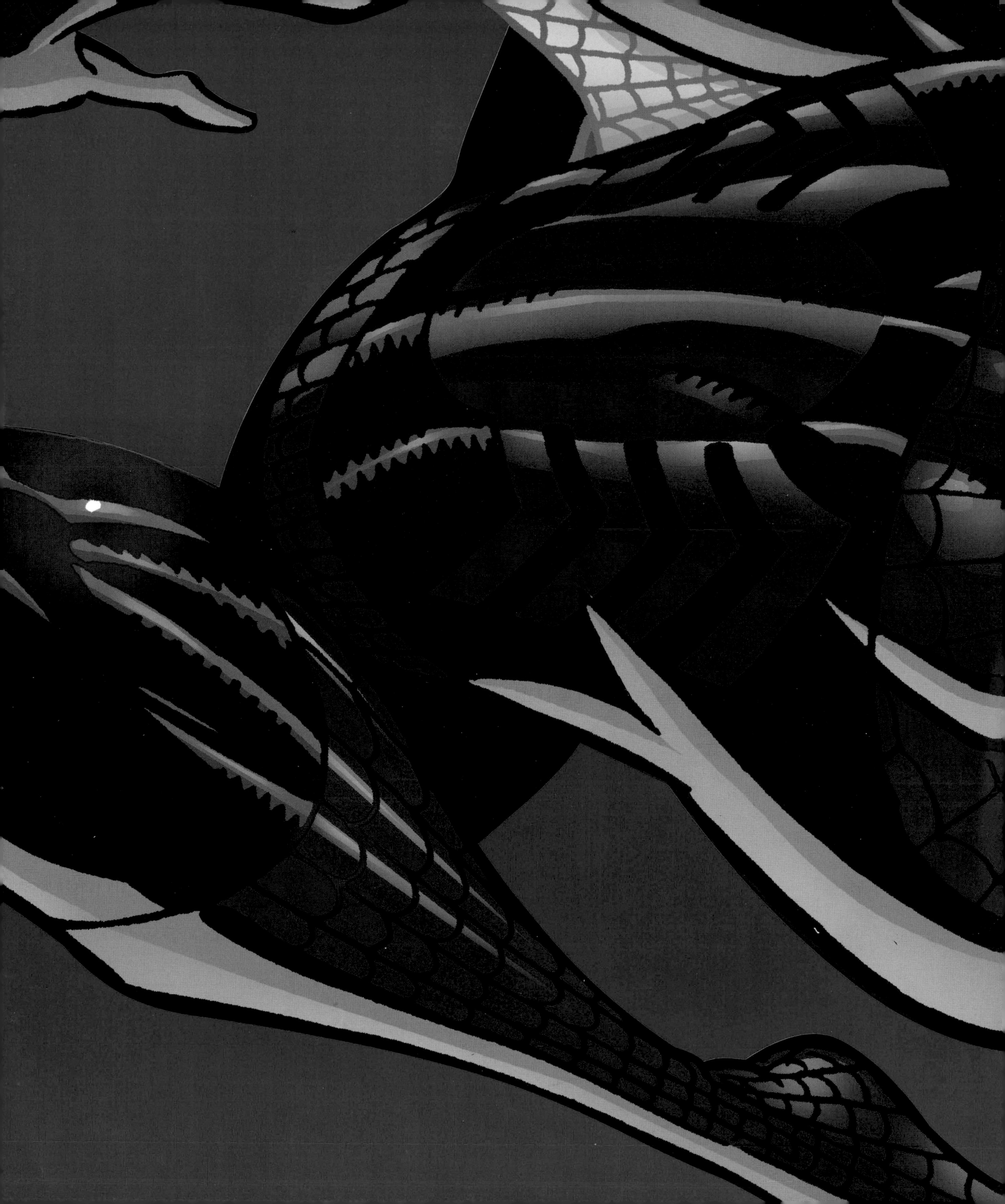

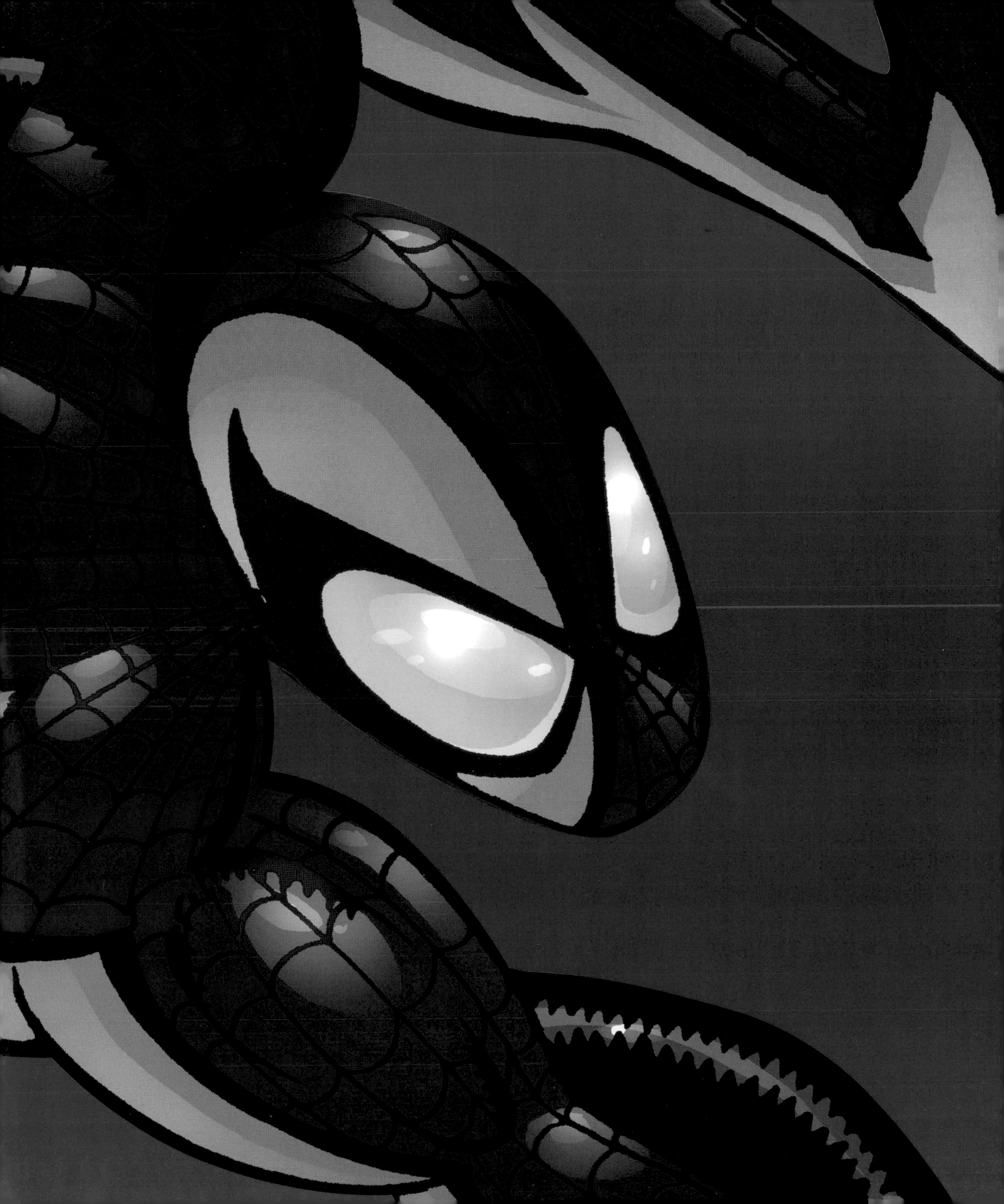

SPIDER-MAN IN THE '80S

MY PERSONAL relationship with Spidey suddenly turned professional during the spring of 1981. I was hired as an editor for Marvel Comics and assigned all three Spider-Man titles, while Mark Gruenwald became my assistant editor.

Other developments included John Romita, Jr. making comic-book history when he began to illustrate his father's former title. Roger Stern intrigued the fans with the mysteries surrounding the Hobgoblin. Bill Mantlo ignited a love affair between Spidey and the Black Cat. And J.M. DeMatteis began to explore the web-head's relationships with his world and himself.

Amazing Spider-Man #252 (May 1984)
First appearance of Alien costume
(Cover art by Ron Frenz)

Spider-Man and his Amazing Friends #1 (Dec. 1981) Onetime publication for new TV series (Cover art by John Romita)

Alas, all good things come to an end. I was promoted and had to give up the spider-titles. But my connection with Spidey wasn't quite over. Given a chance to write The Avengers, Roger Stern decided to leave *Amazing Spider-Man*. Danny Fingeroth, the editor who had succeeded me, offered the book to me. I accepted and was teamed up with Ron Frenz. We plotted "The Saga of the Alien Costume" and added a few new villains.

Meanwhile, the multitalented Al Milgrom was writing and drawing *Peter Parker, The Spectacular Spider-Man*, and Louise Simonson began a wonderful run of stories in the new *Web Of Spider-Man*. David Micheline eventually took over *Amazing*, and was paired with future superstar Todd McFarlane. Their sensational stint included the first appearance of Venom.

THE EIGHTIES

1980

Amazing Spider-Man #200 (Jan. 1980) *Uncle Ben's killer returns*

1981

Amazing Spider-Man #222 (Nov. 1981) *Spidey vs. Speed Demon*

1983

Amazing Spider-Man #238 (March 1983) *The Hobgoblin appears*

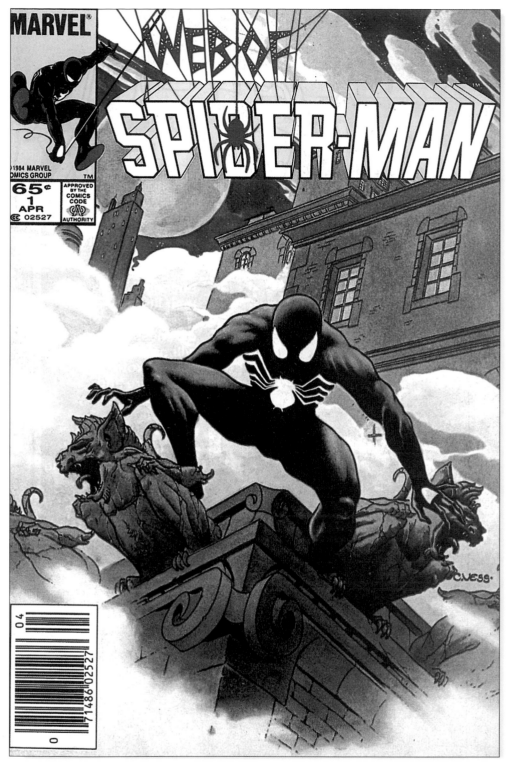

Amazing Spider-Man #300 (May 1988)
Spider-Man first meets Venom
(Cover art by Todd McFarlane)

Web Of Spider-Man #1 (April 1986)
First in a new series
(Cover art by Charles Vess)

1985

Marvel Team-Up
#150 (Feb. 1985)
Final issue in the series

1987

Amazing Spider-Man #290
(July 1987) Peter asks Mary
Jane to marry him

1989

Amazing Spider-Man
#312 (Feb. 1989)
Green Goblin vs. Hobgoblin

NOTHING CAN STOP THE JUGGERNAUT

WHEN CAIN MARKO was a soldier in Korea, he discovered an ancient temple inside a cave. On the lap of an idol was a big ruby with an inscription that read, "Whosoever touches this gem shall possess the power of the Crimson Bands of Cyttorak. Henceforth, you who read these words shall become forevermore a human juggernaut." As soon as he seized the ruby, Cain Marko was transformed into the invincible Juggernaut, a virtually unstoppable engine of destruction.

UNSTOPPABLE AND INDESTRUCTIBLE
The Juggernaut possesses enough strength to lift well over 100 tons, and he can also surround himself with an impenetrable force field that protects him from all harm.

> TAKE IT EASY, CAIN! LIKE I TOLD YE BEFORE, YE'LL SOON HAVE ALL THE ACTION YE CRAVE!

> YOU CALL GRABBING SOME OLD WOMAN "ACTION"? BAH!

> AND HOW MANY TIMES MUST I TELL YOU... I'M *NOT* CAIN MARKO ANYMORE! I HAVEN'T BEEN SINCE THE DAY I BECAME THE *JUGGERNAUT!*

> I NEED A *REAL* WORK-OUT, TOM -- SOMETHING WORTHY OF MY POWER!

Mission: Madam Web
Black Tom Cassidy, an international terrorist, learned of the existence of a psychic called Madam Web. He thought that he could use her power to help defeat the X-Men, and he sent Juggernaut to kidnap the woman.

> SO, I'D SAY THAT A LITTLE SNEAK ATTACK WAS IN ORDER!

> I KNOW I'LL HATE MYSELF FOR THIS IN THE MORNING, BUT--!

FOO

The champion and the challenge
Thanks to her psychic powers, Madam Web knew that the Juggernaut was coming and called Spider-Man for help. Spider-Man quickly learned that his usual tricks were useless against the Juggernaut. When Spidey hurled himself at the massive figure, he just bounced off! Spider-Man knew the odds were stacked against him, but he couldn't abandon a friend— he had to fight the Juggernaut.

> WHAT'S WRONG? YOU HAVING SOME SORT OF FIT?

> YOU BIG, DUMB JERK! SHE'S GOING INTO CONVULSIONS!

BROKEN PRIZE
When the Juggernaut removed Madam Web from her life-sustaining chair, she went into convulsions.

> YOU'RE COMING WITH ME, WEB!

> NO, PLEASE DON'T--!

No winners
Spider-Man was desperate to save Madam Web, but the Juggernaut battered the web-head into submission. Then Marko ripped Madam Web from her life-support system. When the Juggernaut learned that Madam Web would die without it, he grew annoyed that he had come for nothing and casually discarded the dying woman.

Fiery holocaust

After abandoning the helpless Madam Web, the Juggernaut tried to rejoin Black Tom. Spider-Man followed and tried to knock him unconscious by hurling a steel girder at him—but the Juggernaut simply caught it. No matter what Spider-Man threw at the monster, he could not stop the Juggernaut. His frustration growing by the moment, Spider-Man commandeered a tanker truck full of gasoline. He kicked the truck into ramming speed and crashed into his enemy, unleashing a fiery holocaust. The Juggernaut merely activated his personal force field and barely noticed the searing explosion.

A desperate maneuver

The battle moved to a construction site, and Spidey had an idea. Leaping upon the Juggernaut, he wrapped his arms over his enemy's mask and somehow managed to hang on as he guided the wild Juggernaut forward—straight into a recently poured building foundation.

A LONG WAIT
Waiting in a small boat in New York Harbor, Black Tom couldn't understand why his partner had not returned— surely no one could have stopped the Juggernaut!

Still walking

As the Juggernaut stepped into the still-wet concrete foundations, his massive bulk dragged him to the bottom. But thanks to the mystical properties of the ruby of Cyttorak, he does not need to eat, drink, or even breathe—sooner or later, he will break free!

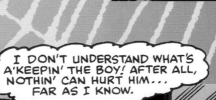

TRAPPED IN HER OWN WEB
Madam Web's special life-support system monitored her health, kept her vital signs stable, and attended to all of her needs.

MADAM WEB

Blind since birth, Cassandra Webb learned of her psychic powers when she was a child. She became a professional medium called Madam Web and used her abilities to help others. However, when she was a young woman, she learned that a mysterious disease had begun to attack her central nervous system. Her husband discovered that she would be completely paralyzed, so he designed an electronic weblike life-support system to keep her alive. Supported by this system, but completely dependent upon it, Madam Web used her psychic powers to learn that Peter Parker was the man behind the Spider-Man costume. She has since secretly aided the wall-crawler on many occasions. Madam Web recently took part in a mystical ceremony called the Gathering of Five that somehow restored her youth. She also became the mentor of Mattie Franklin, the gifted girl who is the current Spider-Woman (*see pages 94-95*).

CLOAK AND DAGGER

CLOAK AND Dagger are runaways: two lonely teenagers who ran away to New York City to seek a better life. Fate, however, had other plans for them. Tandy Bowen grew up in Shaker Heights, Ohio, the daughter of a multimillionaire and his trophy supermodel wife. Her dad abandoned the family while Tandy was young, and her mother was too busy with her career and social life to pay much attention to the girl. Even her boyfriend forgot about her as soon as he went to college. Feeling empty and alone, Tandy boarded a bus for New York City with dreams of becoming a dancer. Tyrone Johnson, or Ty, had a very different background. Ty was raised in the slums of South Boston, Massachusetts, and had been born with a speech impediment—a terrible stutter. When his best friend died because Ty was unable to say the words that might have saved him, the distraught teenager fled Boston.

FAILED EXPERIMENT

Shortly after arriving in New York, Ty saved Tandy from a purse snatcher. But as the two teenagers started to become friends, they were kidnapped and taken to a secret laboratory. Here, Simon Marshall, a pharmaceutical chemist who worked for the gang leader Silvermane (*see page 81*), was developing a synthetic drug, a cheap heroin substitute that could be smuggled into the country easily. He began experimenting on teenage runaways, but most of them died. Only two survived: Tyrone and Tandy. Mysteriously, Marshall's drug transformed them into the superpowered Cloak and Dagger.

Struggle for survival
Ty and Tandy limped out of the laboratory, leaving behind the bodies of the less fortunate victims.

Tyrone's cloak is a piece of discarded cloth that he first wrapped around himself to hide his new powers.

Cloak can project his dark dimension, letting it issue from his cape to envelop anyone or anything he chooses.

GOT TO...STOP THEM!

YOU ARE AN ADMIRABLE OPPONENT, SPIDER-MAN. IT IS A PITY THAT WE HAD TO MEET AS ENEMIES.

CLOAK ENVELOPED DAGGER IN HIS CAPE!

THEY'VE VANISHED!

FAREWELL. I HOPE YOUR PAIN DOES NOT LAST LONG.

UUHNNNHH!

C'MON! YOU'RE NOT REALLY GONNA TRY TO STOP ME BY WAVING A CAPE! THIS ISN'T A BULLFIGHT--AND YOU CAN'T SIDESTEP A GUY WITH SPIDER-SPEED!

WE SHALL SEE...

HEY! WHO TURNED OUT THE LIGHTS?!!

Together, forever

The symbiotic nature of Cloak and Dagger's powers prevents them from ever going their separate ways. Dagger needs Cloak to bleed off any excess energy so that she doesn't become overcharged. Cloak needs Dagger's light daggers to satisfy the never-ending hunger created by his extradimensional void.

A shadow world

Hidden within the folds of Cloak's hooded cape is a dark dimension, an immaterial, featureless, and seemingly endless void that sucks the vitality from anyone foolish enough to enter it. By entering his own dark dimension, Cloak is able to teleport himself and others, including Dagger, anywhere he can visualize.

Light and dark

Cloak feels a constant desire to fill the terrible void of his dark dimension, a hunger that can only be satiated by the vitality siphoned from people who pass into his dimension. Spider-Man has found himself caught in this dimension on more than one occasion, but discovered that he could escape by flailing around until he connected with something solid—namely Cloak's chin!

I DON'T GET IT! THERE'S ENOUGH SPACE IN THIS CAPE TO LOSE A CITY BLOCK!

IT'S FREEZING IN HERE-- AND THE DARKNESS IS SOMEHOW MUTING MY SPIDER-SENSE!

Dagger can mentally control the speed, direction, and power of her light daggers.

REVENGE!
Spider-Man first met Cloak and Dagger when he ran into a terrified Simon Marshall, who was fleeing for his life. Marshall begged the wall-crawler to protect him from the vengeful teens. Spidey tried to convince Cloak and Dagger, but they managed to defeat Spidey and get their revenge.

Let there be light

Dagger has the power to hurl light from her fingertips which can shock enemies into unconsciousness or paralyze them for five minutes. If Dagger desires, these blasts of light can overload a person's nervous system and cause a massive heart attack. They have also been known to cure certain physical symptoms of drug addiction.

ALLIES AND ENEMIES
Spidey sympathizes with Cloak and Dagger, but he is often pitted against them because he can't condone their use of lethal force. When they discovered Silvermane's (see page 81) role in their creation, they added the elderly gang lord to their hit list, forcing Spider-Man to defend his old enemy. Dagger's light projectiles gave the old man a seemingly fatal heart attack. Silvermane's life was saved, however, when his brain was transplanted into a robot body. Silvermane returned to destroy Cloak and Dagger, and Spider-Man suddenly found himself defending them.

OUR GRIEVANCE WAS NEVER WITH YOU-- BUT WE WILL NOT ALLOW YOU TO COME BETWEEN US AND OUR RIGHTEOUS REVENGE.

CLOAK! YOU'RE A TELEPORTER, AREN'T YOU? THAT'S HOW YOU MANAGE TO AVOID ME SO WELL!

YOU CAN SOMEHOW DISTORT SPACE--AND DISORIENT YOUR ENEMIES --BY ENVELOPING THEM IN THAT CRAZY CAPE! THEN DAGGER FINISHES THE JOB!

HYDRO-MAN

MORRIS BENCH was a crewman on a cargo ship that was lowering an experimental generator into the ocean, when he was accidentally knocked overboard by Spider-Man. At that moment the generator began to malfunction, and Morris was exposed to unknown energies, seawater, and underwater volcanic gases. After he was rescued, Morris discovered that he could transform all or part of his body into water. Morris was furious at what had happened to him, and he set out to find those he considered responsible and make them pay—and that included Spider-Man.

VIRTUALLY UNTOUCHABLE
Hydro-Man can allow objects to pass through him without sustaining any injury, and he can fire jets of his liquid with enough pressure to knock a man off his feet.

THE MUD MONSTER

After their first few battles, Spider-Man defeated Hydro-Man by splattering him over an area that was so big that Morris evaporated before he could reassemble himself. But Hydro-Man returned and joined forces with Sandman (*see pages 46-47*) against their enemy, Spidey. They nearly succeeded in killing the web-head, but a freak accident caused the two criminals to merge, transforming them into a giant mud creature.

The Sinister Syndicate
Hydro-Man quickly realized that he wasn't cut out for a solo crime career. He joined with the Beetle, Boomerang, the Rhino, and Speed Demon to form the Sinister Syndicate. They were hired to assassinate Silver Sable, but Spider-Man and the newly reformed Sandman managed to stop them.

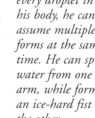

MANY FORMS
Since Hydro-Man has total control over every droplet in his body, he can assume multiple forms at the same time. He can spray water from one arm, while forming an ice-hard fist with the other.

Alone again
Spider-Man and the police managed to dehydrate the mud monster until it crumbled to pieces. It took many months before Sandman and Hydro-Man could disconnect from each other and go their separate ways.

Hydro-Man can hide within any pool of water.

UNIQUE TRAVEL
Hydro-Man can convert the lower part of his body into a blasting stream of water, propelling himself into the air with great force. He can cover a distance of nearly 50 feet with a single leap.

A GAMBLING MAN
Nicholas Powell became Chance because he loves risk more than money. He enjoys putting his life on the line for the thrill of the hunt.

CHANCE

A FORMER PROFESSIONAL gambler, Nicholas Powell combines his new career with his old. Unlike most criminal mercenaries, Chance does not get paid in advance. He bets his services against his fee. Only if he succeeds in his mission does he receive payment. Powell became Chance because he loves the thrill of risking his life for a grand prize. He first met Spider-Man when he was hired to kill a criminal named Andre Bouillon. Chance also wagered his fee at double-or-nothing that he could slay Spidey, too. Powell lost that particular bet and was arrested by the police, but the charges were later dropped due to lack of evidence.

WRIST-BLASTERS
Chance wears gauntlets on both wrists that can fire lasers and powerful blasts. They can also discharge mini-grenades and darts filled with acid that he uses to burn through brick walls.

Other missions
Chance was hired to assassinate casino owner Raymond Trask. But Spider-Man arrived on the scene and drove the mercenary off. A few months later, Trask appeared at Powell's penthouse and offered him another wager. He knew someone else wanted to kill him, so Trask bet Chance $20,000 that the mercenary couldn't keep him alive. Chance took the wager. When Trask tried to double-cross him, Chance outsmarted the casino owner and collected his winnings.

THE LIFE FOUNDATION
A survivalist group called the Life Foundation hired Chance to hijack a shipment of experimental weaponry. But the Life Foundation had other plans, too. They kidnapped Chance and attempted to duplicate his wrist blasters and ankle jets. Still on Chance's trail, Spider-Man was forced to save the mercenary's life. Working together, Spidey and Powell battled and defeated the Life Foundation.

Chance's equipment is powered by a miniaturized power pack that he wears on his back.

The good life
Whenever he isn't working, Nicholas Powell enjoys the good life. He lives in a plush penthouse apartment, surrounded by expensive furniture and objets d'art. He dates a bevy of beautiful women, attends the most prestigious cultural events, and enjoys fine dining. He also jetsets around the world.

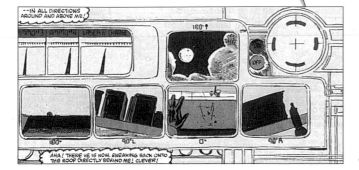

Chance controls his equipment through special cybernetic links that are connected to his helmet. His helmet enables him to see in all directions.

THE ALIEN COSTUME

WHEN HIS spider-sense suddenly flared with the force of an exploding bomb, Peter Parker instantly realized that he was in intense danger. Almost blind with pain, our hero struggled to locate the source of this new threat. He changed into his costume and followed the tingles deep into New York's Central Park. Hidden from view by a forest of trees, Spider-Man was shocked to discover a strange-looking alien structure which rose from the ground. As he approached the unknown edifice, dazzling lights suddenly engulfed Spider-Man and he disappeared within the blinding blaze.

MUST BE THIS ONE! IT LOOKS LIKE IT WANTS TO MAKE ME A COSTUME!

WHAT THE HECK IS THAT--?

AND WHY IS IT MAKING MY SPIDER-SENSE TINGLE?

Into battle
Spider-Man found himself on a satellite in a galaxy far from Earth. Along with other super heroes, such as Captain America, and super villains, including Dr. Doom, Spidey was brought to the satellite by a near-omnipotent being called the Beyonder. The Beyonder wanted heroes and villains to fight a war on a planet called Battleworld. Spider-Man fought many battles, and his costume was left in tatters. Then he found a machine that could replace ruined clothing.

MOVING ON UP
Spider-Man triggered the clothing machine and a round black object sprang from it. It immediately started to spread up Spidey's arm, and didn't stop until it covered his entire body.

KNOW IT ALL
The alien costume always seemed to know what Peter wanted, sometimes even before he did.

THERE WERE SOME BAD MOMENTS IN THE LAST FEW DAYS, WHEN I WAS CONVINCED I'D NEVER SEE THIS OLD HOMESTEAD AGAIN--

--LIKE THAT TIME GALACTUS ALMOST STEPPED ON ME!

OH, WELL, I...

HEY!

THE COSTUME IS RESPONDING TO MY THOUGHTS AGAIN!

Homecoming
After defeating the villains and escaping the Beyonder, the heroes returned to Earth, and Spider-Man took his alien costume with him. He learned that his new supersuit was capable of generating a seemingly endless supply of webbing, and that it could also change its appearance at will.

DIFFERENT LOOK
At first Peter was surprised by his new look, but then he realized that he might have been subconsciously influenced by the design of the new Spider-Woman costume worn by Julie Carpenter (see pages 94-5).

(see pages 94-5)

The spider legs on the spider symbol extended to connect the symbols on the chest and the back.

THIS NEW COSTUME MAY BE FAST AND EFFICIENT!

BUT IT'LL BE A LOOOONG TIME BEFORE--

--I'M READY FOR SERVICE LIKE THIS!

When you wish upon a suit
Peter and his alien costume were always in some kind of psychic contact, even when physically separated. If the costume was in a different room, it came at Peter's mental summons.

TATTERS AWAY
As the alien suit slithered over Spider-Man, it absorbed and dissolved away the tatters of his old costume.

SOON, A TROUBLED SLEEP CLAIMS THE TIRED, BROODING YOUNG MAN. BUT, SHORTLY AFTER IT DOES...

...HIS UNCANNY COSTUME BEGINS TO STIR!

SERPENTLIKE, IT GLIDES ACROSS THE FLOOR, REACHING FOR HIM--

NIGHT TERRORS
Each night while Peter slept, the alien costume secretly slipped over him and took the unconscious Spider-Man wall-crawling at night. The web-swinger awoke each morning with no memory of his nocturnal adventures. All he knew was that he felt more exhausted than before he had gone to bed.

IT CAN APPARENTLY MIMIC ANY OUTWARD APPEARANCE THAT YOU CAN PICTURE IN YOUR MIND! FASCINATING--!

Friend in need
As Peter's fatigue continued to grow, he slept through the entire day and began to have terrible nightmares. So Spider-Man went to Reed Richards, alias Mr. Fantastic of the Fantastic Four, for help.

YOU ARE WEARING A HIGHLY EVOLVED SYMBIOTE-- A SENTIENT BEING WHICH HAS ATTACHED ITSELF TO YOU BOTH MENTALLY AND PHYSICALLY!

YOU MEAN... IT'S ALIVE?!

It's alive!
After an exhaustive series of tests, Mr. Fantastic made a startling pronouncement. Instead of an amazing suit composed of some unknown extraterrestrial fabric, Spidey's new costume was actually a living creature. It was a sentient symbiote who had formed a mental and physical bond with the web-swinger.

TECHNICAL KNOW-HOW
Reed Richards needed all his futuristic technical knowledge to find out what the alien costume was.

Sneak attack
As soon as the symbiote's secret was revealed, it attempted to permanently graft itself to Spider-Man's body. Spider-Man did all he could to escape from the costume, but the symbiote tightened its grip on him, almost crushing Spidey in the process. Luckily, Reed Richards had discovered that the symbiote was vulnerable to certain sound frequencies. Using these sound waves, Richards managed to separate Spidey from the costume. At last our hero was free and the alien was imprisoned.

RISKING DEATH
Peter didn't care that the bells could kill him—he just wanted to be free from the symbiote.

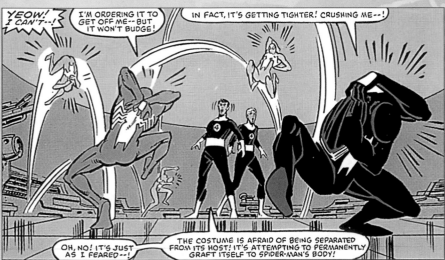

YEOW! I CAN'T--!

I'M ORDERING IT TO GET OFF ME--BUT IT WON'T BUDGE!

IN FACT, IT'S GETTING TIGHTER! CRUSHING ME--!

OH, NO! IT'S JUST AS I FEARED--!

THE COSTUME IS AFRAID OF BEING SEPARATED FROM ITS HOST! IT'S ATTEMPTING TO PERMANENTLY GRAFT ITSELF TO SPIDER-MAN'S BODY!

Escape
Later, the symbiote escaped from the laboratory and pounced on the unsuspecting Spider-Man. In desperation, Spider-Man lured the alien to the bell tower of Our Lady Of Saints Church. He knew that the sound of the bells could free him from the symbiote. The alien, knowing that only one of them could survive the ordeal, sacrificed itself to save Peter.

BONGGG! BONGGGG! BONGGG! BONGGG! BONGGG!

DON'T YOU SEE? I COULDN'T STAND BEING A PUPPET! I'D RATHER DIE!

AND WHAT GOOD WOULD I BE TO YOU THEN?!

SILVER SABLE

THE WORLD'S most famous mercenary is a woman called Silver Sable. Born in the tiny European nation of Symkaria, Silver is the daughter of Ernst Sublinovia. He once ran a group of soldiers who hunted Nazi war criminals. Calling his team the Wild Pack, he gained the tacit approval of the Symkarian government. Sadly, his wife, Silver's mother, was killed by terrorists. Witnessing this horror turned Silver's hair white and made her determined to take over the leadership of the Wild Pack one day.

BUSINESS-MINDED

As the number of war criminals decreased, Silver turned the focus of the Wild Pack toward mercenary endeavors. She formed Silver Sable International and began selling her services around the world. Her clients are wealthy individuals, major corporations, and small countries, and her large fees have become Symkaria's major source of income.

Silver is proficient with over 100 different firearms.

More than a match
Silver Sable's skill in personal combat is so good that she has taken on adversaries like the Punisher, Hydro-Man, and Spider-Man. Her weapon of choice is the chai, a three-pronged throwing projectile of her own design which can stun or disarm an opponent.

Silver Sable usually stays in the local Symkarian Embassy when she travels abroad.

A FRIEND TO THE FREELANCER
With her considerable financial resources, Silver Sable is able to hire freelance operatives whenever she needs specialized assistance. She once employed the Sandman (see pages 46–47) and also formed a team called the Outlaws, which was made up of many of Spider-Man's past associates, such as the Prowler, Rocket Racer, and Will O' The Wisp.

FIRST MEETING
Silver Sable first met Spider-Man when her organization was hired to capture an international jewel thief called the Black Fox. Unfortunately, Spidey took a liking to the elderly rogue and allowed him to escape.

RESPECT?
Despite regarding each other with contempt at the start, both Spider-Man and Silver Sable have come to respect each other's talents and have often worked together.

Silver Sable usually dresses in white or silver, and her clothes are often lined with Kevlar.

Daily workout
Silver Sable sets aside a few hours every day to practice her combat skills. These daily workouts are extremely strenuous, and she tests her abilities to the full, sometimes against several opponents at the same time. She's even been known to hold business meetings while fighting off her sparring partners!

THE PUMA

THOMAS FIREHEART is the guardian of his tribe, the protector of his people. He is also the Puma. Fireheart belongs to a Native American nation whose legends foretold that a being of near-infinite power would threaten the world. In an effort to protect their people, the tribal shamans began a secret program that combined magic and controlled breeding. They produced a line of warriors, of which Fireheart is the latest member.

BUSINESSMAN

Fireheart was bred with the ability to transform himself into a superpowered being, half-human and half-puma. While still a child, he started a lifelong course of training to perfect his enhanced powers. He studied the martial arts, and honed his ability to transform. Believing that his tribe also needed economic protection, he formed Fireheart Enterprises and built it into a huge multinational corporation.

TRANSITION
When Fireheart triggers his transformation into the Puma, his size and weight increase. His eyes change color, fur spreads over his body, and all of his natural abilities are magnified to superhuman levels.

INTERESTED PARTIES
To keep his warrior skills sharp, Fireheart occasionally accepted dangerous mercenary assignments. His talents eventually came to the attention of the Rose (see page 71), one of the Kingpin's lieutenants, who hired the Puma to capture Spider-Man.

Fireheart's closest confidant is his uncle, the tribe's shaman.

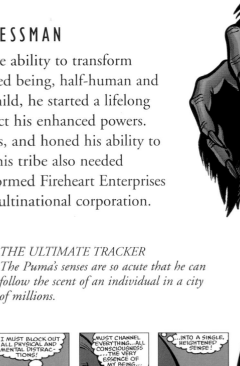

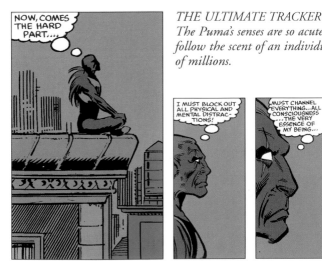 

THE ULTIMATE TRACKER
The Puma's senses are so acute that he can follow the scent of an individual in a city of millions.

Friends or foes?
Though they first met as enemies, Fireheart and Spider-Man have slowly gained a respect for each other. Fireheart paid for Peter and Mary Jane's honeymoon, and also offered his former foe a job with Fireheart Enterprises. The Puma even owned the *Daily Bugle* for a brief time and began a campaign to improve Spider-Man's reputation.

WEIGHTLIFTING
The Puma can lift approximately 12 tons under ordinary conditions.

TOTAL POWER
During a battle with the mystical being called the Beyonder, Fireheart achieved a state of total harmony with the universe and temporarily wielded near-infinite power.

Stronger and faster
The Puma is not only stronger than Spider-Man, his reflexes are also much faster. Even with his spider-sense warning of danger, the wall-crawler found it difficult to avoid Fireheart's first lightning-fast attacks.

TOMBSTONE

Tombstone learned the art of winning through intimidation at school.

LONNIE THOMPSON Lincoln is an albino —he has no pigmentation in his skin, hair, or eyes. He grew up in Harlem, as a classmate of *Daily Bugle* editor Joe Robertson. Taller and stronger than most of the other neighborhood children, Lonnie quickly learned that his fists could get him whatever he wanted. He extorted money from the other kids, brutally beating them into submission if they failed to pay. Dropping out of high school, Lonnie found regular work as a muscle man for various local mobsters. He grew more brutal as the years passed, and his reputation spread across the underworld. Taking the name Tombstone, he became a hitman, and was eventually offered employment by the Kingpin (*see pages 70-71*).

THE ENFORCER

The Kingpin was trying to regain his control over the New York mobs, so Tombstone had plenty of work kidnapping and executing gangland rivals. When Joe Robertson learned that his old classmate was in town, he attempted to gather enough evidence to expose him. Tombstone responded by threatening Joe. Spider-Man finally captured Tombstone, and he was sent to prison. However, during an attempted prison breakout, Tombstone managed to capture the web-head and almost beat him to death. Tombstone later escaped and joined a criminal organization run by Hammerhead and the Chameleon.

NOW IT'S PERSONAL
Though he wanted to protect Joe Robertson, Spider-Man's interest in Tombstone became very personal when the gangster threatened Mary Jane.

School chums?

Tombstone bullied Joe Robertson throughout high school. Years later, Joe gathered enough evidence to prove that Tombstone had murdered a local crime boss. Still completely terrified of the thug, Joe Robertson finally found the courage to stand up to Tombstone and testify against him.

CHILDHOOD FEARS
Joe Robertson has feared Tombstone ever since they went to high school together.

Sweet revenge
When Robertson refused to leave Tombstone alone, the hitman responded by breaking the journalist's spine. Robertson has since recovered, and Tombstone has called off his vendetta against his former classmate.

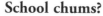

Tombstone stands 6 feet 7 inches tall.

SOLO

JAMES BOURNE was a popular student and a star athlete in high school, but he didn't know what he wanted to be when he grew up. Joining the army after graduation, he discovered that he possessed a natural flair for hand-to-hand combat. While stationed in West Germany, he met an officer named Melinda Wallace. They quickly fell in love, but their happiness ended when Melinda was murdered in a terrorist attack. After her death, James buried himself in his work. A few months later he was selected for a special forces operation called Omega Strike.

Betrayed
Solo eventually learned that three of his former teammates had betrayed Omega Strike in order to form their own terrorist-for-hire organization. He tracked them down and dispensed his own form of justice.

INNOCENT KILLING
Once, one of Solo's bullets passed through a terrorist and killed an innocent bystander. He is still haunted by this terrible accident.

Solo is an expert swordsman.

OMEGA STRIKE

Omega Strike had been created to combat terrorism. Two hundred candidates joined the program, but 10 grueling months later only 12 soldiers graduated. Cyber-chips were implanted in Bourne's brain and linked to his adrenal glands. The chips gave him the incredible ability to teleport at will. On their first mission, Omega Strike was betrayed from within, and Bourne's team was wiped out. Finding himself on his own, he began to go by the name of Solo, and vowed to rid the world of terrorists.

TELEPORTING
There appears to be no limit to the physical distance over which Solo can teleport.

AND WITH A MERE THOUGHT, SOLO TELEPORTS HIMSELF AWAY...

Solo often shouts his personal battle cry, "While I live, terror dies!"

Pouches hold weapons and ammunition.

Different views
Though fate has often cast them together, Spider-Man believes that Solo is a heartless killer. Solo admires the web-head's courage, but thinks he lacks the stomach to deal with the cancer that is terrorism.

His costume is made of bulletproof quilted Kevlar.

Solo's sanctum
Solo works without government sanction.
He supports himself by appropriating funds and equipment from the terrorists he fights. He has a hi-tech secret base in the United States that is equipped with computers that constantly scan all forms of media for any mention of terrorism. From this sanctum, he can teleport anywhere in the world.

THE WEDDING

THE COURSE of true love rarely runs smoothly, especially for your friendly neighborhood web-slinger. Peter Parker had been attracted to Mary Jane Watson from the moment he first saw her. Although he thought she was beautiful and charming, they seemed to have little in common with each other. But as the years passed, their friendship grew and they started dating. Mary Jane knew that Peter was secretly Spider-Man, and she tried to avoid a serious relationship with him. But Peter was persistent. Fate kept drawing them together until the day Mary Jane stopped running...

A prize in every box
When Peter realized that he wanted to marry Mary Jane, he presented her with a box of Crackerjacks, a candy with a prize in every box. He had placed a diamond ring inside, and he proposed to Mary Jane. But Mary Jane returned the ring and soon left town, claiming that she was too much of a free spirit to settle down with one man.

RUNNING SCARED
Though she truly loved Peter Parker, Mary Jane was afraid of marriage. She had seen how it had ruined the lives of both her mother and her sister.

Try, try again
When Mary Jane returned to New York, various friends and relatives tried to revive her romance with Peter.
Although they both resisted at first, Peter and Mary Jane eventually realized that they were only fooling themselves. Peter was unable to deny his feelings any longer, and he asked Mary Jane to marry him for a second time. Once again, she refused, packed her bags, and went to visit her sister in Pittsburgh.

Mary Jane's veil was made of silk and lace.

WEDDING DRESS
Mary Jane's wedding dress was designed by renowned fashion designer Willi Smith.

Family ties
Mary Jane couldn't begin a new life with Peter until she had made peace with her past. On returning to Pittsburgh she discovered that her family life was more of a mess than she'd anticipated. Her father had somehow persuaded Mary Jane's sister, Gayle, to steal a rare manuscript from the museum where she worked. However, Gayle had been spotted on security cameras and arrested. Mary Jane was determined to expose the truth about her father and free her sister. Using the manuscript as bait, Mary Jane got her father to implicate himself and he was arrested.

AND SOON, AT GREATER PITTS-BURGH INTERNATIONAL AIRPORT...
COMFY?
MM-HMM. Y'KNOW, PETE--

-- I'VE GROWN UP A LOT THESE LAST FEW DAYS. I KNOW WHY I'VE BEEN RUNNING AWAY FROM RESPON-SIBILITIES--IT'S WHAT I LEARNED AS A CHILD: MY FATHER RAN AWAY, GAYLE'S HUSBAND RAN AWAY... SO I RUN AWAY.
I WAS SCARED OF LOSING MY DREAMS, BUT MOST OF THEM HAVE ALREADY COME TRUE: MY CAREER'S GOING GREAT, I LOVE MY LIFE-STYLE, I HAVE WON-DERFUL FRIENDS. I'M EVEN TALKING TO GAYLE AGAIN.

ROMANTIC RENDEZVOUS
Mary Jane finally accepted Peter's proposal in the less-than-romantic setting of Pittsburgh airport's departure lounge.

SURPRISE!!
GOOD LUCK PETER!
WE JUST WANTED TO CONGRATULATE YOU, PETE, AND WISH YOU THE BEST IN YOUR UPCOMING MARRIAGE.

SO MAYBE IT'S TIME TO STOP RUN-NING. MAYBE THERE'S NOTHING WRONG WITH MAKING SOMEONE ELSE HAPPY-- AS LONG AS THAT PERSON MAKES YOU HAPPY.
YOU MEAN...?
I MEAN "YES," PETER.
YES...
...I'LL MARRY YOU!

THE LADY SAYS, "YES."
After resolving things with her family, Mary Jane realized that there was nothing wrong with making someone else happy. She finally agreed to marry Peter Parker.

At last...

With her family problems resolved, Mary Jane finally realized that it was time to stop running away from things. So she accepted Peter's proposal of marriage and the two returned to New York. Peter asked his old high school rival Flash Thompson to be his best man. But the problems didn't stop there. As the big day approached, Peter began to have doubts. He remembered Gwen Stacy, and wondered what directions his life might have taken if she hadn't died. Mary Jane also had qualms, and a number of her old boyfriends tried to dissuade her from marrying Peter.

Surprise!

As news of their engagement spread, Peter and Mary Jane were showered with gifts and congratulations. Joe Robertson (*see pages 34-35*) arranged a surprise party for Peter at the *Daily Bugle* and gave Peter a bonus check to help him pay for the wedding.

SORRY I'M LATE, TIGER! I HAD TO MAKE SURE I WAS PERFECT FOR YOU TODA-- TIGER?
I-I'M AFRAID PETER ISN'T HERE, DEAR.

MARY JANE ARRIVES
Mary Jane arrived late for the wedding only to learn that Peter hadn't arrived.

The big day

The wedding was scheduled to begin at noon on the front steps of New York's City Hall. Neither Peter nor Mary Jane arrived on time. As the clock edged toward one, their friends feared that both Peter and Mary Jane had gotten cold feet. Mary Jane was the first to arrive. At first she thought that Peter had jilted her, but he came running down the street a minute later. Mary Jane's uncle, Judge Spencer Watson, performed the ceremony and pronounced them man and wife.

Peter was carrying his shoes as he arrived because he had to resort to wall-crawling in order to reach the ceremony.

WELL, BEING LATE IS FASHIONABLE, SO I FORGIVE YOU-- IF YOU'RE READY NOW!
LADY, I'VE NEVER BEEN MORE READY FOR ANYTHING IN MY LIFE!

FRIENDS AND FAMILY
Surrounded by family and friends, Peter and Mary Jane were married on the front steps of city hall.

KRAVEN'S LAST HUNT

THERE WAS a time when the world marveled at his physical prowess. A period when his courage inspired awe and his exploits drew envy. An interval when he truly was the world's greatest hunter. That was before the environmentalists deserted him, and the animal rights activists condemned him. It was before he met Spider-Man. Before he knew failure and humiliation. Sergei Kravinov was aware that death was coming. He could sense its stealthy approach and could almost see it grinning in the shadows. But Kraven wasn't ready to die. He couldn't rest until he had reclaimed his honor and dignity. Until he had satiated his pride and proven his superiority. Until he had defeated Spider-Man. And so, gathering his strength, Kraven went out on one last hunt...

Fading powers
Kraven was still faster than a panther and stronger than a great ape, but he knew that he was no longer in his prime. Yet he believed that he would never know peace unless he humbled Spider-Man. Formulating a daring plan, he sought to immerse himself in Spider-Man's essence by burying his body within a veritable mountain of spiders and by using jungle herbs and potions to expand his consciousness.

THE CAPTURE
Having recently returned from his honeymoon, Spider-Man was out web-swinging one night when he was suddenly attacked, drugged, and captured by Kraven. As the hunter advanced on his prey, Spider-Man was unconcerned. Until, that is, he saw the rifle and the look in Kraven's eyes. Aiming the rifle at Spider-Man, Kraven shot the wall-crawler right between the eyes.

-- WILL BE RESTORED.

C'MON, KRAVEY-- RIFLES AREN'T YOUR STYLE!

LOOK AT HIS EYES.

THERE'S... SOMETHING IN HIS EYES!

YOU'VE ALWAYS BEEN A *MACHO* MAN!

YOU'VE ALWAYS WANTED TO POUND ME INTO HAMBURGER--

THIS ISN'T THE KRAVEN I KNOW!

--WITH YOUR BARE HANDS!

Masquerade
Kraven took the wall-crawler's body back to his estate, placed him in a coffin, and buried him on the grounds. But it wasn't enough for Kraven to merely slay Spider-Man. The hunter had to prove his superiority. He had to *become* his enemy. So, dressing in a duplicate costume, Kraven assumed Spider-Man's identity.

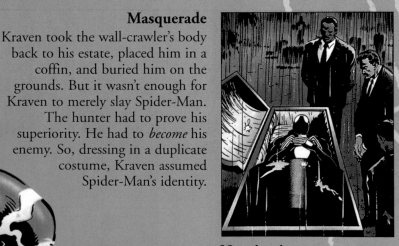

New justice
Kraven began to patrol the city, dispensing his own vicious brand of justice. He even rescued Mary Jane from muggers, but she immediately saw through his disguise.

CONQUER THE SPIDER
Disgusted with the world around him and his own failing health, Kraven vowed to conquer Spider-Man before he died.

Spider imposter
Unlike Spider-Man, Kraven actually killed some of the criminals he came across.

ROWWRRR

THE BATTLE
While Kraven focused on Spider-Man, a ratlike monster stalked the streets of Manhattan. He was called Vermin, and he possessed superhuman strength, speed, and stamina. Kraven used his skills to track the monster through the sewers. Dressed like Spider-Man, Kraven confronted Vermin, beat him unconscious, and took him prisoner.

A rabid beast
More rat than man, Vermin's claws can slash through metal and his teeth are razor-sharp. He has a taste for human flesh, too.

Resurrection
As Kraven claimed victory over Vermin, the real Spider-Man stirred—he had only been drugged by Kraven. Buried deep in the ground, Peter Parker opened his eyes. Desperate to be reunited with Mary Jane, he broke his way free of the coffin and began to crawl upward, clawing his way to the surface. Two weeks had passed since Kraven had buried him alive. After a brief visit to assure his wife that he was still alive, Spider-Man began to hunt the hunter.

THIS... THIS IS THE FINALE, SPIDER-MAN!

YOU EXPECT ME TO *FIGHT* WITH HIM, *DON'T* YOU? FIGHT--FOR YOUR AMUSE-MENT!

NO. FOR MY EMANCIPATION.

WELL, I WON'T DO IT!

PLEASSSSSE-- DON'T HITMEHURTME HITMEHURTMEHITME!

You won't have to.

HONORABLE
When Spidey refused to fight Vermin, Kraven came to realize that his longtime foe was a good and honorable man.

Blood and thunder
Filled with fury, Spider-Man attacked Kraven, who didn't bother to resist. The hunter merely smiled—he had won. He had allowed Spider-Man to live when he could have easily killed him. Kraven had finally proven himself superior to Spider-Man. When the wall-crawler refused Kraven's challenge to fight Vermin, the monster attacked him. Kraven immediately acted to save his old enemy, but released Vermin. Having achieved what he set out to do, Kraven allowed Spider-Man to pursue Vermin. The hunter then committed suicide.

They said my mother was insane.

Compassion not vengeance
Through sheer brutality, Kraven had battered Vermin into submission. He took the monster into custody because he wanted to see if Spider-Man was powerful enough to do the same. But the web-swinger had nothing to prove. He didn't care what the hunter thought and had no desire to inflict pain.

REDEMPTION
Unaware that Kraven had committed suicide, Spider-Man found Vermin and turned him over to the authorities.

Spider-Man trapped Vermin by leading him out of the sewers and into the daylight, where the creature was left dazed and confused.

COSMIC SPIDER-MAN

Wis no slouch when it comes to physical power, he's never exactly been the strongest costumed hero on the block. Iron Man, the mighty Thor, the incredible Hulk, and the ever-loving blue-eyed Thing are all much stronger. It can even be argued that super-villains such as Doctor Octopus, the Sandman, and the Scorpion possess far greater raw power. However, that all changed when a laboratory accident exposed Peter Parker to an unknown energy source. He was transformed into the cosmic Spider-Man.

WEBBING CONTROL
After the accident, Spider-man discovered that he had some amazing new powers. Using his webbing, he could instantly form any complex shape that he imagined, and then manipulate the webbing in whatever way he wanted.

SOME KIND OF SUPER-VISION--

--SHOWING ME NICK KATZENBERG TAKING PHOTOS FROM THE BUGLE'S OFFICE THIRTY STORIES UP!

Exposed
While pursuing his graduate studies at Empire State University, Peter Parker was bathed in unknown energies when an experimental generator exploded. The explosion also caused nearby power lines to overload dangerously. Changing into Spider-Man, Peter spotted a live wire falling toward a young couple. He instinctively caught the wire and was surprised when he wasn't harmed by the massive surge of electricity.

SPIDER-VISION
Spidey's vision was also greatly enhanced. His eyes could now see much farther than any conventional pair of binoculars, and he could look through walls.

FINGER-LICKIN' GOOD
Spidey's new powers included the ability to generate concussive blasts from the tips of his fingers, or combine them into a fist-sized blast powerful enough to shatter an army tank.

Spidey's power blasts could level an entire building complex.

Super-senses
Spider-Man's senses went wild! They had become far sharper than those of Daredevil or the Puma. Suddenly, he could hear a spider crossing a windowpane two blocks away, and smell the fragrance of a potted plant on a distant building ledge. Quickly learning how to filter out the excess noise and smells before they overwhelmed him, Spidey also used his new powers to locate and defeat a super-villain called the Trapster.

Peter was able to push his colleague Professor Lubisch out of harm's way.

CAPTAIN SPIDER-VERSE
Spider-Man's new powers had actually come from a mysterious extra-dimensional entity known as the Enigma Force. It bestowed its Uni-Power on various individuals, turning them into a being known as Captain Universe and giving them superhuman powers long enough to cope with a specific crisis. Spidey was merely the latest Captain Universe.

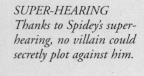

SUPER-HEARING
Thanks to Spidey's super-hearing, no villain could secretly plot against him.

Super-duper battles

As Spider-Man grew more comfortable with his cosmic powers, he found himself fighting a different class of super-villain. During a battle with Magneto, the archenemy of the uncanny X-Men, Spidey eventually drove the master of magnetism away when the villain realized that he couldn't take on the cosmically charged Spidey on his own.

Too much power

With the aid of Doctor Doom, a super-villain named Goliath discovered a way to rechannel Spidey's Uni-Power into himself. Goliath grew stronger and bigger every time the web-head hit him. Realizing that each growth spurt increased the strain on the giant's heart, Spidey kept pounding away. Eventually, Goliath became so overloaded with power, that he collapsed under the pressure.

CAPTAIN
UNIVERSE

The Tri-Sentinel

While Spider-Man didn't particularly like being drafted by the Enigma Force, he realized that he had a responsibility to fight the menace it had foreseen. This menace proved to be in the form of three massive Sentinel robots. In an act of spite, the evil god Loki caused these robots to merge, creating one super-powered robot—the Tri-Sentinel (*see page 131*). Loki then instructed the robot to create as much damage as possible.

Great responsibility

The Tri-Sentinel attempted to cause a nuclear meltdown at a research facility that bordered Manhattan. The web-covered Captain Universe summoned the full power of the Enigma Force and incinerated the Tri-Sentinel in a novalike blast. After the crisis, the exhausted Spider-Man returned to normal.

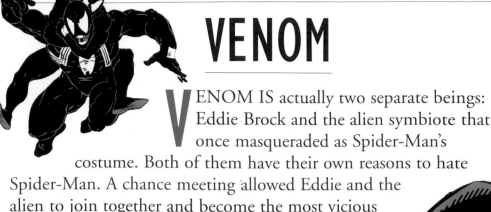

VENOM

Venom can generate his own supply of organic webbing.

VENOM IS actually two separate beings: Eddie Brock and the alien symbiote that once masqueraded as Spider-Man's costume. Both of them have their own reasons to hate Spider-Man. A chance meeting allowed Eddie and the alien to join together and become the most vicious mass of mayhem that Spider-Man has ever faced. Venom possesses all the powers of both Spider-Man and the alien symbiote. He is also far stronger than Spider-Man, and he can use the alien symbiote to disguise himself to look like anything he can imagine.

BONDED IN HATE

Eddie Brock was once a respected reporter who worked for the *New York Globe*, a rival of the *Daily Bugle*. For a while, he was a media star, following his exposé of a man who had confessed to being the serial killer called the Sin-Eater. However, Spider-Man caught the real Sin-Eater—the man Eddie turned in was a compulsive confessor. As a result, Eddie was fired from his job and his wife left him. With his career and personal life shattered, Eddie blamed Spider-Man for his loss. He wandered from church to church, praying for forgiveness for his hatred of Spider-Man. At Our Lady of Saints Church, Eddie's fierce emotion somehow awakened the dormant alien symbiote that had remained in the church after its final encounter with Spider-Man (*see pages 108-109*). The symbiote flowed over Eddie and they joined to become Venom.

STRONG MAN
Eddie Brock could lift almost 700 pounds before he bonded with the alien symbiote, and he became nearly 40 times stronger after they merged.

The symbiote can turn Venom invisible by blending him into any background.

Since the alien symbiote was psychically linked to Peter Parker, Venom knows all of Spider-Man's most intimate secrets.

Nowhere to hide

With his vastly superior strength and the symbiote's additional powers, Venom always had an advantage when battling Spider-Man. Eddie could also stalk Spidey without triggering the wall-crawler's spider-sense (*see pages 22-23*).

FOR THE HATE OF SPIDEY
Sensing a kindred spirit, the symbiote flowed over Eddie, and the two reveled in their mutual hostility for Spider-Man.

Venom victorious

Determined to destroy Spider-Man, Venom lured the wall-crawler to a South Sea island for a final battle. Here Spidey conceived a bold plan and managed to fake his own death. Convinced that his archenemy was no more, Eddie saw no reason to continue being Venom. He and the symbiote decided to remain on the island and live in peace.

SINISTER SIX
Returning to his criminal ways, Venom recently joined the latest incarnation of the Sinister Six (see pages 58-59), and he helped the team track down Spider-Man. In the ensuing fight, the Sandman (see pages 46-47) insulted him, and Venom took a bite out of the sand monster. This action caused the Sandman to lose his ability to hold himself together and may have resulted in his death.

Lethal protector

Eddie has always considered himself to be a defender of the weak and helpless. In his warped mind, he has always believed that he is the hero and that Spider-Man is the monster. After promising to spare the wall-crawler's loved ones in exchange for his freedom, Venom temporarily moved to San Francisco. Here he became the city's "lethal protector," dispensing his own brand of justice to help those he deemed innocent and to punish those he judged guilty.

Venom has always thought of himself as a protector of the innocent.

Exposed

After his battle on the South Sea island, Peter believed that he had finally seen the last of Venom. But this was not to be! When a serial killer called Carnage (*see pages 126-127*) revealed that he had been created by merging with remnants of the alien symbiote, Peter was forced to seek Venom's help against this new super-menace.

Uneasy allies

As with their battle against the serial killer Carnage, Spider-Man and Venom have sometimes been compelled to put their differences aside and join forces against a common foe. However, since neither party trusts the other, these alliances have always been very shaky and have often ended in betrayal.

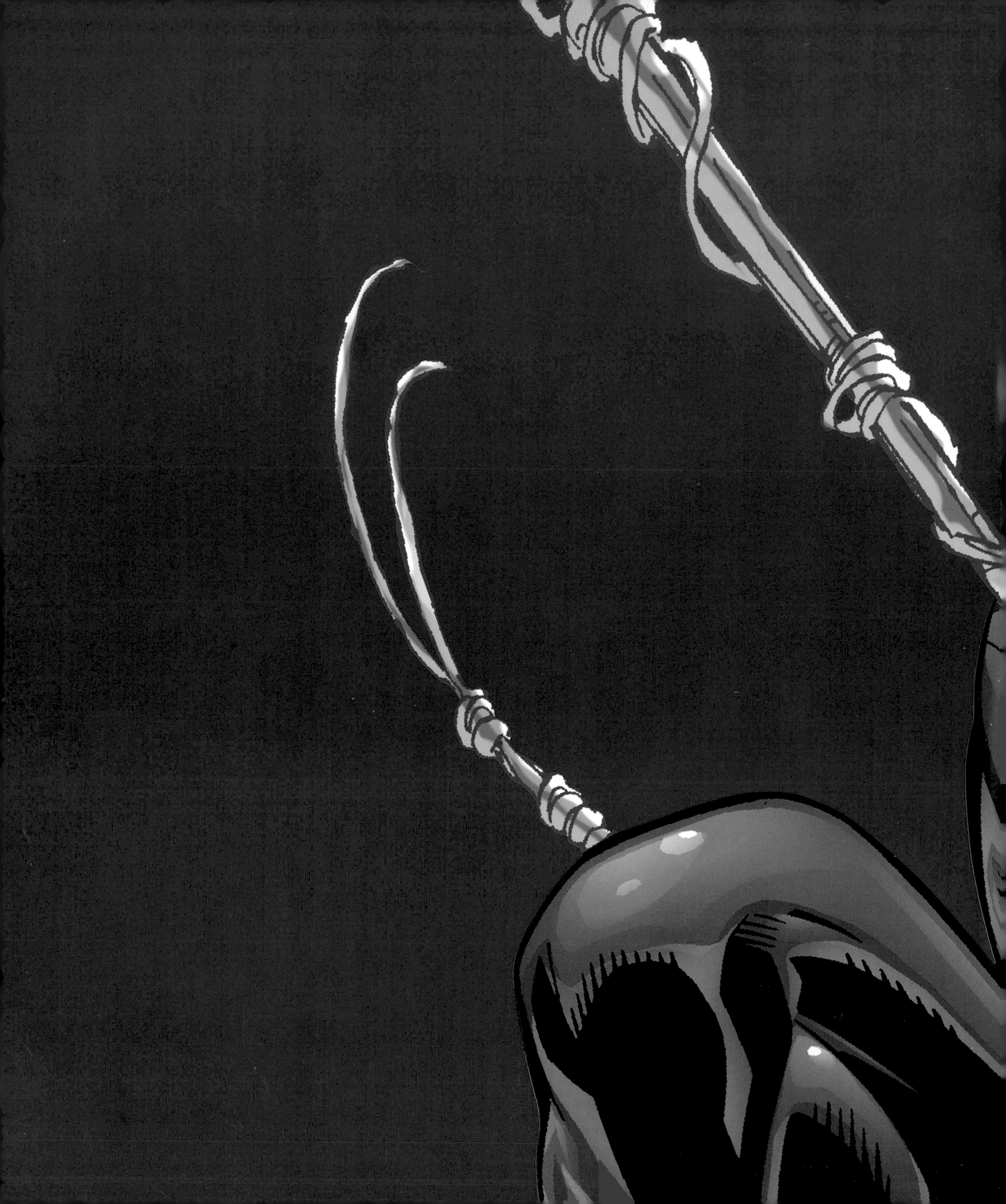

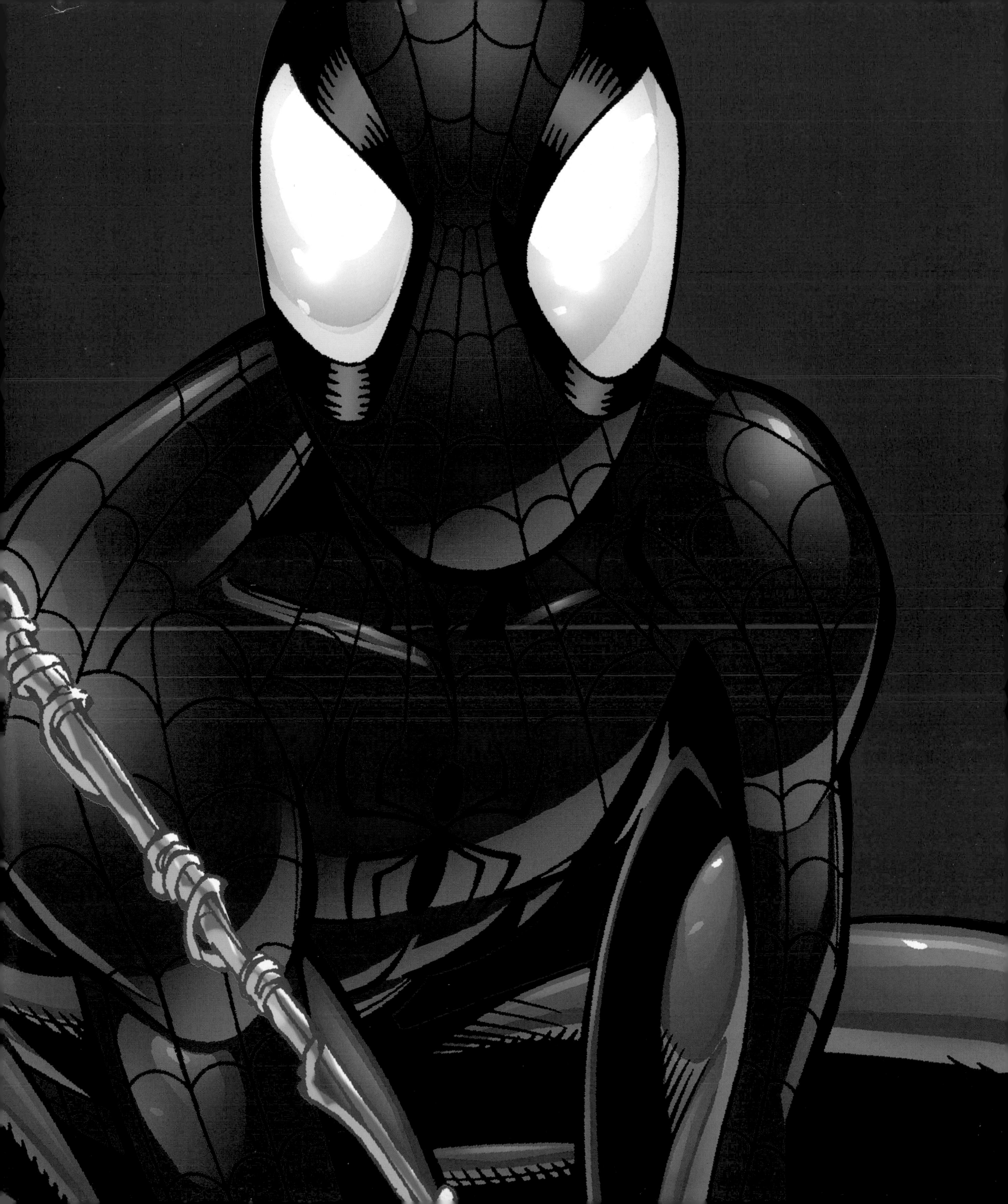

SPIDER-MAN IN THE '90S

AS THE 1990's began, Todd McFarlane left *Amazing Spider-Man* to write and draw a new monthly comic. Simply called *Spider-Man*, its debut issue sold over three million copies.

Marvel also featured everyone's favorite web-head in a series of original graphic novels such as Charles Vess' stunning *Spirits of the Earth*. J. M. DeMatteis and Mike Zeck's haunting *Kraven's Last Hunt* was also published as a hardcover novel.

The list of Spidey's contributors grew to include Erik Larsen, Ron Lim, Sal Buscema, Bill Sienkiewicz, Mike Wieringo, Chris Marrinan, Tom Lyle, Jae Lee, Marshal Rogers, Ann Nocenti, and Todd DeZago. Even I was asked to return!

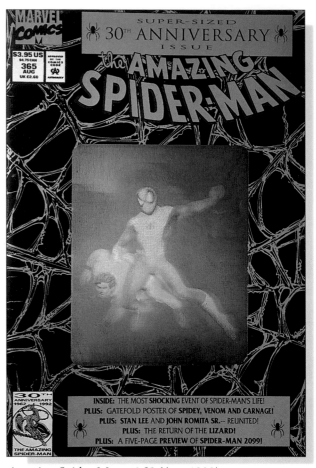

Anxious to spark even more sales, Marvel began to feature big events in the spider-titles. Special foils and printing techniques were added to the covers. Old titles were canceled, and quickly replaced with new ones. Longtime characters experienced major changes, and some were even killed off.

Recalling the Jackal and Spider-Man's clone from Gerry Conway's run, writer Terry Kavanagh proposed a storyline that would rock the very foundation of the Spider-Man mythos—what if the current Peter Parker was actually the clone? So started the Clone Saga.

Having nearly exhausted their supply of big events, the team at Marvel had one last stunt in mind. They decided to cancel all the spider-titles and start the new millennium from the very beginning.

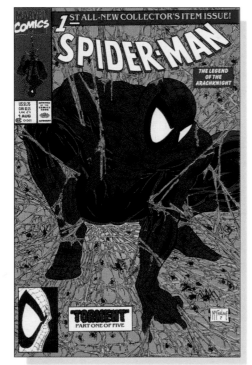

Spider-Man #1 (Aug. 1990)
Sold over three million copies
(Cover art by Todd McFarlane)

Amazing Spider-Man #365 (Aug. 1992)
Spider-Man's 30th anniversary
(Cover is a hologram based on Amazing Fantasy #15)

THE NINETIES

1991

Amazing Spider-Man
#350 (Aug. 1991)
350th issue

1993

Spectacular Spider-Man
#200 (May 1993)
Death of Harry Osborn

1994

Amazing Spider-Man
#392 (Aug. 1994)
Peter stops being Spidey

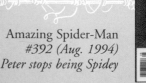

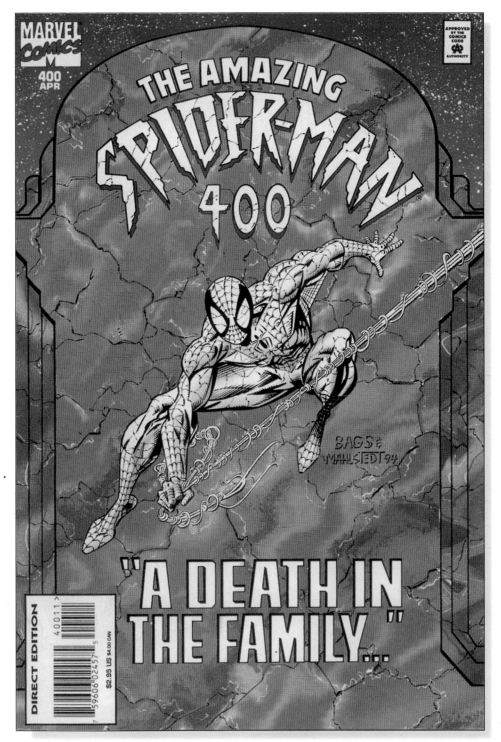

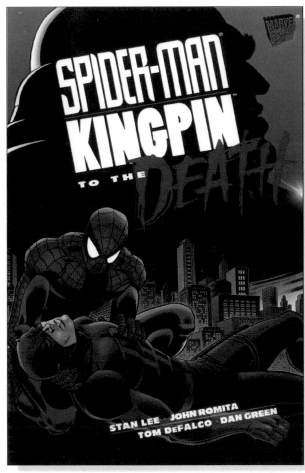

Spider-Man/Kingpin "To the Death" *(1997)*
Original graphic novel featuring Daredevil
(Cover by John Romita)

Amazing Spider-Man #400 *(April 1995)*
The death of Aunt May
(Cover art by Mark Bagley and Larry Mahlstedt)

1996

Sensational Spider-Man
#1 *(Feb. 1996)*
With Ben Reilly as Spidey

1998

Amazing Spider-Man #441
(Nov. 1998)
The end of Amazing Spider-Man

1999

Amazing Spider-Man
vol. 2 #1 *(Jan. 1999)*
Title is relaunched

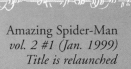

CARNAGE

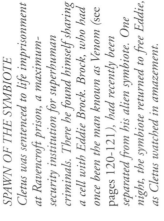
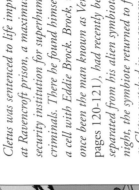

CLETUS KASADY was a notorious serial killer even before he became Carnage. His first victim was his father, and he even claims to have murdered his mother, too. Cletus was raised as an orphan at the St. Estes Home For Boys in Brooklyn. A small and shy child, Cletus was often terrorized by the older residents. He was transferred to another establishment when a fire burned St. Estes to the ground, killing many of his classmates as well as the home's dean of discipline. As Cletus grew older, an alarming number of his acquaintances seemed to die under mysterious circumstances. A girl, who laughed at him when he asked her on date, was pushed in front of a bus, and an alcoholic foster father was found beaten to death in a neighborhood alley. By the time he reached his early twenties, Cletus Kasady had been convicted of eleven murders, but bragged of dozens more.

SPAWN OF THE SYMBIOTE

Cletus was sentenced to life imprisonment at Ravencroft prison, a maximum-security institution for superhuman criminals. There he found himself sharing a cell with Eddie Brock. Brock, who had once been the man known as Venom (see pages 120–121), had recently been separated from his alien symbiote. One night, the symbiote returned to free Eddie, as Cletus watched in amazement.

NO, CLETUS KASADY...

Dangerous spawn

In the aftermath of Eddie Brock's jailbreak, Cletus was left in shock at what he had just witnessed. However, a small part of the alien symbiote that had been left behind merged with Kasady. The combination of the symbiote and Cletus' dangerous mind formed the psychopathic killer called Carnage.

As Carnage, Kasady has pointed teeth and dagger-sharp talons which are actually part of his symbiote.

Shriek

While escaping Ravencroft, Carnage came across the woman of his dreams. Shriek was a mass murderer who could generate sonic blasts. She joined Carnage on his slaughter circuit.

Separate weapons

Though Venom must stay physically linked to his symbiote, Carnage can separate parts of his costume from himself and use them as weapons. He has been known to create sharp objects, such as machetes or spears, and hurl them at his victims. These objects can only maintain their structural integrity for about ten seconds, then they crumble into dust.

Carnage can project a web-like substance from any part of his body.

Kasady has a true symbiosis with his alien costume. It has merged with his bloodstream and is actually part of him.

Carnage vs. Jameson

Once free of the Ravencroft facility, Carnage headed straight for New York and the offices of the *Daily Bugle*. Here, the psychopath confronted J. Jonah Jameson (see pages 34–35), intent on using the publisher as bait to lure Venom. Since then, Jameson and Carnage have met on several occasions. Carnage sees Jameson, the city's greatest crusader for law and order, as the embodiment of all that is wrong in society.

Carnage's hands and feet can stick to any surface.

Superhuman strength

Carnage is stronger than Spider-Man and Venom combined. He can lift over 50 tons, and he never seems to tire. His alien symbiote is constantly supplying him with new energy, and it heals any wounds. Realizing that he was no match for Carnage, Spider-Man was forced to turn to Venom for help. The two former enemies agreed to a temporary truce and successfully defeated the red menace.

Total Carnage

Carnage's alien symbiote suit appears to have gained several powers which Venom's doesn't possess. These include the ability to turn extensions of the costume into solid and powerful stabbing weapons. Also, because the alien symbiote was once joined with Spider-Man, its presence doesn't set off the wall-crawler's spider-sense, allowing Carnage to sneak up on Spidey!

FIRST DEFEAT
Spider-Man was able to defeat Carnage at their first meeting by using the alien symbiote's only weakness—sound. When Carnage appeared at a rock concert, the wall-crawler turned the stage's sound system against the criminal, blasting Carnage with a sound frequency that was high enough and loud enough to knock the alien symbiote unconscious.

SPIDER-MAN'S PARENTS

PETER PARKER was only a young child when he lost his parents. Richard Parker had taken a new job that required him to go overseas for a few months. Since his wife Mary was going with him, he asked his older brother to look after their child while they were gone. Peter's only clear memory of his father is of their farewell at the airport. Peter also remembers that his mother had tears in her eyes when she kissed him goodbye. He never saw them again, because they died a month later. As he grew older, Peter noticed that his Uncle Ben and Aunt May rarely spoke of his parents. They were reluctant to discuss Richard and Mary until one fateful day...

Traitors

While moving an old trunk into the basement, the teenage Peter Parker discovered some old newspaper clippings, which claimed that his parents were traitors who had been plotting against the government. The teenager was racked with confusion. He forced Aunt May to reveal that his parents had died in a plane crash in Algeria under mysterious circumstances.

QUEST FOR TRUTH
Desperate to learn the truth about his parents, Peter changed into Spider-Man and went to Algeria to find out what had happened.

The Red Skull

Arriving in Algeria, Spider-Man searched the Casbah, hunting for the contact his aunt had told him about. His search attracted the attention of the man he sought, who sent out a group of thugs to stop the wall-crawler. Beating them off, Spider-Man discovered the whereabouts of his enemy. Tracking down the hideout, the web-head was shocked to discover that his adversary was none other than the fascist terrorist, the Red Skull!

VINDICATION
The battle with the Red Skull resulted in the destruction of the fascist's headquarters. Spider-Man was able to save the files relating to his parents. As a result he found the proof he needed to clear their names—they had been working as double agents for the United States government and were not traitors after all!

Unexpected return

Many years later, following the collapse of the Soviet Union and the release of political prisoners from behind the old Iron Curtain, a middle-aged couple arrived at JFK International Airport. They took a taxi to Forest Hills, Queens. May Parker almost fainted when she saw them. Richard and Mary had seemingly returned from the dead! According to the Parkers, Russian agents had kidnapped them many years ago, taking them prisoner before they could board the plane.

SPIES LIKE US
Richard and Mary Parker worked as spies for the US government, carrying top secret documents around the world.

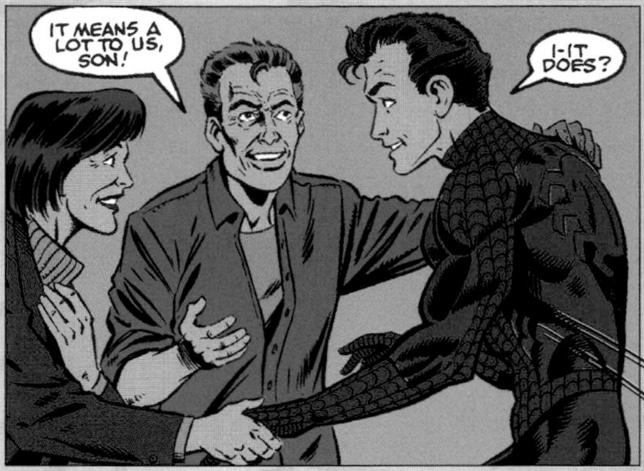
IT MEANS A LOT TO US, SON!
I-IT DOES?

BETRAYED
Spider-Man was shocked when he found his parents with the Chameleon (see pages 40-41) *and the Vulture* (see pages 42-43).

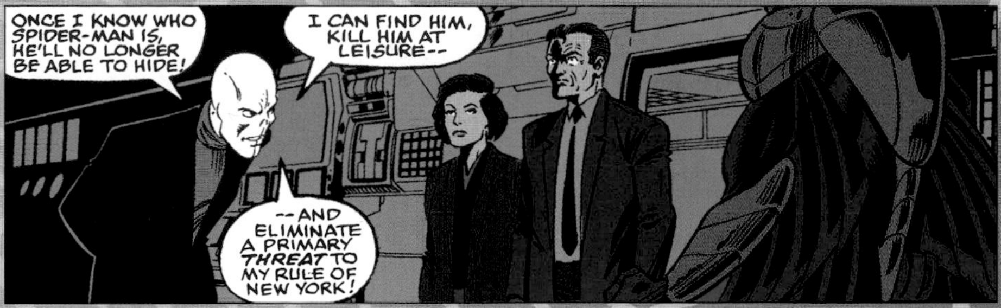
ONCE I KNOW WHO SPIDER-MAN IS, HE'LL NO LONGER BE ABLE TO HIDE!
I CAN FIND HIM, KILL HIM AT LEISURE--
--AND ELIMINATE A PRIMARY THREAT TO MY RULE OF NEW YORK!

His greatest secret

After spending weeks getting reacquainted with his parents, Peter Parker revealed his greatest secret to them.

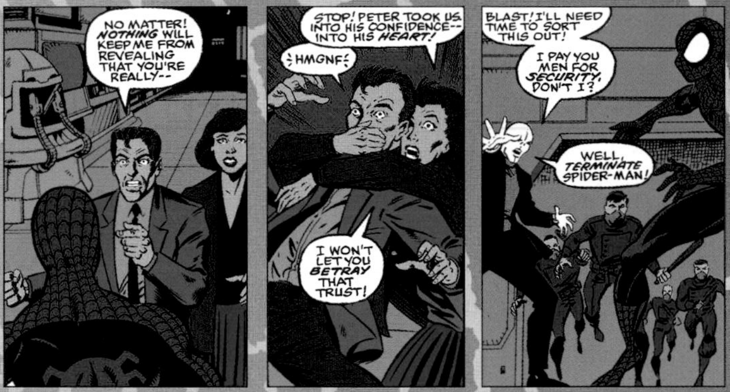
NO MATTER! NOTHING WILL KEEP ME FROM REVEALING THAT YOU'RE REALLY--
STOP! PETER TOOK US INTO HIS CONFIDENCE-- INTO HIS HEART!
HMGNF!
I WON'T LET YOU BETRAY THAT TRUST!
BLAST! I'LL NEED TIME TO SORT THIS OUT!
I PAY YOU MEN FOR SECURITY, DON'T I?
WELL, TERMINATE SPIDER-MAN!

A mother's love

Though Richard was perfectly willing to betray Peter, Mary hesitated. She had been programmed to think of Peter as her own son and had grown to love him. When Spider-Man confronted them, Richard instantly began to morph, transforming into a deadly engine of destruction. Torn between her conflicting programs, Mary stopped Richard from revealing Spider-Man's true identity and was forced to terminate her robot husband.

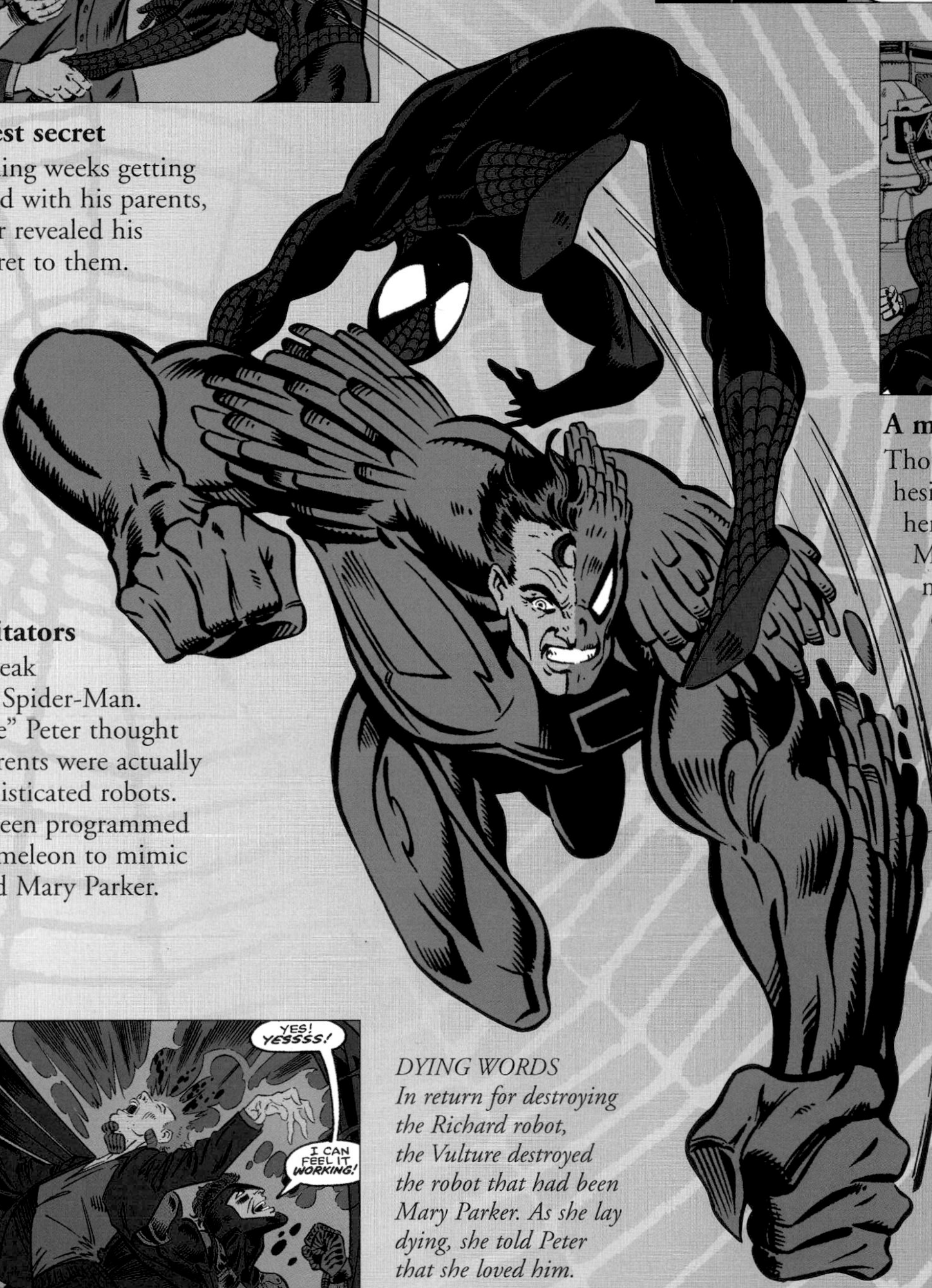

Richard Parker was in reality a killer-droid who could extend his steel-plated limbs and mold them into sharpened spikes.

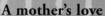

Robot imitators

But heartbreak loomed for Spider-Man. The "people" Peter thought were his parents were actually highly sophisticated robots. They had been programmed by the Chameleon to mimic Richard and Mary Parker.

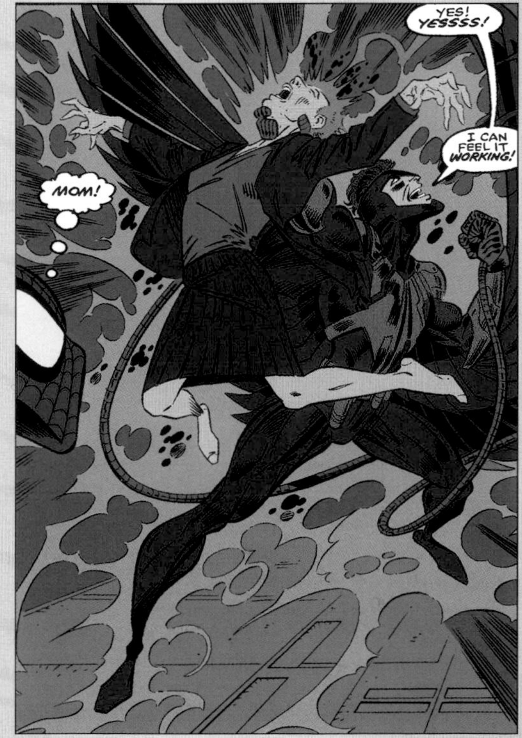
YES! YESSSS!
I CAN FEEL IT WORKING!
MOM!

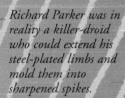

DYING WORDS
In return for destroying the Richard robot, the Vulture destroyed the robot that had been Mary Parker. As she lay dying, she told Peter that she loved him.

Game over

Devastated and furious by the deception, Spider-Man pursued the Chameleon and eventually captured him. That's when the web-head learned that someone else had encouraged the Chameleon to create the Parker robots, supplying the criminal with all the necessary information. The Chameleon, the Vulture, and the robots had all been pawns of Harry Osborn, the Green Goblin (*see pages 54-55*).

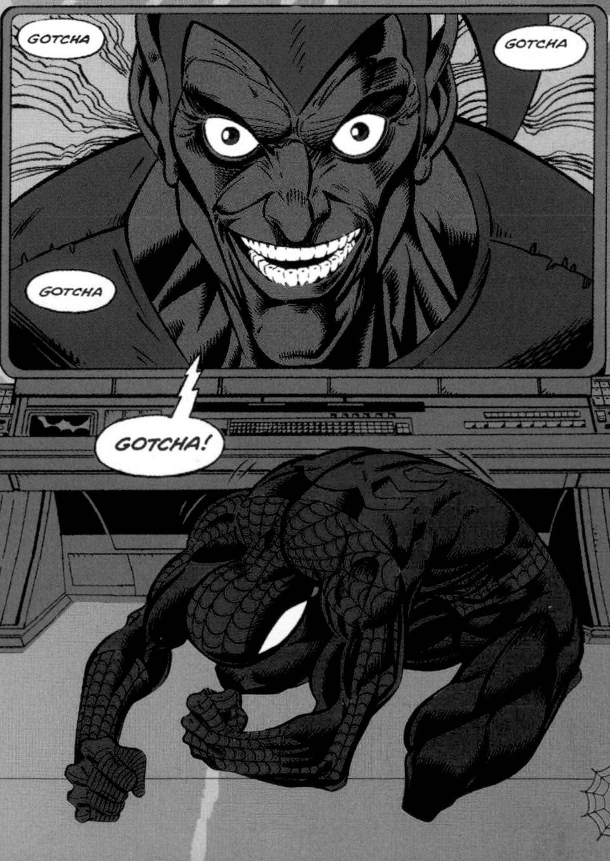
GOTCHA
GOTCHA
GOTCHA
GOTCHA!

CARDIAC

CARDIAC IS a man torn by conflict. As Doctor Elias "Eli" Wirtham, he is a dedicated physician and surgeon who has vowed to uphold the Hippocratic oath. While still a child, Elias' older brother, Joshua, died of a rare and incurable disease. Elias decided to become a healer. After graduating from medical school, he learned that a chemical company had produced a new drug that could have saved his brother. The company had kept the drug off the market until the economic climate was more favorable. Though the company was innocent of any wrongdoing in the eyes of the law, its corporate greed had killed Joshua. Since someone had to bring such immoral practices to a halt, Elias took on the role of Cardiac.

THE BIO-VIGILANTE

Cardiac never intended to fight Spider-Man. He actually admires the web-head and believes that they are working on the same side. They first met while Spidey was investigating Sapridyne Chemicals. He had heard a rumor that the company was creating perfectly legal chemicals which were needed to process cocaine, and was exporting them to South America. Spidey came to shoot a few incriminating photos and to expose the company to the public. Cardiac, on the other hand, came to destroy the place.

Other adversaries
Spider-Man isn't the only superpowered foe that Cardiac has battled. He has taken on the Rhino (*see pages 66-67*) and a pair of assassins called Styx and Stone. He even clashed with Chance (*see page 107*) when they both tried to kill a businessman who produced sonic enhancers that caused serious side effects.

Man into machine
Elias Wirtham underwent a series of extremely painful operations in order to become Cardiac. His heart was surgically replaced with a compact beta particle reactor. His entire body was encased within a layer of vibranium-mesh pseudoskin that was specifically designed to channel beta particles into his muscles and weapons.

DAMAGE TO PSEUDOSKIN IS EXTENSIVE.

Cardiac often uses a remote-controlled, beta-propelled stingray hang glider that attaches to his pulse staff.

Cardiac's pulse staff can fire concussive blasts, or be used as a fighting staff. It can also contract to the size of a baton.

An imperfect world
Cardiac knows that he doesn't live in a perfect world. He wants to save lives, but often has to take them. He is haunted by every death he causes. But he cannot stop his crusade—his compassion makes him ruthless, and his desire for justice compels him to break the law.

WHAT A MAN!
Cardiac's physical alterations have also given him superhuman strength, speed, and stamina.

Cardiac's costume is made of a padded stretch fabric. It contains numerous pockets and pouches that hold assorted chemicals and additional weapons.

TRI-SENTINEL

ALTHOUGH THE Spider-Slayers were built for the sole purpose of destroying a certain web-head, the Tri-Sentinel was made by people who couldn't have cared less about Spider-Man. They just wanted to hunt mutants. Mutants are people who have been born with a genetic difference that usually gives them special powers, such as the ability to read minds. The highly sophisticated Sentinel robots were created to eliminate these mutants. When three new, heavily armed Sentinels came off the assembly line, Loki, the Asgardian god of mischief, used his magic to merge them into a single monstrosity. The terrifying Tri-Sentinel.

DAY OF ITS RETURN

Spider-Man defeated the Tri-Sentinel the first time they fought (*see pages 118-119*). The second time he wasn't so lucky. Spider-Man and the superpowered teenager Nova were trying to locate some highly dangerous Antarctic vibranium that had been stolen from Empire State University. They tracked it to a mountain retreat where they discovered a well-funded survivalist group called the Life Foundation. The Foundation had rebuilt the Tri-Sentinel for its own purposes; but, once activated, the robot rejected its new programming and renewed its efforts to destroy Spider-Man.

Unstoppable

When magic merged it into a single entity, the Tri-Sentinel appeared to be a virtually indestructible engine of destruction. It stood nearly 300 feet tall, and each of its six hands was equipped with a blaster array that could fire electronic beams, lasers, knockout gas, and clouds of hot steam.

UNITED IT STANDS
Each of the three individual Sentinels that comprised the Tri-Sentinel was a living weapon which had been specifically designed to fight the uncanny X-Men.

Each fist is larger than an adult person.

The Tri-Sentinel can easily lift over 100 tons.

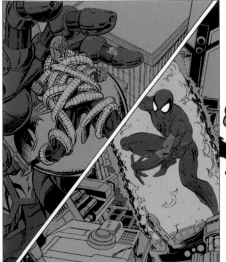

DEACTIVATE
Spider-Man and Nova stopped the Tri-Sentinel by melting its central processor.

BACK FOR MORE
Sentinels learn from their mistakes, and they are programmed to regenerate... so Spidey probably hasn't seen the last of the Tri-Sentinel.

THE DEATH OF HARRY OSBORN

PETER PARKER and Harry Osborn met in college and became the best of friends (*see pages 14-15*). Their friendship became strained when Harry turned to drugs. It degenerated even further when Harry learned that his father was the first Green Goblin and that Peter was Spider-Man. Soon after his father's apparent death, Harry became the second Green Goblin (*see pages 88-89*). But Peter Parker refused to abandon his former roommate. He kept trying to find a way to help his old friend, until the Osborn legacy eventually led to Harry's death...

Mary Jane Parker feared for her life when the Green Goblin kidnapped her.

A TIME TO DIE
Harry Osborn finally decided that either Spider-Man or the Green Goblin had to die.

Descent into madness

Harry Osborn seemed to settle down after he married Liz Allen. He stopped being the Green Goblin, and became the president of Osborn Industries. His wife eventually gave birth to their only child, Normie, and it seemed like Harry Osborn was finally destined to live happily ever after. But the memories of his painful childhood slowly began to resurface. Seething with hatred, he donned the guise of the Green Goblin once again and vowed to destroy Spider-Man. To create the maximum impact, he kidnapped Mary Jane.

A solemn promise

Dressed as the Green Goblin, Harry took Mary Jane to the bridge where his father had killed Gwen Stacy (*see pages 82-83*). Mary Jane assumed that she was about to die, but she refused to beg Harry to spare her. Harry was completely taken aback by her reaction. She was one of his dearest friends, and he promised her that he would never harm her. He only wanted to kill Spider-Man.

Stalking the spider

Peter frantically searched the city for his missing wife. He eventually found her back at their apartment with the Green Goblin. Both Peter and Mary Jane attempted to make peace with Harry, but he refused. Over the next several days, the Green Goblin stalked Peter Parker. Whenever he left his apartment, dropped in at the *Daily Bugle*, or stopped for lunch, the Goblin was hovering nearby.

HIS MORNING ROUNDS
Claiming there was no law against soaring around town in a colorful costume, the Green Goblin began to follow Peter Parker wherever he went.

THOOM!

I!!

MY FATHER'S STRENGTH-EN-HANCEMENT FORMULA HAS CHANGED ME, PETEY-O! I'M NOT JUST YOUR *EQUAL*-- --I'M YOUR *SUPERIOR!*

Building suspense

Tired of the constant harassment, Spider-Man struck back. He attacked the Green Goblin, who merely laughed in his face and threatened to make a formal complaint against him for assault. Though Harry intended to kill Spider-Man, he wasn't sure just when he would get around to it. He liked tormenting Peter and keeping him in suspense. In addition, Harry had taken a strength-enhancing potion to overwhelm Spider-Man once he decided to attack. Time and strength were on his side, or so he thought.

THROUGH THE ROOF
Spider-Man was on the roof of the townhouse when the Green Goblin suddenly exploded through a skylight to begin their final battle.

Other targets

Peter Parker wasn't Harry's only target. He also planned to get revenge on everyone who had ever betrayed his father. Harry announced the formation of a new charitable organization, The Norman Osborn Foundation. He purchased a townhouse and prepared to launch his new charity with a major gala. The guest list included celebrities, politicians, and business leaders. All were former associates of Norman Osborn. Harry secretly wired the townhouse with enough explosives to level a city block—because he intended to kill them all.

SECRET TOUR
Spider-Man feared that Osborn was getting more dangerous, so he decided to take a secret tour of the Osborn Foundation's new townhouse.

WE'RE COMING--

Final plea

Spider-Man had no idea that his wife, Mary Jane, was also visiting the townhouse with Harry's son Normie. Mary Jane begged Harry to get help to try and cure himself, but as he began to waver, an alarm suddenly sounded— Spider-Man had arrived. Realizing that the time had finally come to finish their war, Harry left to murder his former best friend. In the fight that followed, he and Spider-Man exchanged bone-breaking blows. But when brute strength failed to overwhelm Spidey, Harry resorted to drugging his old enemy. Then he activated a timer that would cause the whole building to explode, forgetting that both Mary Jane and his son were inside as well!

"SO GO, HARRY!"

FLYING TO SAFETY
While Spider-Man lay drugged and helpless, Harry Osborn rushed to get his son and Peter's wife from the house.

Redemption

Once Mary Jane and Normie were safe outside the building, Harry came to his senses and realized that he had left Peter to die. With only seconds remaining on the timer, Harry reentered the townhouse and emerged with Spider-Man in his arms. Peter and Mary Jane tried to thank him when, suddenly, Harry began to convulse. His strength-enhancing formula was poisoning his system.

The ambulance arrived to take Harry to hospital, but there was nothing the medics could do. Harry Osborn died with his best friends at his side.

MAKING PEACE
As Harry Osborn lay dying, he finally made his peace with Spider-Man.

AUNT MAY'S DEATH

MAY PARKER always held a very special place in Peter's heart. She and her husband Ben welcomed the young child into their home after the tragic death of his parents. After the murder of Uncle Ben, Peter and his aunt grew even closer. He could always depend on her for sympathy, support, and advice. But May's health was frail, and her condition continued to degenerate over the years. She began to experience dizzy spells and eventually collapsed. The hospital doctors feared the worst, but May recovered slightly and insisted on returning home for one final week with her nephew and his wife.

SHE KNEW...
Peter couldn't believe his ears when Aunt May revealed that she was aware of his secret. He had kept the truth from her for many years, fearing that it would be too much for her weak heart.

A surprising revelation

Over the next week, Peter spent many hours with his aunt. May asked him to take her to the top of the Empire State Building, where she used to go with Ben when they were dating. As they gazed at the view, Aunt May asked Peter how it felt to swing over the city, and she revealed that she had always known that her nephew was secretly Spider-Man.

The circle of life

Aunt May was delighted that Mary Jane was expecting a baby. She knew the experience would enrich the Parkers' lives, but it would also give Peter even more responsibility to shoulder.

INTUITION
As soon as she saw Mary Jane, Aunt May instantly realized that Peter's wife was pregnant. May congratulated the couple, and recalled how hard she and Anna Watson had worked to get them together.

Her time

After their trip to New York, Aunt May grew weak. She developed a fever and had to take to her bed. Peter could see that her health was rapidly deteriorating and he wanted to rush her back to the hospital, but she refused to go—she didn't want to see any more doctors. She just wanted to spend the time she had left with her nephew. Aunt May had realized that their last week together had been a gift, a chance for them to say goodbye. She had had a good and happy life, but now she had to take her final journey—it was time.

YOU'VE NEVER BEEN VERY GOOD...AT LETTING GO, PETER. LOSING YOUR PARENTS THE WAY YOU DID... MADE IT SO HARD FOR YOU.

NO, AUNT MAY--

YES. BUT NOT ALL LEAVE-TAKING IS BAD. I'VE HAD A GOOD LIFE. A LONG LIFE.

BUT I'M TIRED, PETER. IT'S MY TIME.

IT'S MY TIME.

"--AND STRAIGHT ON TILL MORNING."

Letting go

As his aunt lay dying, Peter reminded her how she used to read *Peter Pan* to him as a child. Peter quoted lines from the book as his aunt passed away.

Remembering May

After May's funeral, the mourners gathered at Peter and Mary Jane's home to share their grief and remember a remarkable woman. Though this loss would haunt him for years to come, Peter was also brimming with gratitude over all the gifts his aunt had given him. He recalled May's wry humor, her unconditional love, her stubbornness, and the way she had mollycoddled and fussed over him. He pictured her uncanny ability to bounce back from tragedy and the zestful manner in which she embraced life.

SHARING ETERNITY
May Parker was finally laid to rest beside her cherished and adored husband Ben.

THE CLONE SAGA

SHORTLY AFTER Aunt May fell into her final coma (*see pages 134-135*), Mary Jane received a phone call from a young man who claimed to be an old friend of the family. She immediately informed him of May's condition, but he hung up before she could catch his name. The man then packed his meager belongings,

Ben and Peter first met on a rooftop in New York.

mounted his motorcycle, and began the long trek to New York City. He had secretly been in contact with May Parker for the past five years, and he was determined to see her before she died. He called himself Ben Reilly, and he was the clone of Peter Parker (*see pages 86-87*).

BEN REILLY

Contrary to what Peter believed, the Spider-Clone hadn't been killed in the explosion that took the life of Professor Miles Warren, alias the Jackal. Instead, the clone had regained consciousness in the smokestack where Peter had left him, and he went off to make a new life for himself. Armed with Peter's memories and spiderlike powers, he took the name Ben Reilly; Ben, after the uncle who had taught him so much about responsibility, and Reilly because it was Aunt May's maiden name. For five years, he wandered the country, using his powers to help people whenever needed. But now he was returning home, and Peter Parker's life would never be the same.

Once a hero
Though he only came to New York to say goodbye to Aunt May, Ben Reilly couldn't resist playing the hero. When he learned that Peter Parker was in danger, Ben immediately donned a makeshift costume and went out to save his double.

THE WANDERER
As he traveled across America, Ben Reilly would often use his spiderlike powers to help those in need.

Peter and Ben had developed very different personalities during the five years they had been separated.

Peter had greater experience and skill as a crimefighter, but Ben actually seemed to enjoy it a lot more.

WHAT FOLLOWS OVER THE NEXT FEW MINUTES SEEMS MORE LIKE A CAREFULLY ORCHESTRATED BALLET THAN A BLOODY BATTLE--

--AS TWO AGILE FIGURES MOVE IN PERFECT HARMONY--

--STRIKING, DARTING, DODGING, RICOCHETING--

--DELIVERING BLOW AFTER PUNISHING BLOW!

CLOSER THAN BROTHERS
Peter and Ben possessed the same memories and powers. They slowly grew to rely on one another, and teamed up against foes like Carnage, Judas Traveller, and Kaine.

CONGRATULATIONS, TIGER! YOU HIT ANOTHER JACKPOT!

WE'RE HAVING A BABY!

YOU'RE ABOUT TO BECOME A FATHER!

Questions, questions
When Peter Parker first saw Reilly, he was convinced the man was a fake, another trick masterminded by Harry Osborn. He had to be some kind of other-dimensional doppelganger or another state-of-the-art robot built by the Chameleon (*see pages 40-41*). As Peter finally started to accept the fact that Ben was the Spider-Clone that had been created by the Jackal, an intriguing question emerged. Was it possible that Peter was the clone and Ben the original?

I DON'T KNOW, PETE, YOU'VE BEEN SPIDER-MAN LONGER THAN I HAVE. YOU'VE BUILT A LIFE HERE.

A STARTLING REVELATION
After months of uncertainty, Ben and Peter finally determined who was the original Parker.

PETER, I AM SO VERY SORRY!

YOU'RE THE CLONE!

I...I'M THE ORIGINAL!

The greatest responsibility
When Mary Jane revealed that she was pregnant, Peter's priorities suddenly changed. Raising a family was an awesome responsibility. Not only did he need to get a better-paid job so that he could provide a stable environment for his child, but he also began to wonder if it was finally time for him to hang up his webs.

JACK'S BACK
Soon after Ben reentered Peter's life, the Jackal also returned. He emerged from a secret laboratory with a genetically altered body and new superhuman abilities. Determined to replace mankind with an army of clones that he had grown from Spider-Man's cells, the Jackal pitted Ben against Peter. He played with their minds, feeding them lies and swearing to each that they were the original Parker. Only by working together could Peter and Ben defeat the Jackal and crush his mad plan.

IT'S GOTTA BE A LIE!

YOU CAN'T DO THIS TO ME!

YOU CAN'T STEAL MY LIFE!

A new Spider-Man in town
After months of uncertainty, Ben and Peter finally decided to conduct their own tests to determine who was the clone. Peter was driven to the brink of insanity when the results indicated that Ben was the original. With Mary Jane's help, however, Peter came out of his depression, and realized that everything had worked out for the best. He voluntarily gave up his life as a costumed crimefighter and moved to Portland, Oregon, where he and Mary Jane planned to start a family. Meanwhile, Ben stayed in New York and took on the role of Spider-Man.

SEEING DOUBLE
New York didn't need two Spider-Men. So Peter eventually gave up his life as the masked web-slinger.

SCARLET SPIDER

A FTER HIS first reunion with Peter Parker (*see page 136-137*), Ben Reilly decided to stay in New York for a few days before moving on. He visited some old haunts and even stumbled upon a robbery in progress. Though the police arrived before anyone could be hurt, Ben immediately realized that it was only a matter of time before he would be forced into action. Thinking of all he had missed over the years, Ben journeyed to the warehouse where Peter Parker had cornered the burglar who shot Uncle Ben. He remembered Peter's vow to use his power to protect the innocent and realized that he also had a great responsibility.

In an attempt to distance himself from Peter Parker, Ben began to dye his hair blond.

AN OLD ENEMY
Ben Reilly was surprised to learn that Kaine, an enemy from his past, had followed him to New York City.

A NEW LIFE

So Ben became the Scarlet Spider and used this identity for the period when both he and Peter were in New York. However, after Peter left for Portland (*see pages 136-137*), Ben became Spider-Man, a role he continued to fulfill until his death (*see pages 142-143*).

New weapons
The Scarlet Spider invented impact webbing, which encased a target within a web cocoon, and stingers, which were miniature web-missiles that exploded on contact.

Ben's costume included a sleeveless T-shirt bought at New York's Museum of Natural History.

Unaware of Spider-Man's truce with Venom, the Scarlet Spider pulled out all the stops to capture him.

Back in the swing
As Ben pondered his future, he learned that Venom was in town. Wondering why Peter had never been able to defeat this madman, Ben quickly threw together a makeshift costume and went hunting for him. Venom seemed to have the advantage at first, but then Ben introduced some new weapons into his spider-arsenal. With the aid of his new impact webbing and his stingers, the Scarlet Spider finally managed to capture Venom and turn him over to the authorities, succeeding where Spider-Man had so often failed.

KAINE

TO THE WORLD at large, he is a cold-blooded killer, a remorseless assassin-for-hire who leaves his distinctive brand on the faces of his victims. But few know the truth about Kaine.

He is actually a clone of Peter Parker, the first of Professor Warren's re-creations to reach maturity (*see pages 86-87*). However, since Professor Warren was still perfecting his cloning technique, Kaine soon developed a condition called clone degeneration, the symptoms of which have left him horribly scarred.

MORE MONSTER THAN MAN

Warren considered Kaine a failure and discarded him. Forced to fend for himself, Kaine turned to crime, using his spiderlike strength and agility to brutal effect. Kaine believed that Ben Reilly was the original Parker and secretly stalked him across America. He hated Ben, and did everything in his power to spoil the quality of Ben's life. He even followed Ben to New York, where he came across the original Peter Parker.

STOPS YOU COLD, DOESN'T IT? COLD AS THE GRAVE.

WHAT HAPPENED? THAT MARK ON YOUR FACE IS THE SAME AS—

THE SAME AS THE MARK FOUND ON THE BODIES OF DOCTOR OCTOPUS AND THE GRIM HUNTER.

*THE MARK OF KAINE
Kaine often rips the flesh from his victims' faces, and leaves a hideous scar.*

Due to complications with the cloning process, Kaine is taller, stronger, and faster than Peter or Ben.

*SECOND SIGHT
Possessing a weird variation of Peter's spider-sense, Kaine has the ability to receive precognitive visions.*

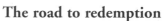
Kaine's special bodysuit prevents further clone degeneration.

The road to redemption

After seeing the life that Mary Jane and Peter Parker had carved out for themselves, Kaine fell into a deep depression. He eventually became filled with guilt and self-pity, and tried to goad Ben Reilly into ending his suffering by killing him. When that failed, Kaine turned himself over to the authorities. He intended to pay for his crimes and spend the rest of his life in jail. However, when word reached him that one of Spider-Man's greatest enemies had seemingly returned from the grave, and having learned the fate of Peter and Mary Jane's baby, Kaine broke out of prison.

*OBJECT OF ANGER
Believing that Ben Reilly was the original Peter Parker and the reason for his misery, Kaine would do anything to make his life miserable.*

JUDAS TRAVELLER

Judas Traveller's team consisted of Chakra, Boone, Mr. Nacht, Medea, and Scrier (not shown here).

DOCTOR JUDAS Traveller was a world-renowned criminal psychologist and a noted philosopher. He claimed to be a powerful mutant and believed that he was immortal. While visiting Ravencroft, a maximum-security institution devoted to the study of superhumans who were insane, Traveller's powers appeared to teleport the hospital's personnel off the grounds and seemed to surround the institute with an unbreakable force field. He then challenged Spider-Man, claiming that he intended to kill all the inmates, including Shriek and Carnage. Spider-Man responded but was soon captured. Traveller then began to peel away the layers of Spidey's mind. He would have been left a mindless shell if Ben Reilly (*see pages 136-137*) hadn't come to the rescue.

SECRET WORK
Unknown to Traveller, the Host secretly answered to Scrier. Only Chakra remained loyal to the Doctor.

TRAVELLER'S HOST

Judas Traveller was always accompanied by a band of assistants that he called his Host. Boone was a skilled hunter who claimed that he could track a single snowflake in a blizzard. Medea was a sharpshooter and master of various martial arts. Mr. Nacht was a weasel of a man who took constant notes, recording the suffering of Traveller's victims in gruesome detail. Chakra had the ability to teleport herself and others. Scrier was the final member of Traveller's band, and also the most mysterious.

It's a lie

Spider-Man later learned that everything he believed about Traveller was a lie. But Traveller truly was a mutant with limited psionic powers; his primary talent lay in his ability to alter people's perceptions of reality and make them think they saw his lifelike illusions. But Traveller wasn't the only one capable of playing tricks. Instead of working for Traveller, his Host was actually guarding and manipulating him. When the Host eventually turned on Traveller, it was left to Spider-Man and Ben Reilly to rescue him.

Since the betrayal by his Host, Judas Traveller has been on the run; but Spider-Man believes that he will return some day.

A MASTER ILLUSIONIST
Using his mutant ability to affect perceptions, Traveller was able to separate Cletus Kasady from his alien symbiote (see pages 126-127), and he also managed to convince both of them that they were powerless to harm him.

SCRIER

ALL THE SAME
Every Scrier wears the
same mask and costume.

H E MOVES among the shadows, seemingly able to appear and disappear at will. He claims to have been a faithful servant of Judas Traveller, and his sole confidant for hundreds of years. He lies. Centuries-old and very exclusive, Scrier is actually the name of a secret cabal. It is dedicated to accumulating wealth and power. Inspired by an ancient mythical being of immense power, the Brotherhood of Scrier is a worldwide criminal organization much like the Maggia and Hydra. Its members dress in identical costumes, wear the same mask, and call each other Scrier. They are well-trained, well-funded, well-informed, and well-armed.

Judas Traveller mistakenly believed that Scrier was his most trusted friend.

The goal

The Rose, a masked criminal with ties to the Kingpin (*see pages 70-71*), learned that Scrier was more than he appeared. Scrier was the name of an organization, not an individual. This organization, the Brotherhood of Scrier, is one of the world's most powerful secret organizations with the ultimate goal of dominating all humanity. Recently, however, the Brotherhood fell on hard times. But the rise of a new, mysterious leader has since boosted their power.

Pawns

The Scriers new leader has turned out to be one of Spider-Man's greatest enemies. Using his worldwide network of informants, this individual has secretly kept tabs on the wall-crawler for years. He ordered the Scriers to supply Professor Miles Warren (*see pages 86-87*) with all the funding and expertise he needed to perfect his cloning technique. He sent operatives to follow Ben Reilly, and helped Kaine (*see page 139*) establish himself as a criminal mercenary. At his request, Judas Traveller was sent to Ravencroft and directed toward Spider-Man. This mysterious manipulator turned out to be Norman Osborn, back from the dead and determined to destroy Spider-Man.

MODERN AND MYSTICAL

Though they have taken on many of the trappings of a quasi-religious cult, the Scriers are a modern organization with access to the very latest technology and the most sophisticated armaments. Their annual budget for weaponry exceeds that of most small nations and they employ state-of-the-art devices for gathering intelligence. Every operative is a master of the martial arts, and would rather die than betray this sacred brotherhood.

REAL SCRIER
The Brotherhood is based on an ancient religion that worshiped a mythical godlike being called Scrier. This ancient being was recently revived and even battled the Silver Surfer to a standstill.

REVELATIONS

PETER AND Mary Jane Parker truly believed that they would live happily ever after—they were young, in love, and about to have their first child. Peter now believed that he was the clone and had retired from crime fighting (*see pages 136-137*). He turned his webs over to Ben Reilly, who was doing a fine job as the new Spider-Man. Though the job in Portland hadn't worked out, Peter and Mary Jane were content to return to the old Parker house in Forest Hills. While Mary Jane went shopping with Aunt Anna, Ben Reilly stopped over to help Peter clean the attic. They planned to meet Anna and Mary Jane later for dinner and thought they had a quiet evening ahead of them. They were wrong...

Deadly diversions
On their way to join Mary Jane and her Aunt Anna, Peter and Ben passed an abandoned building and noticed some children playing inside it. Suddenly, an armor-clad madman attacked them. As Peter tried to usher the kids to safety, he discovered they were really robots that had been programmed to kill him. To make matters worse, his pager began to buzz—Mary Jane was having the baby.

Induced labor
While she and Aunt Anna waited at the restaurant, a waitress named Alison Mongrain slipped something into Mary Jane's food. Moments later, Mary Jane began to experience intense pain. Something was wrong with her baby. Paramedics were called, and she was rushed to the nearest hospital. Aunt Anna immediately paged Peter, assuming he would drop everything and meet them in the delivery room. She didn't know that he was engaged in a desperate fight for his life.

WHERE'S PETER?
As soon as Mary Jane went into labor, Aunt Anna started paging Peter Parker. She couldn't understand why he didn't respond.

Torment
When she arrived at the hospital, Mary Jane was rushed into the delivery room. Her pain was increasing by the moment, and the grim faces of the hospital staff only added to her fear. She prayed for the life of her baby, but her prayers went unanswered. Silence greeted Mary Jane when she asked why her baby wasn't crying. The Parkers had suffered the greatest loss of all.

Shock follows shock

Unaware of the terrible tragedy that had just occurred, Peter and Ben managed to defeat the killer robots. They then learned that the armored man was an old enemy called Mendel Stromm, the Robot Master. Peter left Ben to web up the bad guys and raced to the hospital. Soon after Peter's departure, Ben was suddenly attacked again. Wondering why his spider-sense had failed to warn him, he turned to face his assailant. Beneath his mask, his eyes grew wide with disbelief—the man who stood before him was dead. Ben had *seen* him die.

Norman lives

BACK FROM THE DEAD
Seemingly returned from the grave, Norman Osborn resumed his role as the Green Goblin.

Amazingly, Norman Osborn had actually survived his final battle with Spider-Man. The chemical formula, which gave him the superhuman strength to become the Green Goblin, had also come with a healing factor that enabled him to recover from almost any wound. He awoke within the city morgue, and learned that his son Harry had protected his secret identity by removing his costume. Norman decided to give Harry a chance to prove himself and moved to Europe, where he eventually became the undisputed leader of the Brotherhood of Scrier (*see page 141*).

NO GREATER LOVE
Even though he still believed that Peter was a clone who had been grown by the Jackal, Ben Reilly heroically sacrificed himself to save Peter's life.

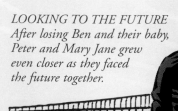

THE FINAL PROOF
Seconds after Ben Reilly died, his body crumbled into dust, proving beyond all doubt that he had always been the clone.

Night of the Goblin

Over the years, Norman Osborn had secretly used his Scriers to follow, torment, and manipulate both Peter Parker and Ben Reilly. He was now ready for his ultimate revenge. With Ben already his prisoner, Norman abducted Peter and revealed that he had already stolen everything that Peter had ever held precious—Gwen Stacy, his baby, and Peter's very identity. Osborn disclosed his connections to the Jackal and the cloning experiments. He also informed Peter that he was the original Parker, and that Ben had actually been the clone.

Peter and Ben joined together and eventually overwhelmed the recently revived Green Goblin, but they won their victory at a terrible cost. Ben was killed during the battle, still believing that he was the real Peter Parker.

LOOKING TO THE FUTURE
After losing Ben and their baby, Peter and Mary Jane grew even closer as they faced the future together.

IDENTITY CRISIS

The Hornet could fly at nearly 50 miles per hour.

SHORTLY AFTER his unexpected resurrection, Norman Osborn set out to clear his name. He produced evidence to prove that he wasn't the Green Goblin. He also used blackmail to gain a controlling interest in the *Daily Bugle* and goaded Spider-Man into assaulting him, capturing it all on video which he released to the media. A few days later a thug named Joey Z was found murdered, suffocated by a substance that appeared to be web fluid. Through the *Daily Bugle*, Osborn issued a five million dollar reward to capture Spider-Man. With every bounty hunter in the world now gunning for him, Peter Parker needed a new secret identity...

Though the jetpack was far too heavy for a normal man to carry, Spider-Man had no trouble with it.

THE HORNET

BEATING THE ODDS

Peter knew that other costumed heroes had temporarily adopted new identities in the past, but they were always exposed. He wanted to beat the odds and decided to adopt more than one. Realizing that it would be difficult to juggle different personas at the same time, he decided that each one would reflect some aspect of his real personality or powers. With a little help from his friends, Peter Parker began to create four new costumed identities.

WISECRACKER
The wisecracking Ricochet seemed to be a less than law-abiding member of society.

The Hornet
Peter, dressed as Spider-Man, went to visit his old friend Hobie Brown, an electronics wizard and inventor who was also the Prowler (*see pages 72-73*). Hobie had recently invented a cybernetically controlled jetpack. This was perfect for Spider-Man's new identity. Using his science background to design some additional weapons, Peter became the Hornet.

RICOCHET

SPIDER SPY
As Dusk, Spider-Man spied on the underworld by pretending to be a criminal mercenary.

DUSK

Dusk's costume could blend into shadows, making him a monstrous creature of the night.

Ricochet
While searching through the used clothing at a local thrift shop, Mary Jane discovered a leather jacket with a distinctive letter "R" on its back. Using that insignia as her starting point, she designed another new costume for her husband.
Peter used his spiderlike agility to pretend that he was a superathlete called Ricochet.

Dusk
Spider-Man had visited an alternate dimension called the Negative Zone a few weeks earlier and had acquired a costume that allowed him to merge with shadows and become practically invisible. To this he added a utility belt that contained gas, smoke, and stun grenades. Peter decided to call this dark and mysterious persona Dusk.

TAKING CHARGE
Mary Jane took an active part in Peter's super hero life during his identity crisis. She helped him brainstorm ideas for different types of heroes, designed some of his costumes, and enjoyed every moment of it.

As Prodigy, Peter Parker wore facial makeup, including an artificial nose.

PRODIGY

Prodigy was dressed in gold armor.

Prodigy

Conceived and designed entirely by Mary Jane, Prodigy was the consummate costumed hero. He possessed superhuman strength, a bulletproof costume, and could leap from one rooftop to the next with a single bound. He advocated strong morals, and was unfailingly polite and modest. He claimed that he had powers and abilities far beyond most normal men, and that he wanted to use them only to help people. He immediately became a media darling, achieving all the fame and respect that had always eluded Spider-Man. Even Norman Osborn seemed to admire Prodigy. In so many ways, he became the costumed champion that Peter Parker had always wanted to be. Prodigy was an old-fashioned good guy, exactly like the comic book archetypes of Peter's youth.

MISTAKEN IDENTITY
Not realizing who was wearing the costume, the Human Torch confronted the Hornet and warned him against harming Spider-Man.

Vindicated

Using his various new identities, Spider-Man was able to discover and expose the real killer of Joey Z. He even took a page out of Osborn's book and manufactured evidence that seemed to prove that the Spider-Man on Norman's videotape was actually an imposter. Once Spider-Man had been exonerated of any wrongdoing, the *Daily Bugle* quickly withdrew its reward. Since Prodigy had been such a big a hit with the public, Mary Jane thought Peter should keep that identity. But while it was fun to pretend to be someone else, Peter Parker knew that he had been born to be Spider-Man.

SLINGERS

A few months after Spider-Man retired his four new identities, someone else reactivated them.

Dan Lyons was an old man who had once been a costumed crime fighter known as the Black Marvel. He gathered four young misfits and gave them the identities and powers once used by the web-swinger. Eddie McDonough, a shy freshman at Empire State University, gained the enhanced strength and cybernetic exoskeleton of the Hornet. Richie Gilmore, an egotistic college student with dreams of glory, was soon encased within the bulletproof costume of Prodigy. Johnny Gallo possessed his own hyperactive agility and assumed the mantle of Ricochet. Cassie St. Commons, a poor little rich girl from Connecticut, took on the guise of Dusk.

RELAUNCH

AFTER MORE than 38 years, the powers-that-be at Marvel Comics decided it was time to give Spidey an update. A lot had changed since the first Spider-Man story back in August 1962. Now a new millennium was on the horizon, and their flagship character had to be ready to face it. To curb the flood of monthly spider-material, *Sensational Spider-Man* and *Spectacular Spider-Man* were canceled. *Amazing Spider-Man* and *Peter Parker, Spider-Man* ended their first series and started second volumes with new first issues. Howard Mackie, John Byrne, and John Romita, Jr. were entrusted with the daunting task of recreating one of the world's most popular icons.

UNITED ORIGINS
In Spider-Man: Chapter One, *Peter Parker became Spider-Man in the same accident that created Doctor Octopus.*

SPIDER-MAN, NO MORE (AGAIN)

Marvel's old Spider-Man titles concluded with Peter Parker realizing that he could not have a normal life as Spider-Man. So he burned his costume and vowed to end his web-slinging career. The new volumes took on the story showing him adapting to his new life as a civilian. At the same time, a new title, *Spider-Man: Chapter One*, reworked the origin of Spider-Man and his early adventures, adapting it to suit a new audience. The idea was to move the wall-crawler's early days from the Sixties and into the present day where he belonged.

The accident
The new *Chapter One* series tweaked and polished elements of Spider-Man's story, including Spider-Man's origin. Attending a demonstration on radioactivity presented by a certain Doctor Otto Octavius, Peter suddenly found himself an innocent bystander in a freak accident. The presence of a tiny spider inside Doctor Octopus' radiation chamber triggered an enormous explosion, killing many and exposing the survivors to radiation. In the aftermath of the explosion, Peter has to cope with the bite of the radiation-soaked spider.

TRANSFORMATION
The combination of the explosion and the spider bite transformed Peter into Spider-Man.

Amazing recovery
Peter spent weeks in the hospital where doctors were amazed at his recovery—they had written him off as another casualty of the fatal explosion. One day after leaving the hospital, Peter was amazed when he leapt to avoid a car and found himself 15 feet up the side of a building, able to scale that wall as easily as walking down the street!

Crusher Hogan

Once he realized he possessed spiderlike powers, Peter immediately thought about using them to fight evil. He wondered if the Fantastic Four could use a new member. It was only later, after joking with Uncle Ben, that Peter decided to meet Crusher Hogan in the ring and to direct his efforts toward show business.

The burglar

In *Chapter One* the burglar who killed Uncle Ben reveals himself to Spider-Man. Believing that Spidey was a fellow cat burglar, the man deliberately robbed the Parker house because he hoped to run into the web-head and become his partner in crime.

*SUPERMODEL
Peter's new apartment was financed by Mary Jane, who was now a successful supermodel.*

A return to the webs

Though retirement seemed to agree with the Peter, he eventually resumed his responsibilities and returned to the role that he was born to play. Spider-Man went back into action and fought new villains such as the Ranger, Shadrac, and Captain Power. While many of his life's details had changed, Spider-Man was still the same old friendly neighborhood web-slinger.

MARY JANE

Glamorous life

While *Chapter One* was retelling the story of Spider-Man's origin, the other Spider-Man comics picked up the story with Peter renouncing his role as a crimefighter to focus on leading a normal life. He now lived in a luxury apartment with Mary Jane and Aunt May, whose death had actually proved to be a hoax created by Norman Osborn. Peter worked part-time for the Tricorp Research Foundation, a private brain trust that served as a playground for the country's brightest scientific minds.

*ANOTHER SURVIVOR
Captain Power, a new foe for Spider-Man, proved to be another survivor from the nuclear accident in* Spider-Man: Chapter One.

New takes on old villains

The relaunch also affected many of the established members of Spidey's rogues' gallery. Characters like the Vulture, Electro, and the Scorpion were given new costumes and their backstories were altered.

Venom, Mysterio, Electro, the son of the original Kraven, the Vulture, and the Sandman made up the new Sinister Six.

CAPTAIN POWER

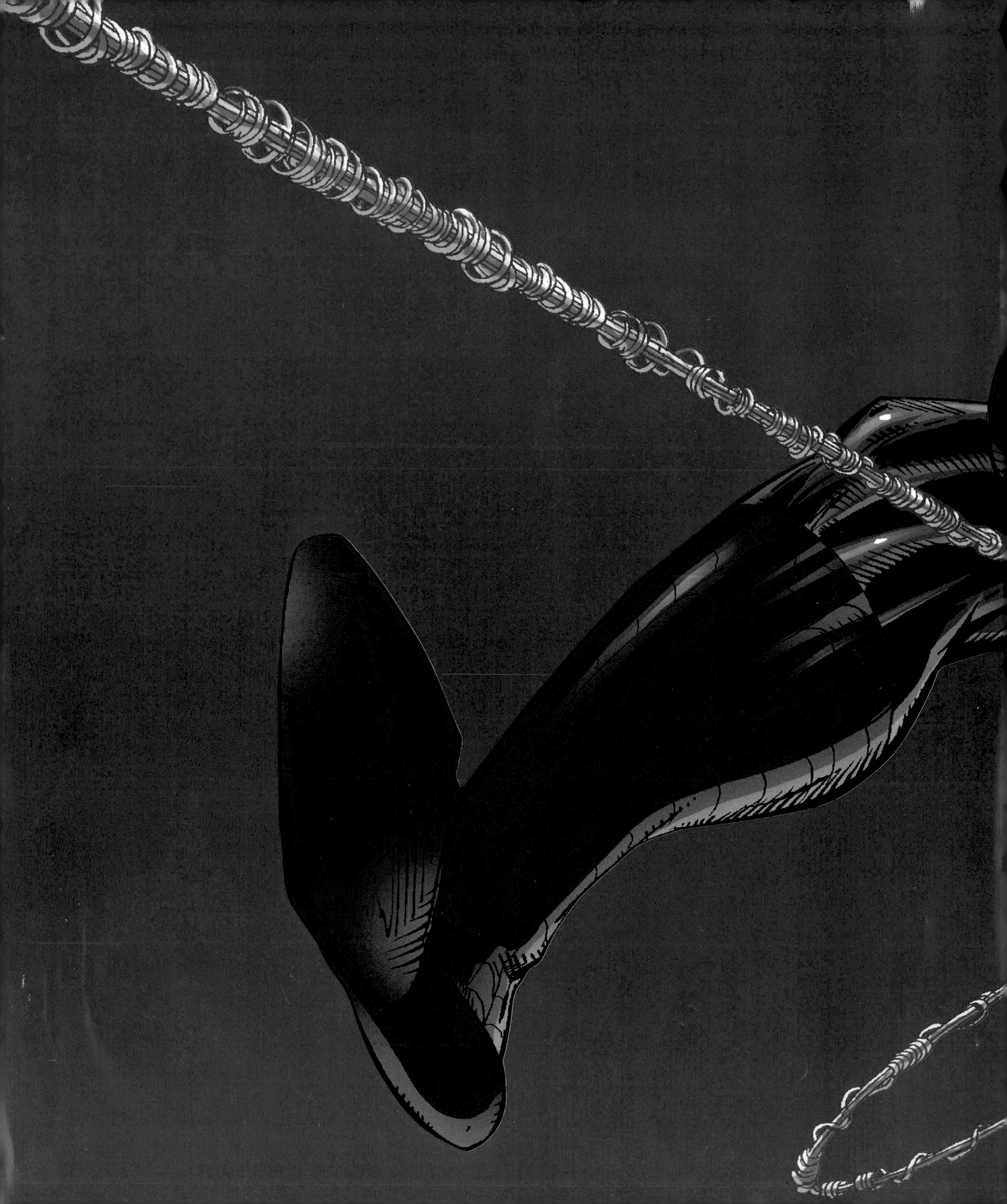

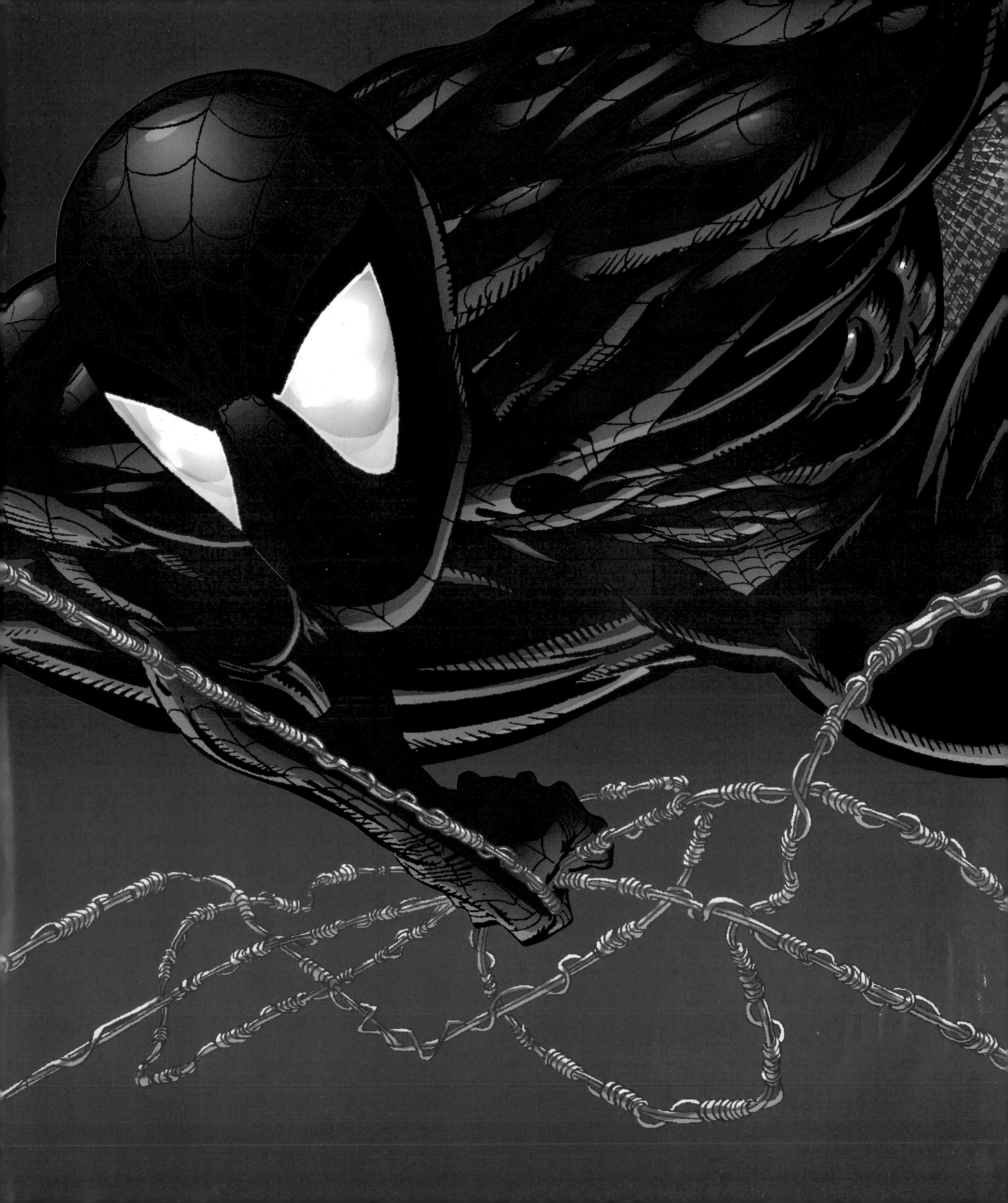

SPIDER-MAN 2000

SPIDER-MAN BEGAN the new millennium with a bang. A big one! Friction had developed between Peter and Mary Jane when she found out he had secretly returned to web-spinning. She also realized that someone was stalking her. To get away, Mary Jane accepted a modeling assignment in the small east European country of Latveria. However, her airplane exploded en route, and people feared the worst. Only Peter refused to believe that Mary Jane was dead. The people in his life had a habit of returning from the dead, so he lived in a state of complete denial for many months. He distracted himself by challenging the Hulk to a fight, and later traveled to Latveria. But as time passed and Mary Jane didn't return, Peter grew to accept the grim reality of his wife's death.

Mary Jane Parker was presumed dead after the plane she was in exploded.

DOWNWARD SPIRAL

Peter eventually lost his job at Tricorp and learned that Mary Jane's savings had been embezzled. Unable to afford their luxury apartment, Aunt May moved back to Forest Hills, and Peter started to share a rundown bachelor apartment with Randy Robertson. His life continued to make some unexpected twists and turns, and he started to explore alternative avenues, trying things that he'd never had the time or the nerve to do before. This included taking his sharp wit onto the stage at an open mike night. Unfortunately, the results of this were not encouraging for a future career in comedy.

ROOMMATES
Peter Parker was broke again, so he moved in with Randy Robertson, the son of Daily Bugle *editor Joe Robertson (see pages 34–35).*

HULK ATTACK
Desperate to escape those who were chasing him, the Hulk fled to New York, only to run into your friendly neighborhood wall-crawler.

THE END?
After months of trying to deny the truth, Peter Parker finally accepted the reality of Mary Jane's death.

Living in denial

While those around him mourned the loss of Mary Jane, Peter refused to accept her death. After all, Aunt May had returned after her apparent death, and even Norman Osborn had returned to haunt Peter—so why couldn't Mary Jane? His feelings were confused even more when he received a simple phone call of two words; "She's alive!" Without hesitating, Peter left for Latveria, hoping to find his missing wife.

Despite the difference in size and strength, Spidey was still able to hurt the Hulk.

Doomed

Believing that Doctor Doom had somehow staged the plane crash in an elaborate plot to kidnap his wife, Spider-Man traveled all the way to Latveria in a desperate attempt to rescue Mary Jane. Unfortunately, the plot only existed in the web-head's mind, and Doom knew nothing of Mary Jane Parker.

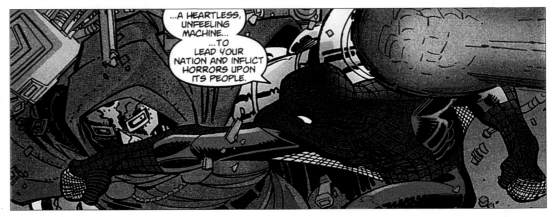

...A HEARTLESS, UNFEELING MACHINE... ...TO LEAD YOUR NATION AND INFLICT HORRORS UPON ITS PEOPLE.

ROBOT IMPOSTER
Instead of the real Doctor Doom, Spidey was shocked to learn that a lifelike robot had been ruling Latveria during its master's absence.

Twists and turns

Spider-Man's life was growing more complicated at this time. The new Spider-Woman (*see pages 94-95*) wanted to date him. Venom (*see pages 120-121*) absorbed Carnage's symbiote (*see pages 126-127*) and turned against the other members of the Sinister Six (*see pages 58-59*). Cletus Kasady temporarily escaped police custody. The Green Goblin (*see pages 54-55*) even made a surprise reappearance, and Norman Osborn attempted to brainwash Peter Parker into becoming his heir.

I... I GUESS THAT'S THE HARD PART ABOUT TH' HERO GAME, HUH? KEEPIN' IT TOGETHER.

LAST REQUEST
Poisoned by a bite from Venom, the Sandman (see pages 46-47) knew that he was dying when he searched out Spider-Man. He begged the wall-crawler to say goodbye to his mother for him.

Carnage dreamed of defeating both Venom and Spider-Man, even without the alien symbiote.

Onward...

Having finally accepted Mary Jane's death, Spider-Man soon learned that he had been right all along. She was still alive. Drugged, then smuggled off the plane before it took off, she had been held prisoner by her stalker. Spider-Man eventually rescued her, but that didn't necessarily mean that Peter and Mary Jane got to live happily ever after. Life has never been easy for everyone's favorite web-head, and it probably won't improve.

HISTORY REVISITED
Even as he dealt with his recent tragedies, the web-head recalled the death of Captain Stacy (see pages 82-83) in a limited series titled, Death And Destiny by writer/artist Lee Weeks.

Spider-Man screamed his denial of Mary Jane's death while delivering a flurry of punches to the Hulk. When the green giant heard the wall-crawler's predicament, the Hulk took pity on him and ended the fight.

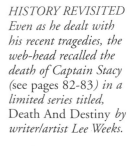

Remember with great power comes great responsiblity. Rember Peter

ULTIMATE SPIDER-MAN

WHEN THE Spider-Man relaunch (*see pages 146-147*) was greeted with less than thunderous applause, the powers-that-be at mighty Marvel went back to the drawing board. A major motion picture was on the horizon, and they expected a veritable flood of new readers. They wanted to make absolutely certain that their flagship character would appeal to the current generation. Bill Jemas, Marvel's President of Publishing and New Media, conceived of a bold new direction. Instead of merely revamping the web-slinger as they had done with John Byrne's *Spider-Man: Chapter One*, Bill decided that the time had come to completely overhaul the origin of Spider-Man.

The new Peter Parker had unruly hair and distinctive round glasses.

Brainy Jane
Mary Jane Watson was now a science nerd, and one of Peter's classmates. Peter seemed oblivious to her obvious crush on him!

TOTAL MAKEOVER

Fan favorite and critically acclaimed writer, Brian Michael Bendis was hired for the daunting task of recreating an American icon. Working closely with Bill Jemas, Bendis took Stan Lee and Steve Ditko's original 11-page origin story and expanded it into an epic that played out over 150 pages. Mark Bagley, whose distinctive art style practically defined Spider-Man in the 1990s, was brought in to visually reinterpret the characters he knew so well.

AUNT MAY
No longer in failing health, Aunt May was now an internet-savvy woman who often surfed the net for medical advice.

The new Peter Parker
The new Peter Parker wasn't just a shy and unassuming social misfit. He was now an exceptionally clumsy 15-year-old, who spent his days in total terror of being humiliated by Flash Thompson and his friends. Barely able to speak to his fellow classmates, Peter cowered behind his books and came across as a total dork. He was still an honor student and still had a close relationship with his Aunt May and Uncle Ben—who had gained a ponytail and the laid-back personality of a former hippy!

HARRY OSBORN
Rich and popular, Harry Osborn was now a member of the in-crowd who took a special interest in Peter Parker. He often tried to discourage Flash Thompson from picking on Pete, and Peter returned the favor by doing Harry's homework for him.

NO HOLDS BARRED
As with the original story, Peter designed his costume to wear in the entertainment business. However, instead of going on TV, Peter started in the world of professional wrestling.

Norman Osborn

Employing the greatest scientific minds that money could buy, Norman Osborn was a ruthless entrepreneur whose company was a world leader in scientific research. He masterminded a revolutionary new wonder drug called Oz.

STRANGE NEW POWERS
Instead of being radioactive, as in the old origin story, the spider that bit Peter is now a test subject that has been injected with the Oz formula. After the arachnid bites Peter, he begins to display spiderlike speed and agility.

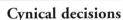

The spider's bite infected Peter with the Oz drug.

Cynical decisions

After the incident in their laboratory, Osborn Industries lawyers feared a lawsuit from the Parker family and advised Norman to accept no responsibility for the accident. But Osborn shocked the legal minds by opting to play a more dangerous game.

He ordered them to pay for Peter's medical bill and to keep a close eye on the teenager.

The new origin

Unknown to Norman Osborn, the special test spider escaped from its containment jar. The following day, Peter's class was on a tour of Osborn Industries. It was during the visit that the escaped spider bit Peter.

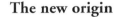

AIN'T IT COOL
Peter Parker was delighted when he learned that he could now crawl up walls and hang from ceilings.

Personal tour

Shortly after Peter first began to use his new powers, Norman Osborn treated the boy to a special tour of his lab under the pretext of an apology for the accident. In fact, Norman was secretly anxious to obtain a sample of Peter's blood and discover any effects of the spider's bite.

Test subject

After obtaining a sample of Peter's blood, Osborn discovered that the teenager's blood cells had become stronger and more spiderlike. He realized that his Oz formula was the cause, and immediately decided to test it on himself, after consulting with one of his most trusted scientists, Doctor Otto Octavius.

Chaos unleashed

When Norman tested Oz on himself, the results were even more spectacular than in Peter's case. Norman was transformed into a demonic monster which proceeded to destroy the Osborn Industries building and then went on to burn down his own home. Not content with this destruction, Norman hunted down Peter, and the two battled as Spider-Man and the Green Goblin.

SPIDER-MAN 2099

IN AN alternate future timeline, governments have given way to multinational corporations that now rule the Earth. The year is 2099, and many things have changed in New York. People with jobs and money live in the upper levels of the inner city, where they are constantly watched by the Public Eye, a private police force hired to enforce the corporate laws. Miguel O'Hara was a geneticist who worked in the bioengineering division of Alchemax, one of the largest and most influential corporations. He was assigned to the Corporate Raider program, and it was his job to find a way to enhance human performance and produce the ultimate superspy. Inspired by the legend of the original Spider-Man, Miguel devised a procedure to rewrite a subject's DNA, giving him the proportionate strength, speed, and agility of a spider.

ALWAYS A JOKER
Though he was one of Alchemax's most brilliant scientists, Miguel O'Hara was a wise guy with little respect for authority.

POISON
Miguel has fangs that pump out a venom which is strong enough to temporarily paralyze a grown man.

RAPTURE

Miguel was ordered by his boss to test his new procedure on a human guinea pig. But the geneticist was sickened by the result and tried to resign. To force Miguel to stay, his boss gave him a farewell drink laced with Rapture, a highly addictive and expensive drug whose distribution was controlled by Alchemax. Since Rapture bonds with its victims on a genetic level, Miguel attempted to cure his addiction by using his own experimental procedure to restore his original DNA. But at the last moment, a jealous coworker changed the imprint sequence, and Miguel received the Spider-Man process instead, giving him the powers that turned him into the Spider-Man for a new generation.

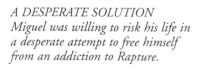

A DESPERATE SOLUTION
Miguel was willing to risk his life in a desperate attempt to free himself from an addiction to Rapture.

Roommates
Miguel lives in the east wing on the 252nd floor of Babylon Towers in New York. His fiancée, Dana D'Angelo, also lives there. She is employed by Sythia East and helps to develop new food resources for the overpopulated world of 2099.

GABRIEL
Born with an artistic soul, Gabriel is Miguel's younger brother. He makes his living as a freelance virtual reality artist. Gabriel hates the fact that Miguel worked for Alchemax and frequently tried to serve as his brother's conscience.

Holographic maid

Miguel O'Hara's closest confidante is Lyla, who is actually a computer-generated hologram. She has been programmed with nearly three hundred different appearances and personalities, and is completely capable of running his computerized household by herself.

Villains 2099

Like his namesake, Spider-Man 2099 has had to battle a horde of colorful super villains, including Venture, a cyborg bounty hunter hired by Alchemax to capture the new web-slinger. Other villains include a sword-wielding, futuristic Samurai called the Specialist and an evil doppelganger of the new wall-crawler called Flipside.

Miguel has retractable talons that can slice through metal.

PUNISHER 2099

SPIDER-MAN 2099

RAVAGE

DOOM 2099

Other heroes

Spider-Man isn't the only costumed hero in 2099. Ravage is a former garbage man who gained superhuman strength along with an inhuman appearance. This era also has its own version of the Punisher, Doom, the Fantastic Four, and a virtual reality Ghost Rider. It even has a new team of X-Men.

STRANGE 2099
The sorcerer supreme of Earth in 2099 is a young woman who secretly shares her body with a monstrous demon.

Doom 2099

Though he could not recall how he had been mysteriously transported into the future, Doom 2099 claimed to be the original Doctor Doom. Found by a band of cyber gypsies, he sought to free his beloved Latveria from a dictator called Tiger Wylde, who was a former employee of Alchemax.

Miguel's costume is made from a synthetic fabric called lite byte which acts like an airfoil to allow airborne flight.

VENOM 2099

VENOM 2099
Possessing many of the same powers as the original, the Venom of 2099 also has the ability to secrete a flesh-melting acid.

STRANGE 2099

EVERY MAN IN HERE WISHES HE LOOKED LIKE YOU RIGHT NOW, PETER. / BELIEVE IT, TIGER...

SPIDER-GIRL

SPIDER-GIRL LIVES in an alternative timeline, a future that might have been. In her reality, Peter and Mary Jane are still married, still living happily ever after, and their baby, named May, survived. During his final battle with Spider-Man, the original Green Goblin was killed and Peter Parker lost his right leg. So Spider-Man retired from crime fighting, and Peter eventually got a job as a forensic scientist for the New York City Police Department. The family moved back into Aunt May's house in Forest Hills, and May grew up without learning that her dad had once been the friendly neighborhood web-slinger. Then one day May discovered she had inherited some very special powers…

LEGACY

May "Mayday" Parker was already a teenager in high school when her powers first began to manifest themselves. Their timing couldn't have been better. Normie Osborn, the son of Harry and grandson of Norman, had recently taken over the family business and become the newest incarnation of the Green Goblin. Blaming Peter for the deaths of his father and grandfather, the new Goblin tried to goad Peter into resuming his costumed identity so that he could have the honor of killing Spider-Man.

Mary Jane took Mayday into the family attic and told her about Peter's past. So, donning Uncle Ben Reilly's old costume, May Parker became Spider-Girl. She defeated Normie and managed to save her father.

SURPRISE SHOT
Peter and Mary Jane Parker were shocked when their daughter made a spectacular 15-foot leap during a basketball game. They realized that she was finally showing signs that she had inherited her father's amazing spider-powers.

Athlete and nerd
Unlike her father, Mayday Parker is quite popular in high school. Possessing both Mary Jane's winning personality and Peter's brains, Mayday is a top student, a member of the science club, and a star athlete. She gets along with the computer geeks as well as the school jocks. Her friends include Davida Kirby, Courtney Duran, and Nancy Lu.

HIGH SCHOOL STAR
May "Mayday" Parker is the star of her high school basketball team.

Spider-Girl can "magnetize" an object that she is holding so that it sticks to anything it touches.

Spider-Girl can also forcibly repel an object which she is stuck to.

FOE TO FRIEND
Although Normie Osborn originally wanted to destroy Peter, Mayday has convinced him to retire from crime. He is now one of her closest friends.

With a little help from her friends

Fearing for May's safety, her parents tried to discourage her from continuing as Spider-Girl. But Mayday was undaunted and enlisted the aid of Phil Urich who worked in the forensic laboratory with Peter. Phil had also enjoyed a brief career as an incarnation of the Green Goblin (*see page 89*) and missed the excitement. He trained Mayday on how to use her spider-powers.

The Fantastic Five

Having changed with the times, what used to be the Fantastic Four now consists of five members. Their leader is John Storm, the Human Torch. The other team members are John's shape-shifting wife Lyja Storm, who is also called Ms. Fantastic; Reed Richards, who was injured in a terrible accident and now calls himself Big Brain; Franklin Richards, known as Psi-Lord; and, of course, Ben Grimm, The Thing.

Ben Grimm,
The Thing

Reed Richards,
Big Brain

May's powers are
likely to become even
more powerful as she
grows older.

Though she only possesses about half
the super-strength her father did in
his prime, Spider-Girl can easily
match him when it comes to
acrobatics and agility.

John Storm,
The Human Torch

Lyja Storm,
Ms. Fantastic

Franklin
Richards,
Psi-Lord

Rogues' gallery

As well as battling the Green Goblin, Spider-Girl has fought with the Venom symbiote and the man called Kaine. She has tangled with Mr. Nobody, a gun-toting killer who can dematerialize at will, and she has taken on Killerwatt, a former rock roadie with electric powers. She has also aided the Fantastic Five on more than one occasion.

THAT JAMESON BOY
Jack Jameson is the grandson
of J. Jonah Jameson. JJ,
as Jack is called by his
friends, currently lives with
Jonah and attends Midtown
High with Mayday.
However, he also has a secret
identity as the crimefighter
known as The Buzz.

THE BUZZ

SPIDER-MAN AROUND THE WORLD

Mary Jane inherited a small cottage in the Scottish Highlands from a distant relative.

Scottish Highlands

• Liverpool
• London
• Berlin

While he and Mary Jane were spending their honeymoon in a private villa in the south of France, the Puma invited Peter to Marseille and offered him a full-time job with Fireheart Enterprises.

• Marseille

• Crete

After the death of her father, Gwen Stacy went to visit her uncle in London. Peter made his first trip to England to find Gwen, but ended up in a fight with the incredible Hulk.

JAPAN

ETHIOPIA

Europe

Though Spider-Man spends most of his time in the New York area, he has traveled to Europe on a few occasions. Silver Sable was born and is based in Symkaria, a small Balkan nation. She once recruited the web-slinger to help quash a rebellion in the neighboring kingdom of Latveria, the home of Doctor Doom. Peter Parker also attended an international conference on cloning in the Swiss Alps, and he helped Hercules on a mission to Crete. The web-head also joined Wolverine to track down the killers of Ned Leeds, who was murdered in Berlin.

Japan

Thomas Fireheart spent many years in Japan, both as a businessman and as a student of the martial arts. When the Puma first confronted the mysterious Beyonder in New York, he was suddenly teleported to Tokyo against his will to confer with his old sensei.

Ethiopia

Learning that a band of mercenaries was running a kidnapping ring, Spider-Man joined with the Punisher to investigate their leader. The web-swinger was eventually captured and imprisoned in a detention camp located in Ethiopia. Spidey escaped with the Punisher's help. They freed the hostages and turned the kidnappers over to the authorities.

OUT OF THIS WORLD
Spidey has even left the planet on rare occasions. He once aided the Avengers and the Fantastic Four, who had teamed up to prevent Thanos, a godlike being with incredible power, from destroying all life in the universe. The wall-crawler has also journeyed to the Moon.

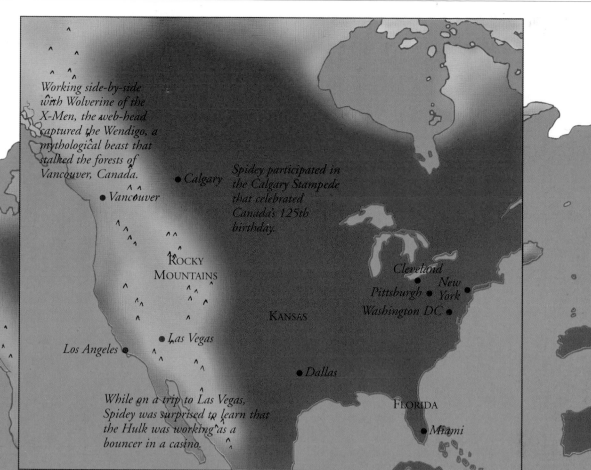

Working side-by-side with Wolverine of the X-Men, the web-head captured the Wendigo, a mythological beast that stalked the forests of Vancouver, Canada.

Spidey participated in the Calgary Stampede that celebrated Canada's 125th birthday.

While on a trip to Las Vegas, Spidey was surprised to learn that the Hulk was working as a bouncer in a casino.

United States

Thanks to his job as a freelance photographer for the *Daily Bugle* and his crime-fighting chores, Peter Parker has traveled extensively around the US. He first met the Lizard in the Florida Everglades while on a business trip with J. Jonah Jameson. In Imporia, Kansas, Spidey made the acquaintance of Wes Cassady, a man who had been bitten by a radioactive lab specimen and gained the proportionate leg strength and speed of a jackrabbit. When Eddie Brock was imprisoned in the Vault, a maximum security prison for superhuman criminals that was built into the Rocky Mountains, Spider-Man and Daredevil traveled to Colorado for the trial of Venom. During a visit to the state of Connecticut, the web-slinger was temporarily transformed into a Spider-Hulk. He also helped the Vision and the Scarlet Witch, two members of the Avengers, oust Doctor Doom from a base he had established in Salem, Massachusetts. While waiting in the airport in Pittsburgh, Mary Jane Watson finally agreed to marry Peter Parker.

Mexico

When a robot version of Spider-Man was discovered in the ancient temple of Tipod in Mexico, the real web-head had to form an alliance with Iron Man and the Avengers to prevent Kang, a menace from the far future, from unraveling the myriad webs of time.

The Caribbean

Venom lured Spider-Man to an island in the Caribbean for their final battle. The web-head managed to escape by convincing his enemy that he had perished in an explosion. Unfortunately, when Carnage began his first slaughter spree, Spidey was forced to return to the island, where he revealed his deception and begged Venom to help him against Cletus Kasady.

The Savage Land

Gwen Stacy and J. Jonah Jameson accompanied Peter Parker when he first trekked to this legendary land-that-time-forgot on a photo assignment for the *Daily Bugle*. Peter was surprised to find Kraven the Hunter waiting for him.

South America

The Black Tarantula, an international criminal mastermind that some people believe is immortal, lives in a castle somewhere in the jungles of Bolivia. He first fought Spider-Man when Norman Osborn offered a five-million-dollar reward for the web-head's capture. Spidey later dropped in on the Tarantula's home turf and handed him his first real defeat.

159

GAZETTEER

COMIC BOOK TITLES

AF—*Amazing Fantasy*
ASM—*Amazing Spider-Man*
ASMA—*Amazing Spider-Man Annual*
BC—*Black Cat*
CA—*Captain America*
HL—*Hobgoblin Lives*
MM—*Machine Man*
MS—*Marvel Spotlight*
MSHSW—*Marvel Super Heroes Secret Wars*
PPSSM—*Peter Parker, The Spectacular Spider-Man*
PP—*Peter Parker, Spider-Man*
SSM—*The Sensational Spider-Man*
SPEC—*The Spectacular Spider-Man*
SLI—*Slingers*
SU—*Spider-Man Unlimited*
WSM—*Web Of Spider-Man*
WF—*What If*

CHARACTER	FIRST APPEARANCE
Alien symbiote	
(Spider-Man's living costume)	MS HSW #8
Allen, Liz	
(friend of Peter Parker)	AF #15
Arvad, Jackson	
(Will O' The Wisp)	ASM #167
Avril, Sally	
(high school friend of Peter Parker)	AF #15
Baker, William	
(Sandman)	ASM #4
Bannon, Lance	
(photographer at *Daily Bugle*)	ASM #208
Barrison, Francis Louise	
(Shriek)	SU #1
Beck, Quentin	
(Mysterio)	ASM #13
Bench, Morris	
(Hydro-Man)	ASM #212
Black Cat	
(Felicia Hardy)	ASM #194
Black Marvel	
(Dan Lyons)	SLI #1
Boone	
(one of Traveller's Host)	WSM #117
Bourne, James	
(Solo)	WSM #19

Bowen, Tandy	
(Dagger)	PPSSM #64
Brant, Betty	
(girlfriend of Peter Parker)	ASM #4
Brock, Eddie	
(Venom)	ASM #299
Brown, Hobie	
(Prowler)	ASM #78
Cardiac	
(Dr. Elias Wirtham)	ASM #344
Carnage	
(Cletus Kasady)	ASM #360
Carpenter, Julia	
(Spider-Woman #2)	MSHSW #7
Castiglione, Frank	
(AKA Frank Castle) Frank	ASM #129
Castle, Frank	
(Punisher)	ASM #129
Chakra	
(one of Traveller's Host)	WSM #117
Chameleon	
(Dmitri Smerdyakov)	ASM #1
Chance	
(Nicholas Powell)	WSM #15
Chang, Philip	
(college friend of Peter Parker)	ASM #184
Cloak	
(Tyrone Johnson)	PPSSM #64
Connors, Billy	
(son of Curt Connors)	ASM #6
Connors, Dr. Curt	
(Lizard)	ASM #6
Connors, Martha	
(wife of Curt Connors)	ASM #6
Dagger	
(Tandy Bowan)	PPSSM #64
Dillon, Max	
(Electro)	ASM #9
Drago, Blackie	
(Vulture #2)	ASM #48
Drew, Jessica	
(Spider-Woman)	MSL #32
Dusk	
(AKA Spider-Man)	PP #90
Dusk #2	
(Cassie St. Commons)	SLI #0
Electro	
(Max Dillon)	ASM #9
Fireheart, Thomas	
(Puma)	ASM #256
Fisk, Richard	
(son of Kingpin)	ASM #83
Fisk, Vanessa	
(wife of Kingpin)	ASM #70
Fisk, Wilson	
(Kingpin)	ASM #50
Franklin, Mattie	
(Spider-Woman #3)	ASM #441
Gallo, Johnny	
(Ricochet #2)	SLI #0
Gargan, Mac	
(Scorpion)	ASM #19
Gilmore, Richie	
(Prodigy #2)	SLI #0

Grizzly	
(Mark Markham)	ASM #139
Hardy, Felicia	
(Black Cat)	ASM #194
Hardy, Walter	
(father of Black Cat)	ASM #195
Hammerhead	
(real name unknown)	ASM #113
Harrow, Dr. Jonas	
(underworld surgeon)	ASM #113
Hobgoblin	
(Roderick Kingsley)	ASM #238
Hopkins, Steve	
(college friend of Peter Parker)	PPSSM #36
Hornet	
(a.k.a. Spider-Man)	SSM #27
Hornet #2	
(Eddie McDonough)	SLI #0
Host	
(agents of Judas Traveller)	WSM #117
Hydro-Man	
(Morris Bench)	ASM #212
Ionello, Jason	
(high school friend of Peter Parker)	AF #15
Jackal	
(Professor Miles Warren)	ASM #129
Jack O'Lantern	
(Jason Macendale)	MM #19
Jameson, J. Jonah	
(publisher of *Daily Bugle*)	ASM #1
Jameson, John	
(son of J. Jonah Jameson)	ASM #1
Johnson, Tyrone	
(Cloak)	PPSSM #64
Juggernaut	
(Cain Marko)	XM #12
Kafka, Dr. Ashley	
(director of Ravencroft)	PPSSM #178
Kaine	
(first clone of Peter Parker)	WSM #119
Kane, Marcy	
(college friend of Peter Parker)	PPSSM #32
Kasady, Cletus	
(Carnage)	ASM #344
Kingpin	
(Wilson Fisk)	ASM #50
Kingsley, Daniel	
(identical twin of Roderick)	HL #1
Kingsley, Roderick	
(Hobgoblin)	PPSSM #43
Kraven the Hunter	
(Sergei Kravinov)	ASM #15
Kraven #2	
(Alyosha Kravinov)	SPEC #243
Kravinov, Alyosha	
(Kraven #2)	SPEC #243
Kravinov, Sergei	
(Kraven the Hunter)	ASM #15
Leeds, Betty	
(a.k.a. Betty Brant)	ASM #4
Leeds, Ned	
(reporter at *Daily Bugle*)	ASM #18
Lincoln, Lonnie Thompson	
(Tombstone)	WSM #36
Lizard	
(Dr. Curt Connors)	ASM #6

Loop
(friend of Black Cat) BC #2

Lyons, Dan
(Black Marvel) SLI #1

Macendale, Jason
(Jack O'Lantern) MM #19

Madam Web
(Cassandra Webb) ASM #210

Manfredi, Silvio
(Silvermane) ASM #74

Man-Wolf
(John Jameson) ASM #124

Markham, Mark
(Grizzly) ASM #139

Marko, Cain
(Juggernaut) XM #12

Marko, Flint
(Sandman) ASM #4

Marshall, Simon
(creator of Cloak and Dagger) PPSSM #64

Martin, Chip
(college friend of Peter Parker) PPSSM #36

McDonough, Eddie
(Hornet #2) SLI #0

McKeever, Tiny
(high school friend of Peter Parker) AF #15

Molten Man
(Mark Raxton) ASM #28

Morbius, Dr. Michael
(Morbius the vampire) ASM #101

Mysterio
(Quentin Beck) ASM #13

Nacht, Mister
(one of Traveller's Host) WSM #117

Octavius, Mary Lavinia
(mother of Dr. Octopus) SU #3

Octavius, Otto
(Dr. Octopus) ASM #3

Octavius, Torbert
(father of Dr. Octopus) SU #3

O'Hara, Miguel
(Spider-Man 2099) ASM #365

Osborn, Harry
(Green Goblin #2) ASM #31

Osborn, Liz
(a.k.a. Liz Allen) AF #15

Osborn, Norman
(Green Goblin) ASM #23

Parker, Ben
(uncle of Peter Parker) AF #15

Parker, Mary
(mother of Peter Parker) ASMA #5

Parker, Mary Jane
(wife of Peter Parker) ASM #25

Parker, May
(aunt of Peter Parker) AF #15

Parker, May "Mayday"
(daughter of Peter Parker) WF #105

Parker, Peter
(Spider-Man) AF #15

Parker, Richard
(father of Peter Parker) ASMA #5

Powell, Nicholas
(Chance) WSM #15

Prodigy
(AKA Spider-Man) SPEC #256

Prodigy #2
(Richie Gilmore) SLI #0

Prowler
(Hobie Brown) ASM #78

Puma
(Thomas Fireheart) ASM #256

Punisher
(Frank Castle) ASM #129

Raxton, Mark
(Molten Man) ASM #28

Red Skull
(ordered death of Peter's parents) CA #1

Reilly, Ben
(clone of Peter Parker) WSM #115

Rhino
(real name unknown) ASM #41

Ricochet
(a.k.a. Spider-Man) ASM #434

Ricochet #2
(Johnny Gallo) SLI #0

Robertson, Joe
(editor of *Daily Bugle*) ASM #51

Robot Master
(Professor Mendal Stromm) ASM #37

Rose, The
(Richard Fisk) ASM #253

Sandman
(William Baker a.k.a. Flint Marko) ASM #4

Scarlet Spider
(Ben Reilly) WSM #118

Schemer
(Richard Fisk) ASM #83

Scorpion
(Mac Gargan) ASM #20

Scrier
(agents of Norman Osborn) WSM #117

Shriek
(Francis Louise Barrison) SU #1

Silvermane
(Silvio Manfredi) ASM #74

Silver Sable
(Silver Sublinovia) AMS #265

Sloan, Dr. Morris
(college teacher of Peter Parker) PPSSM #32

Smerdyakov, Dmitri
(Chameleon) ASM #1

Smythe, Alistair
(son of Spencer Smythe) ASMA #19

Smythe, Professor Spencer
(creator of Spider-Slayers) ASM #25

Solo
(James Bourne) WSM #19

Spider-Girl
(Mayday Parker) WF #105

Spider-Man
(Peter Parker) AF #15

Spider-Man 2099
(Miguel O'Hara) ASM #365

Spider-Slayers
(killer robots) ASM #25

Spider-Woman
(Jessica Drew) MS #32

Spider-Woman #2
(Julia Carpenter) MSHSW #7

Spider-Woman #3
(Mattie Franklin) ASM Vol. 2 #5

Stacy, Arthur
(uncle of Gwen Stacy) ASM #93

Stacy, Capt. George
(father of Gwen Stacy) ASM #56

Stacy, Gwen
(girlfriend of Peter Parker) ASM #31

St. Commons, Cassie
(Dusk #2) SL #0

Stillwell, Dr. Farley
(creator of Scorpion) ASM #20

Stromm, Professor Mendel
(Robot Master) ASM #37

Sublinovia, Silver
(Silver Sable) ASM #265

Thompson, Flash
(friend of Peter Parker) AF #15

Tombstone
(Lonnie Thompson Lincoln) WSM #36

Toomes, Adrian
(Vulture) ASM #2

Traveller, Judas
(leader of the Host) WSM #117

Tri-Sentinel
(killer robot) ASM #329

Venom
(Eddie Brock) ASM #299

Vermin
(Edward Whelan) CA #272

Vulture
(Adrian Toomes) ASM #2

Vulture #2
(Blackie Drago) ASM #48

Warren, Professor Miles
(Jackal) ASM #31

Watson, Anna
(friend of May Parker) ASM #25

Watson, Gayle
(sister of Mary Jane) ASM #259

Watson, Madeline
(mother of Mary Jane) ASM #259

Watson, Mary Jane
(a.k.a. Mary Jane Parker) ASM #25

Watson, Philip
(father of Mary Jane) ASM #259

Webb, Cassandra
(Madam Web) ASM #210

Whelan, Edward
(Vermin) CA #272

Will O'The Wisp
(Jackson Arvad) ASM #167

Wirtham, Dr. Elias
(Cardiac) ASM #344

Whitman, Debra
(girlfriend of Peter Parker) PPSSM #36

AFTERWORD

WHEN I WAS first offered this assignment, I thought it would be fun. It gave me a justifiable excuse to pull out my old comics and spend some quality time with my good friend Pete Parker.

Another friend of mine, Peter Sanderson—author of similar books such as *Ultimate X-Men* and *Marvel Universe*—warned me that a project like this was always a lot harder than it looked.

Seems we were both right.

Let's talk about the fun part first. I've known Pete Parker for the majority of my life, and I really like the guy. He struggles, equivocates, whines, screws up, and knows heartache—just like a real person! Unlike most real people, though, you can always count on him to do the right thing simply because it *is* the right thing.

I might have wanted to be Superman, the Phantom, or John Carter of Mars when I grew up, but I've always had a lot more in common with Pete. I can identify with his money problems, his constant struggle for acceptance, and his desperate attempts to juggle personal happiness with duty and responsibility.

Pete has always been a major source of inspiration for me. Whenever I confront a seemingly overwhelming obstacle, I picture him buried under that mountain of rubble in the Master Planner's hideout, striving to free himself as the water rises around him. I recall his sense of humor in the face of adversity, his humility in the aftermath of victory. And I try to keep an eye out for future problems that may be running past me in the hall.

As for the hard work part, rereading old comics can be a real delight, but paging through 15 or 20 books in a desperate (and often futile) search for a single arcane fact or a specific image gets rather old after the first few hours. (Especially when you're a writer like me who is usually paid to make things up!)

And now, some recognition is in order…

While I truly enjoyed the trip down memory lane, I never would have completed this book without a little help from my friends. The original comics may have provided the basis of my actual source material, but I also relied rather heavily on the work of people like Mark Gruenwald, Peter Sanderson, Elliot Brown, Mark Bernardo, Bob Budiansky, Tom Brevoort, Eric Fein, and all the others who contributed to *The Official Handbook Of The Marvel Universe* (all three editions) and *Spider-Man Unmasked*. George Olshevsky's *The Official Marvel Index To The Amazing Spider-Man* and Roger Stern's *Spider-Man: The Secret Story Of Marvel's World-Famous Wall Crawler* also came in very handy.

Peter Parker wouldn't exist without the creative genius of Stan Lee and Steve Ditko. Nor could Spider-Man have retained his popularity without the contributions of the talented writers and artists who followed, people like John Romita, Sr., Gil Kane, Ross Andru, Roy Thomas, Gerry Conway, Len Wein, Roger Stern, Bill Mantlo, Al Milgrom, David Michelinie, Todd McFarlane, and so many others.

I am also deeply indebted to all those who collaborated with me on my own spider-work, most especially Ron Frenz, Pat Olliffe, Sal Buscema, Mark Bagley, Ron Lim, Al Williamson, Marc DeMatteis, Todd DeZago, Danny Fingeroth, Ralph Macchio, and all the rest.

I owe Ben Abernathy for conning me into signing on for this project, and will forever be grateful to my editor Jon Richards for his guidance and patience.

I would also like to express my gratitude to you, my reader, for being a spider-fan just like me.

Thanks for being there!

Tom D.

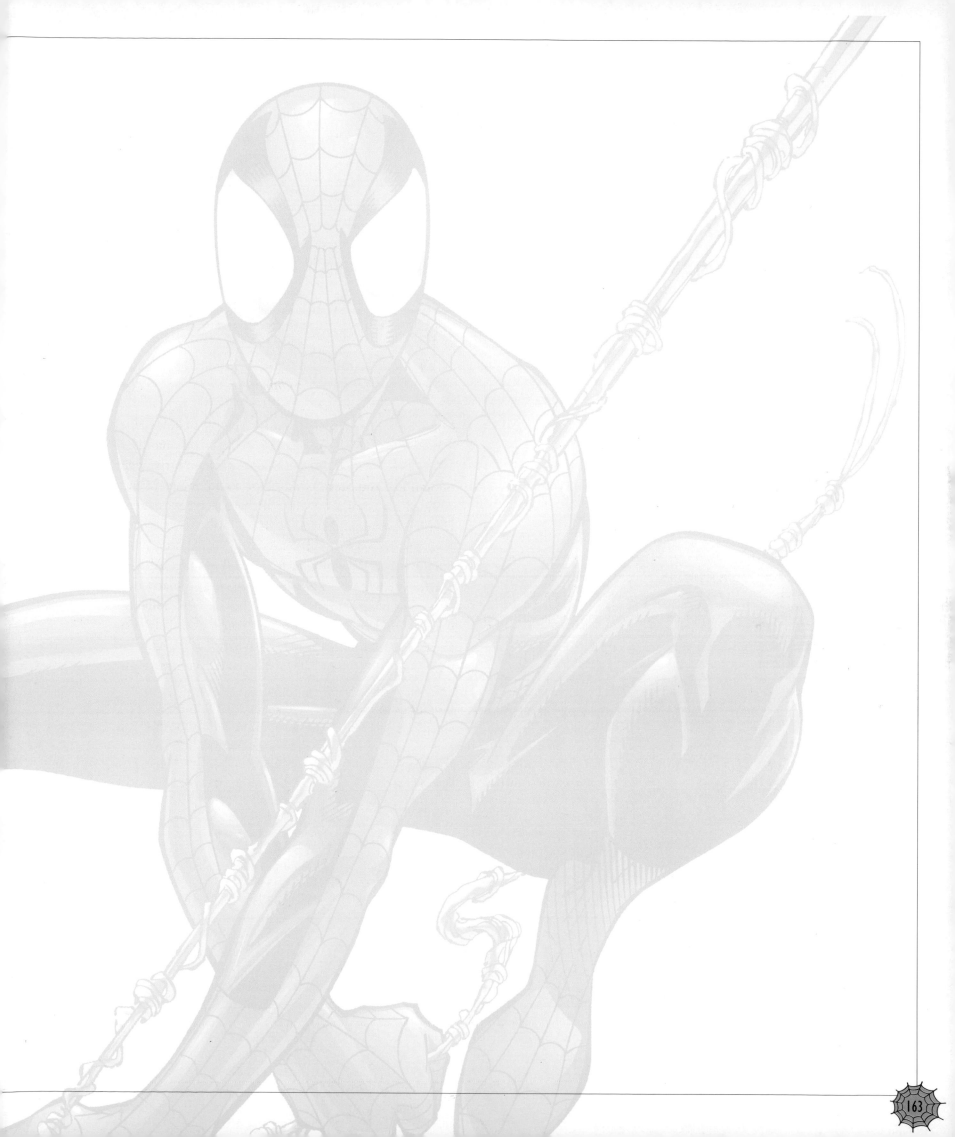

INDEX

Main entries are in **bold**.

T U V

W

X Z

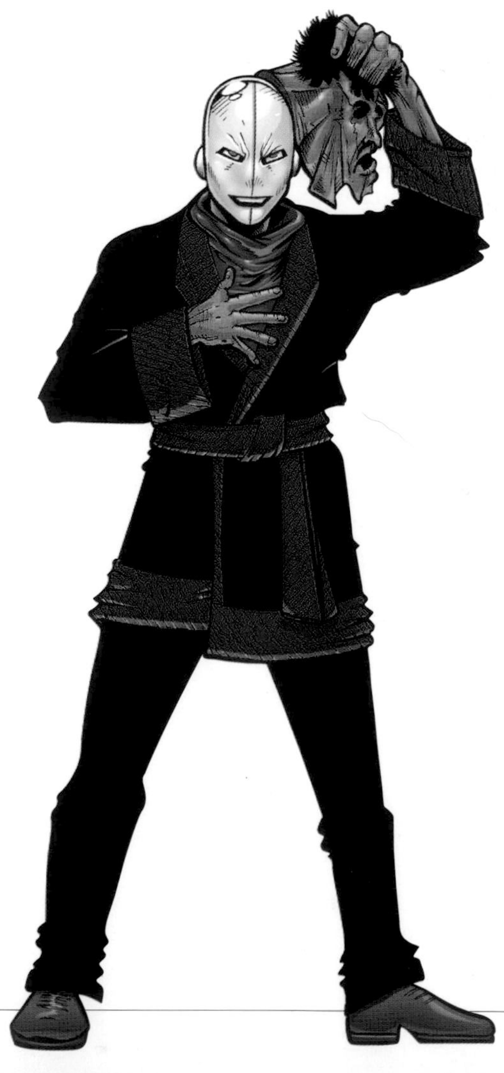

LONDON, NEW YORK, DELHI, PARIS,
MUNICH, and JOHANNESBURG

SENIOR EDITOR Jon Richards
SENIOR ART EDITOR Nick Avery
EDITORS Simon Beecroft and Rebecca Knowles
DESIGNERS Guy Harvey and Gary Hyde
PUBLISHING MANAGER Cynthia O'Neill
ART DIRECTOR Cathy Tincknell
PRODUCTION Nicola Torode
DTP DESIGN Jill Bunyan

First published in Great Britain in 2001 by
Dorling Kindersley Limited
80 Strand, London WC2R 0RL

Dragon

A CIP catalogue record for this book is available from the British Library.

ISBN 0-7513-2017-X

Color reproduction by Media Development in the UK
Printed by Mondadori Printing in Italy

ACKNOWLEDGMENTS

Dorling Kindersley would like to thank the following people:

Brian Miller at Hi-Fi Design, Gerard Murphy at VLM.
Sabrina Gilbert, Ben Abernathy, Adam Cichowski, Chris Dickey, Mikhail Burtnik,
Andrew Leibowitz, Gregg Schigiel, Scott Elmer, Axel Alonzo, Ralph Macchio,
John Miesaeges, and Elizabeth Maya at Marvel Enterprises, Inc.
Stan Lee and Holli Schmidt.

See our complete
catalog at
www.dk.com